CW01095503

SLAUGHTERED LIKE ANIMALS

by

Edward Browning

Grosvenor House
Publishing Limited

This book is published by
Grosvenor House Publishing Ltd
28-30 High Street, Guildford, Surrey, GU1 3EL.
www.grosvenorhousepublishing.co.uk

A CIP record for this book
is available from the British Library

ISBN 978-1-908596-01-7

DEDICATION

To the Royal Irish Constabulary and its successors

A Detailed Examination of the killing of 17 Members of the Royal Irish Constabulary

Auxiliary Division by the IRA in an ambush at Macroom, County Cork,

28 November 1920

and similar notorious incidents in that period.

SLAUGHTERED LIKE ANIMALS

THE KILMICHAEL AMBUSH

Look up Kilmicheal in West Cork on the internet and you will only be told "The village is located on the R587 regional road between Macroom and Dunmanway".

Search for "Kilmicheal ambush" and you will find hundreds of pages about an incident on 28 November 1920, just a mile and a half away that put the village on the world map. The 17 men who died there were the largest single loss the government suffered in the period.

The standard heroic IRA account of the ambush as told in most histories is quite simple. A group of British Auxiliary police, specially recruited to fight the IRA, had been amusing themselves by terrorising the countryside of West Cork, beating up and robbing innocent civilians.

Determined to protect the people from foreign mercenaries and to further the cause of Irish freedom, the IRA leadership ordered that the Auxiliaries be ambushed.

Under the leadership of Tom Barry, a former British soldier, between 35 and 40 IRA men with no military experience and only a week's training, set up an ambush on one of their regular patrol routes.

When the usual two lorries with 18 men appeared pretty much all accounts, including Barry's own, say that he stood in the road in uniform and flagged them down. As they got close, he threw a grenade into the cab of the first lorry killing the driver and at that moment the main ambush party opened fire.

At this point most accounts tell how the second lorry arrived on the scene and was engaged by another section of the IRA ambush group.

It is claimed that realising they were trapped and losing the fight, the British shouted, "We surrender!" at which point the IRA say they ceased fire.

When the IRA left their positions to accept the surrender and take the prisoners the British treacherously opened fire on them, killing three men. Realising he had been tricked, Barry ordered his men to open fire and keep firing until all the British were dead.

Many accounts then relate how Barry's inexperienced men were so shaken by what had happened that he was obliged to form them into a column on the road and drill them for some minutes until their nerves had settled down.

I intend to show that this account is largely untrue.

What took place was actually a premeditated massacre. At least half the men who died were victims of what would normally be considered a war crime.

I also contend that this has been common knowledge, not only in County Cork where the ambush took place, but was/is known to the Irish and British Governments.

Now read on.

INTRODUCTION

Whenever I start to read a book my impatience is such that I resent long introductions, so I shall keep this one to a minimum.

This book examines an ambush that took place on what is still a quiet country road at Kilmicheal, County Cork in Southern Ireland on 28th November 1920.

Two lorries carrying 18 British "Auxiliary Police" - soldiers in all but name - were attacked by a group of between 36 and 40 young men calling themselves the West Cork flying column of the IRA.

Three IRA died but there was only one, seriously wounded, British survivor. According to legend, the IRA were led by one Thomas Barry, the 25-year-old son of a retired policeman and until eight months before, a regular soldier in the British Army's Royal Field Artillery where he was a Bombardier (Corporal).

This was the greatest loss the Government forces suffered in one incident and consequently every history book on Ireland at this time makes reference to it. Depending on the sympathies of the writer, it is anything from a serious blow to the Government to a quite glorious victory in Ireland's long struggle for freedom.

It demonstrated the efficiency and fighting prowess of Irishmen and the IRA because a group of mainly teenagers with only a week's training, outfought and destroyed a patrol of former officers all of whom had years of combat experience.

The question, which is rarely asked about such events is - What actually happened?

It is beyond dispute that 17 of the 18 "police" were killed, together with three members of the IRA.

But is there anything that merits investigation behind the bald facts of: ambush; 17 British, three IRA dead?

Good historians are honest enough to admit they cannot explain everything and certainly not every incident.

Politicians, on the other hand, usually have an interest in misleading when they are not engaging in outright lying. Poets and writers turn lying into an art form. Because of the many elements involved in reporting news, not least the pressure of time, journalists' accounts are superficial and should be largely ignored.

I am not attempting to write literature, but to examine a well-known event as honestly as possible.

It is therefore more akin to presenting the findings of an inquiry, taking into account technical details that no writer or historian has understood or perhaps known, but did not care to make public.

The greatest question about any event is 'Why?'

When investigating we must examine every aspect otherwise we cannot hope to explain why.

I have learned that to properly understand anything in life or history requires a wide range of apparently obscure social and technical information that few are interested in reading.

This is a fact of life. When I worked in English Local Government, a matter about which I had considerable knowledge attracted press attention. But when I contacted a national paper with a view to informing their reports on it, the response from one journalist was typical of them all: "Oh that's just a lot of boring detail."

You should understand that this book could also be dismissed as "just a lot of boring detail", but if you trouble to read it, these details will provide a foundation that will help you analyse similar events.

You will hopefully be more inclined to ask – 'Why?' and then be better able to reach an informed conclusion.

Thanks to all who helped in particular Gwen Browning and Ged Dunkel for reading and preparation and to Jim Turner for his design

REFERENCES

In the course of this book, I quote various people. To avoid the constant use of footnotes I will outline briefly the purpose of the reference here and afterwards refer to them by the author's name.

The Making of Modern Ireland 1603-1923 by JC Beckett
   This is more or less the standard work on Ireland for the period and while it is a very fair book he follows the normal - and historians' - line regarding the 1916 Rising and The Troubles of 1920-21.

The Green Flag and Volume 3 by Robert Kee
   Journalist and author Robert Kee wrote this highly regarded series of three books in the 1970s. This was at the height of another IRA campaign and he had the obvious intention of being as scrupulously honest and even-handed as possible. The interesting thing is that at several points he asks whether the IRA campaign of 1920-21 was really necessary, but as an Englishman cannot come out and categorically say it was not.

The Men I killed by General Crozier
   This book makes only passing reference to Ireland, but General Crozier is a great favorite of the Republicans because he resigned as commander of the Auxiliary Police in a protest over their indiscipline and specifically the assassinations of suspected IRA members. For a man

who was a clear sighted and outstanding Brigadier in the First World War he is incredibly naive and he is probably not trusted by historians for that reason.

What is apparent is that although he was from a military background and destined for the army from childhood he was more sensitive and questioning than most people, let alone his contemporaries.

His attitude to the situation he found in Ireland is all the more remarkable because he tells how during the war he not only had the only son of a widow shot for walking out of the battle area but stage managed the execution for maximum effect. Commanding a battalion made up mainly of Ulster Unionists, he also accepted that in battle his officers stood behind their men with revolvers ready to shoot any man who tried to run away. His later indignation that some of his men adopted the same approach as the IRA is a shift in attitude that requires psychoanalysis - which does not imply in any way that he was insane, because he certainly was not.

No matter, this book should be a standard reading for everyone, because it is mainly his introspective discussion of the phenomenon whereby soldiers and other military men talk endlessly about their experiences but never about the men they have killed.

Curious Journey by Kenneth Griffiths

Kenneth Griffiths was a Welsh character actor, TV documentary maker and a lifetime supporter of the IRA and all things Republican so this book is a hymn of praise to them. However another historian described him as "just a groupie" which is quite fair. Reviewing one of his television documentaries the Australian-born critic Clive James described him as a "daft Taff actor" which is also very fair.

Nevertheless this book was published in 1982 and contains many interviews with IRA members from the 1920-23 period. His undoubtedly sincere and completely uncritical approach to the interviewees encouraged them to speak openly and say things they might have otherwise concealed. This gives a fascinating insight into their minds and quite unintentionally provides some shatteringly original information.

The Recollections of Riflemen Bowlby by Alex Bowlby

Alex Bowlby was a public schoolboy, who unusually for the British Army, was not commissioned as an officer but served in the ranks of an infantry battalion in Italy from 1943- 45.

His book is considered to be one of the most honest histories of the war and tells the outlook of the majority of infantry soldiers. While it relates the death of good friends it contains no accounts of bloody combat, but portrays the attitudes of a group of men, mainly Londoners but with the occasional Irishman. He describes his battalion as "the men who made the numbers up", ordinary men whose prime objective in The Great War for civilisation was just to get out of it alive and go home.

With a Machine Gun to Cambri by George Coppard

This short book was written in the 1960s and has no mention of Ireland, but it is one of the few soldier's memoirs to come out of the war. Coppard joined up when he was just 16 and was to be promoted to Sergeant on the day he was wounded during the battle of Cambri late in 1917.

The wound was so serious it kept him out of the remainder of the war and he accepted that he was lucky to keep his life and his leg. His open, honest, account of his service in the Machine Gun Corps is untroubled by doubt or regret and has become a standard reference for anyone wishing to know what the ordinary soldier experienced and thought.

His attitude to the death of friends, killing and the casual way the men accepted the horror of everyday life and death in the trenches would be the attitude of the veterans who formed the Black and Tans.

A Terrible Beauty is Born by Ulick O'Connor

A writer and author well known in Ireland, he is an unstinting admirer of the IRA and all its works. This short book published in 1981 is an account of the period 1916-1923 and refers to many interviews with IRA veterans.

It follows the standard line for this period adopted by many professional historians and is of course completely uncritical. Nevertheless, as with Griffiiths' book, it is of interest to anyone who wishes to understand the way these people justified their actions.

The IRA by TP Coogan

TP Coogan has written extensively on the IRA and its activities for more than 40 years but it is still worth looking at his book to see how such a well-known and distinguished writer can overlook critical details.

The Virgin Soldiers by Leslie Thomas

I make passing reference to Welsh author Leslie Thomas's semi autobiographical novel based on his experiences as a National Serviceman and army pay clerk in Singapore in the 1950s. While he was almost two years in Malaya at the height of the guerrilla campaign it suggests that his experience of the war consisted of a few days duty with a riot squad and being caught in a brief but quite serious train ambush.

The Easter Lily by Sean O'Callaghan

Sean O'Callaghan was an officer in the Irish Regular Army who had been a member of the IRA in the 1930s. It is an interesting glimpse into the thinking of the Irish farming class who made up the bulk of the rural IRA.

The IRA and Its Enemies by Dr Peter Hart

I have to admit it that I have not read this book but it provoked a quite ferocious controversy when it was published in 1998. His view of the events at Kilmichael was that Barry's account had changed considerably over the years after 1922 and it was "riddled with lies and evasions".

He also concluded, and in my view correctly, that it was the intention that the entire patrol should be massacred. I would agree with this but as we shall see I question whether Barry was aware that this was the intention or whether he was actually in charge. His research was based on interviews with individuals whose testimony was given on the understanding that they would not be identified. Sufficient to say that this alone was enough for Irish patriots to call him a liar and in the course of a considerable correspondence in the Irish Times some patriots went so far as to threaten him with violence.

Police Casualties in Ireland 1919-1922 by Richard Abbott
Richard Abbott is a serving inspector in the RUC, now the Police Service of Northern Ireland. This book lists in chronological order the casualties suffered by the Royal Irish Constabulary, including the Auxiliaries in the period and has become a standard work of reference.

Apart from the casualties suffered in ambushes and other attacks, it is interesting to note the number of police killed while unarmed and off duty. In many cases the circumstances are such that had the victims been the IRA and the killers the Black and Tans there would have been universal condemnation.

One could perhaps cite the case of two English constables, Smith and Webb, who were fishing near Castlemartyr in Cork when they were surrounded by 12 armed heroes and shot.

Had they been IRA, their deaths would be the subject of books, poems and articles laying bare the wickedness of the English and the bright shining characters of the victims.

An Irish patriot told me in no uncertain terms that as the author was a member of the RUC none of his work is to be trusted. So I have no doubt that fuller research would prove that Smith and Webb were in fact notorious torturers responsible for the death of many patriots and killing (sorry executing) them was only justice.

The Secret Army, The IRA by Dr J Bowyer Bell

I quote from this painter and writer's obituary in the *The Independent*, Britain's leading liberal newspaper.

'The Secret Army was published, with good timing, in 1970 and has been in print ever since (the latest edition appearing as *The IRA, 1968-2000: Analysis of a Secret Army* in 2000), making Bell a leading spokesman on the subject...'

It continued: 'Indeed he was often **suspected** of Republican bias...'

Also: 'His books were held in reverence, not least by harder-line Republican elements. In the words of the Sinn Fein vice-president Des Long: "He was the first historian to link the modern IRA with the Republican struggle from 1916".'

This suspicion would seem reasonable, given that the Irish writer Malachi O'Doherty noted in his book *The Trouble with Guns*, that Dr Bowyer Bell was given access for his research to all levels of the IRA by its army council.

Suspected? Suspected?

To write that Bowyer Bell was 'often suspected of Republican bias' is akin to writing "Papal encyclicals are often suspected of being sympathetic to Catholicism.

As an American, an academic and a Protestant, his value as praise singer of Irish Republicanism is incalculable. Nevertheless, his writings are a valuable source because, like Kenneth Griffiths, his unstinting admiration of the

IRA meant they gave him open access for his research. But that is all.

As a source he is very useful, but emphatically not as a professional historian. Like Hitler, the world would be a better place if men like him were not taken seriously and they had stuck to painting.

For my part I shall content myself to referring to him occasionally as "Boywer Bull". Bull as in "bull——".

Most importantly - not a book but a web posting.

In matters of military training, human reactions to combat and military planning I quote from Pierre Reinfret's reminiscences, posted on the web in 2000, generally headed "The Joke Called Infantry Training".

Reinfret was a 19-year-old Private when the US Army sent him into combat in 1944. After the war he went into politics and eventually stood for Governor of New York.

He set down his experiences 55 years later in one of the most unequivocally critical memoirs of an army and it's training that I have ever read.

What is of interest is not his training in the US Army, or rather the lack of it, but what he learned in combat. To give some insight into the realities of infantry fighting I include the 22 essential points he learned as a frontline infantryman. He attributes his survival to remembering these, together with a lot of luck.

Pierre Reinfret's self-taught rules for infantry combat

Never, but never, expose yourself to the enemy.

Never walk along or stand on a skyline.
Never get out of your foxhole.
Change firing positions as often as possible
Never run standing up, run in a crouch.
Throw hand-grenades from prone, if possible.
To do not follow trails, if possible.
Always make sure there is a round in the rifle chamber.
Never, but never, group up.
Camouflage everything and anything.
Move in the utmost silence possible.
Get rid of noisy gear.
Never issue verbal commands, if possible.
Use tracer ammunition only if absolutely necessary.
Avoid any and all contact with enemy material.
Never approach a fallen enemy, do not take your eyes off him, be ready to kill him.
Stay hidden as long as possible and as much as possible.
Bury everything you don't want.
Don't display command insignia.
If you take prisoners strip them to the buff.
If you get lost in the dark, freeze where you are until dawn breaks.
Lay down as much firepower as you can; fire, fire, fire and then fire some more

He concludes;

"Much as I hate to say it the fact of the matter is that far too many men lost their lives due to command stupidity, their own carelessness and most of all their lack of training. Stupidity, obvious stupidity, ignorance, arrogance and lack of training may well have accounted for most losses in combat."

CHAPTER 1

BACKGROUND

The purpose of this book is to try to inform and educate, not just about the particular incident at Kilmichael or even about Irish history. Social detail, technical data and background information are seldom mentioned in history but they are the essential raw material of the conclusion we call "the truth".

I seek to put into the reader's mind a body of basic technical knowledge which can be retrieved and applied whenever necessary.

A craftsman will keep a box of 50 tools but only use 10% of them every day, the rest are kept ready for use on the inevitable occasions when their properties are required - so it is with technical details. For this reason I refer several times to details and events because if you're educating someone, and we are all being constantly educated, it is essential to repeat information so it is permanently retained.

It is important when dealing with matters of history and patriotism to remember that the reaction of people in England, Scotland, Ireland and Wales to these things is quite different.

I outlined my findings about Kilmichael to a fellow Irishman who had lived in England most of his life, married an Englishwoman and made a comfortable living there. As I did so he became increasingly incoherent with rage exclaiming: "That's the English version!" To which I quietly replied: "No, it's the truth." He became even more outraged and kept repeating: "That's the English version! That's the English version!" again and again until he had to leave the room to calm down. We were not invited to his home again for some time.

Millions of words have been written about the Kilmichael ambush/massacre and there is not much point in examining who said what, to whom and when. Dr Hart is the only man who has come anywhere near the truth with his statement that the intention from the beginning was that the patrol was to be wiped out.

This sparked outrage throughout Ireland at the very notion that such a great hero as General Barry could do such a thing. The gist of the argument is that Irish patriots are always true, chivalrous and humane except when driven beyond reason by the treacherous British. To suggest otherwise one is to be a traitor, a fool and a liar if you are Irish, and just a liar and a fool if you are not.

English patriotism is quite different as I discovered when I had been at secondary school in England for just three days. The entire school was marched down to the cinema on Friday afternoon to watch a special showing of *The Dam Busters*. In my delight and innocence I asked my new classmates: "Do you go to the pictures every Friday afternoon in England?" Of course not, it was a special showing arranged by the authorities who thought it the sort of film patriotic English boys ought to see. As I was in a racial minority of one, I was not consulted, but in any case I was delighted at the prospect of going to the pictures instead of school and, better still, it was free! The main feature had not quite finished at 4 o'clock when virtually the entire school, some 500 plus boys, rose to their feet and walked out. I was in an absolute panic. *The Dam Busters* hadn't quite finished and I wanted to see the second feature. I anxiously asked the boys walking past me: "Do we have to leave at 4 o'clock?"

The answer was of course no, but 4 o'clock was "home time". They were not obliged to stay after that and patriotic film or not they were going home. For them history was a matter of take it or leave it. In official school time they were prepared to take it but when it was their own time they left it.

History has been a lifetime fascination of mine. I was always near the top of the class and around the bottom of it in maths and I learned that in history, as in life, we see through a glass darkly.

I read any well-written history, military, industrial, social, because all these "specialisations" are interlinked and to fully understand anything requires an ability to notice the links. Too much "history " is concerned with a particular field and consists of assumptions based on a few facts, and these few are at best only half understood.

Irish history provides one excellent example of this and the way modern political and social thought combine with ignorance of pre-industrial military logistics to produce, on the one hand, a historic grievance and on the other, self-righteous guilt.

Every Irish history notes that one of the restrictions placed on Catholics by the penal laws of the late 17th century was that they were forbidden to own a horse costing more than £5. A British journalist wrote that this was "quite bizarre" and an eminent British civil rights lawyer considered it a terrible example of social oppression. Another Englishman told his readers that ownership of a horse was after all the mark of a gentleman in European society and by denying the right to Irish Catholics they were deliberately denying them social status. In all cases these opinions can be summarised thus – as absolute rubbish.

Put simply, the purpose of this law was precautionary and intended to stop a group who were considered politically unreliable from collecting a large number of warhorses.

These were an indispensable part of any insurrection or foreign invasion and cost about £8 each at that time. As the majority of workers then seldom earned £5 a year, a law forbidding them to own a horse costing that much, for which they had no practical use and which they could not afford to maintain, was only theoretically oppressive.

There is also clear evidence that in practice nobody minded Catholics owning expensive horses, but they ran the risk of Protestant wide-boys invoking the clause in the law compelling them to sell them to Protestants for £5. In short, if the law was invoked, it was enforced but this was done by individuals on the make and not by the state intent on repressing the majority.

On the other hand historians should not be ridiculed for missing something they could not understand by reason of their time and social background. When it was first proposed to legalise homosexuality in Britain in the 1950s the Home Secretary of the day rejected it, because "most people in Britain do not know what a homosexual is" and he was quite right.

One should remember this when considering Hedley McCoy's biography of Patrick Pearce, leader of the 1916 rebellion, which was published in the 1960s, in which he recounts how Pearce's sister told him her brother had a wonderful sense of humour. As a teenager he would borrow her dresses to go around Dublin, but he gave it up because it was no fun. He was such a good looking boy people thought he was a girl! McCoy later tells how when Pearce and some friends set up St Edna's school where boys would be educated by young men as he believed was the custom of Celtic warriors, he requested a school chaplain be appointed on no less than three occasions. It was a minor mystery why the Dublin diocese had not replied to any of his letters even though Pearce was known to be a devout Catholic.

The key to discovering things in history is the ability to cross-reference new information with something you may have read years earlier

One line in Richard Abbot's book *Police Casualties in Ireland 1919-1922* triggered such a train of thought.

Sergeant Armstrong, a man with 21 years service in the RIC, was shot near his barracks at Ballina, County Mayo in July 1920. As he lay dying he said: "I do not think any Ballina man would do this to me."

I remembered reading something in Sean O'Callaghan's book; *The Easter Lily* 40 years before. An Irish army officer, O'Callaghan was in the IRA in the 1930s and in The Troubles his father was leader of the local IRA. When his father was ordered to attack the local police barracks it was a problem for him as he had no wish to kill any of the police - foreign hirelings or no. The Constables were ordinary Irishmen and part of the community, one was courting a local girl and the Sergeant in charge was a personal friend. He solved the problem by calling at the police station and together with the Sergeant he *staged* a battle, ensuring no one on either side got hurt. The station was evacuated and the powers that be on both sides were apparently satisfied.

I thought the IRA leader Michael Collins would undoubtedly hear about this, appreciate such mock battles would not serve his purpose and in future ensure that the police were attacked by men from a village too far away for them to know the victims personally. This seems to be what generally happened as, quite apart from the motivational aspect, there was a need not to implicate local men who could be identified in local attacks/killings. It would make an interesting piece of historical, social and psychological research to discover how far from a police station or victim Irishmen needed to live before they would kill other Irishmen. Regrettably, in some cases it does not seem to have been too far.

This initial reluctance to kill one's own people seems to be a working class thing, as even SS men did not like shooting German Jews who were for the most part ordinary Germans like themselves and SS officers admitted it caused "morale problems". This is quite understandable, but educated people do not appear to have a problem with it. By contrast, in Argentina's Dirty War of the 1970s university students would befriend the children of leading politicians or businessmen so they could get past security and kill their "friends"' parents.

There was another recorded instance described on the Irish Radio station, RTE a few years ago of this reluctance to kill neighbours and known people. In this case the reporter said how in the 1970s he met an old gentleman farmer who told him that in 1914 Ireland was a united country. On the outbreak of war, in common with many men of the area, he joined one of the great Irish Regiments and while still a very young man he had reached the rank of Major by 1918. Leaving the Army he returned after the war and carried on with his life when the "War of Independence" unfolded around him. As a former officer, the IRA considered he was bound to be a traitor/spy/informer so one night they sent a vanload of men to his house to kill him. But he was unusually lucky. When he got in the back of a van to be taken away and shot - sorry, executed - as a traitor/spy/informer, it chanced that one of the IRA men had served with him in France. When he recognised his voice he exclaimed with shock and outrage: "That's the Major you've got there!" They had served together in the trenches for four years and he was so appalled at the prospect of them killing his old commanding officer that he protested vigorously enough that the IRA were obliged to let him go.

The only thing I would say about politics is that I was cured of them during my work in English local government, when I saw commonsense, professional integrity and a clear public interest being placed subordinate to political theory.

The Pirate King in Gilbert and Sullivan's supposedly comic opera The Pirates of Penzance now sums up my view of politics. I say supposedly comic because like most of Gilbert's writing it is savagely satirical. When he is accused of being a murdering cutthroat who sinks ships, the Pirate King agrees, but replies by singing:

"There is many a King on a first class throne who has much dirtier work to get through if he wants to call his throne his own".

This has always been true. Compared to politics, piracy with its cutting throats and sinking ships is a pretty clean business.

In the matter of policing, compared to the practical organisation of the RIC in Ireland with its centralised training and national responsibilities, policing in England has always been a crazy hotchpotch.

They have always seen the absence of a national police force as a sign of freedom. There was very serious resistance to the formation of police forces in the English counties in the 1830s and most people thought that a couple of elderly constables employed by each town was all that was necessary. Indeed, there seems to have been a perception that because the first national police force was organised in Ireland it was proof positive that police forces were a tyrannical institution. One could go on at considerable length about this but when the first eight County policemen arrived in the Lancashire township of Colne, then and now a backwater, they had to be rescued by the military. The General commanding the district thought that opposition to the police was such that they would have to be armed. Paradoxically, the people told him that they did not mind the army imposing order but would not have the police under any circumstances. Such was the feeling that at a time when hanging for murder was almost routine, two Lancashire policemen were killed in riots and those convicted were merely sentenced to transportation. However, a more typical attitude is a letter to the local paper from an "old farmer" saying that he "could not believe we were paying for 500 of these men to parade about in their fine suits and accoutrements with nothing to do". He concluded, "they would be better employed repairing the roads as their present spy business was about as low as a man could get".

It is interesting that when it was first formed, no less than one third of the Lancashire County Police, were Irish. One could speculate whether they were recruited because they were ex-Irish Constabulary and therefore properly trained.

Rebellion is assumed to be an Irish or Scottish pastime, but Englishmen are blissfully unaware that in the 30 years after the French Revolution, the government took the precaution of surrounding Britain's industrial cities with defended military barracks. These were still in existence until the 1960s, although they were no longer required for their original function.

In common with many British military establishments, most have long been sold off for housing and industrial estates. But I was passing one several years ago when I saw something which taught me how one's thinking is conditioned by the state's education system.

Little remained of the old barracks except a wall about seven metres high with an earth bank at the bottom and a sort of projecting turret at the corner with two rifle slits to allow fire along the top of the wall. I could well understand why they had a high wall but with my lifelong interest in military architecture I could not make sense of the two rifle slits. Not only were they inadequate for defensive purposes they were in completely the wrong place. A couple of cannon shots would flatten the wall so what use would be two rifle slits firing along the top of it?

Military practice at the time was to put what we would now call a pillbox in a dry ditch in front of the wall, sited to allow the defenders to fire along it. The pillboxes (called camponiers then), being below ground level would be impossible to hit with cannon fire.

No, however I thought about it, it just did not make sense. Then I read in a classic social history published in 1917 about the barracks constructed around British towns 100 years previously and the strange defences made sense.

They were not protection against a foreign army but against the people of the town! While the purpose of the high wall was obvious, what of the earth bank at the bottom and the rifle slits? The bank was to prevent ladders been placed close to a wall at the correct angle to allow an ascent, but just in case anyone did make it to the top, the two rifle slits which allowed firing along the top of the wall would be enough to stop them getting further. It simply never occurred to me that a British Army barracks would need to be defended from the British people; there was nothing in the education system to make us think the government would ever consider such a precaution necessary.

It was the formation of the Irish Constabulary that actually allowed the British Army to pull out of Ireland to watch English cities. So next time some smug English historian says, "The Irish Constabulary was formed to watch the rebellious Irish peasantry", you can say, "True because they pulled the Army out of Ireland to watch you."

Ignorance of this military redeployment is occasionally the cause of academic discussion. Historians have asked themselves why the numbers of Irishmen serving in the British Army fell sharply during the 19th century from something over half the army's strength to less than a third.

The usual reasons suggested are increasing national confidence, political awareness and the growth of nationalism. I would suggest a much more obvious and less political reason. Armies always recruit from the area in which they are stationed and this has been true of every regular army from Rome onwards.

As the British Army was increasingly moved to Britain it naturally started to recruit from the areas of the mainland where it was stationed. This was recognised in the 1881 army reforms when regiments that had only been *numbered* for 200 years or more were given *names* appropriate to their home garrison area. It was also a sound political move, allowing the people of the area to identify with its "local" regiment. Hence the Prince of Orange's Irish Regiment which became the 5th Foot when it was placed on the English establishment in 1751, was renamed the Royal Northumberland Fusiliers in 1881. It is interesting that the regiment remained proud of their Irish origins to the end of their days.

As an Irishman in England I must always remind myself that my approach to life is different and our now English families recognise this. My brother and I have daughters who refer to us, I hope affectionately, as "having a weird Irish sense of humour" while my late wife thought Irishmen were hard to live with, but compensated for it by being intelligent and interesting.

If you wish to be taken seriously in England you must have Doctor, Professor, Director of... before your name to be allowed to speak on technical matters. Otherwise to know your job or even worse someone else's job is to be a "nerd" and to be placed in the same category as a man who spends his time collecting the numbers of railway engines.

I have no time or patience for heroes and have never desired to have a one-to-one conversation with any "great" man or women. They are for the most part people with a bit more than average intelligence but a great deal more than the average share of luck – chancers who get away with it.

Someone does not have to be "great" to have a clear grasp of reality which is why I must mention two of the "ordinary" people who have had a profound influence on my thinking.

The first was a teacher at my secondary school in England when I was 11. So far as we could tell he had been an officer in an infantry regiment during the fall of France in 1940 and later served in the 1944/45 campaign in North West Europe. One day when we were working our way through a poem about the Second World War whose author was killed, he suddenly broke off.

I can still see him sitting on his desk one knee drawn up to his chest and a book of poems in his right hand. Suddenly out of the blue he looked at us and said: "War isn't the way you read about it in your comics you know!" Then he stood up and walked down the centre of the class, the book by his side, and the expression on his face told us he was no longer in the room. He was back on some horrible battlefield 10 years previously as he told us just what war was like. I cannot remember what he said after the first sentence, but I remember the last sentence clearly. With obvious revulsion he said: "And when you go in after flame-throwers there is the awful smell of burnt flesh." He then recovered himself, returned to the front of the class and continued the lesson.

The second profound influence was a wood machinist I met five years later. Tommy had served with the Manchester Regiment in North West Europe and the Parachute Regiment in what was then Palestine. He was a man of considerable intelligence, but like so many of his generation and class this had never been developed by the English education system. I could not say he suffered any great trauma as a result of his military service but like many ex-soldiers he did not speak of his more unpleasant experiences. As a 15 year-old brought up on gung-ho 1950s comics and war movies I was forever asking him about his service and posing hypothetical questions about the army and war, to which he would reply a with exasperation, but great patience: "But it's not like that!" When I was older and had read a lot more I understood what he was trying to say.

I will always be grateful to these two very different Englishmen who said in very different ways: "It's not like that!" Because whenever I am presented with information, "one-off" facts "proving" instant simple conclusions, I hear them saying: "But it's not like that!"

So forget what you have been told, forget what you have seen in the movies. Clear your mind of all preconceptions and when reading history start with an open mind. Collect, file and collate "boring detail" and, above all, remember: "But it's not like that!"

Chapter 2

WHAT IS AN AMBUSH?

The word ambush is often used to describe a surprise action in any field of activity. Thus a businessman who outmaneuvers a rival in a deal, or a politician who produces facts to which his opponents have no answer is said to have ambushed them.

To describe an ambush in the context of war, it is simply one group of well-armed and well-concealed men lying in wait for another group to come close enough to kill them before they have any chance to fight back. I do not know who first stood by with a stopwatch, but in a successful ambush 90 per cent of the victims are killed or wounded in the first 10 seconds.

Armies studied and refined ambush techniques to a high degree in the 20th century, but the ambush is as old as war itself, because lying in wait to surprise and kill passing enemies is the most basic, as well as the safest, form of warfare.

The Roman Legions, moving along paved roads, understood that they were particularly vulnerable to ambushes. The most notable occurred in Germany in 9AD when three complete legions were caught on a road and systematically slaughtered. As a result the Romans never again tried to expand north of the Rhine and this is probably the most significant ambush in European history.

It was to prevent such disasters that legion regulations required all forest and vegetation be cleared for two bowshots on either side of the road. If they moved through mountains or broken country the Legion commander would have Cavalry and light troops investigate and, if necessary, garrison likely ambush sites until his Legion had passed. When possible this is still the standard military practice, showing that in 2000 years the technology of warfare may have changed, but basic military tactics have not.

Such precautions obviously require large numbers of men and these are not always available when a unit moves through hostile country, so, if attacked, troops must fight their own way out or hold on until their support troops get to them. Therefore most ambush victims are in small, isolated groups who can be killed quickly enough to allow the ambusher to escape before the support troops can retaliate. It was a leading member of Britain's wartime SAS who simply and honestly summed up the unit's basic tactic as "butcher and bolt".

As with all warfare, there is seldom anything heroic or glamorous about it. The ambushers lie well concealed, waiting for the victims to come within 50 50 metres, but preferably less because at that range even the worst marksman in the world cannot miss. Once within range, the commander decides whether the enemy is weak enough to be massacred and if so he opens fire. If not he lets them pass.

All ambushes depend on intelligence and the route and strength of the victims must be known in advance. Even then most ambushes come to nothing. A competent enemy will vary his routes and timing to the extent that ambushers can lie in wait for days until they are compelled to withdraw at the limit of their physical endurance. At Kilmichael due to inaction it is said the Auxiliaries had grown careless and a member of the Company said individual patrol commanders had settled into a routine of using the same routes on the same days to a predictable schedule. There is also a report that on the day they were killed they knew a unit from the Essex Regiment was operating in the area and by having some of their men wear British uniforms the IRA lured them into a trap.

In the Hollywood version of war the script lays down that the good guys have sharp-eyed scouts who spot the ambush and allow their side (the good guys) to creep around and surprise their would-be killers (the bad guys). Complete nonsense of course, because a moving group of men is at an enormous disadvantage compared to concealed riflemen and machine gunners.

In long grass, let alone forest or jungle, a soldier is more likely to discover his enemy by tripping over him than by seeing him. Usually, his first indication of an ambush is when he and his comrades are being shot to pieces.

Even in conventional warfare when fully alerted troops are moving forward and supported by heavy weapons they are at a terrible disadvantage facing a concealed enemy. To give just one example from the experience of the United States Marines in the Pacific War, consider an account by Sergeant A C Bordages taken from the book *The Sharp End of War*.

Only snipers shot at the Marine Scouts as they moved across the creek, feeling their way through the thickets... more marines followed, but jungle exploded in their faces. They hit the deck trying to deploy in the bullet lashed brush and strike back - marines died there firing blindly cursing because they couldn't see the men who were killing them ......all day Marine detachments felt for a gap or soft spot in the enemy positions They'd be blasted by invisible machine guns and leave a few more marines dead in the brush as they fell back, then they'd do it all over again

There was nothing else they could do .... when the enemy is dug in and your orders are to advance you don't know where the enemy is. His pillboxes are so well camouflaged that you can usually only find them when they fire at you.

One cannot allow this quote to pass without saying that the courage of the US Marines in such a situation is incredible.

It can be reasonably said that every modern military action begins with an ambush. The advances in weapon technology in the second half of the 19th century rendered set-piece battle with massed bodies of troops manoeuvring like pieces on a chess board impossible. Until then battles had been close range affairs with inaccurate and unreliable smoke belching muskets fired from as little as 40 metres. Soldiers could often see the enemy artillery a few hundred yards away load and fire the iron cannonballs that would knock them over like skittles. Indeed one artillery technique was to ricochet the iron shot off the ground so it bounced through the enemy ranks like a ping-pong ball.

All this ended with the advent of precision engineered rifles and smokeless powder that allowed a soldier to shoot accurately from a concealed position several hundred yards away. Likewise, rifled artillery could now fire high-explosive shells accurately over several miles making the manoeuvring of mass formations in the open, suicidal.

Battles now begin with the attacking force advancing on a well dug in and concealed enemy whose location only becomes known when he fires on the leading troops. It is then the task of the attacker to assess the strength of the defence and make the necessary counter moves using artillery, tanks and aircraft as available. At this point the ambush stops and the battle begins.

Incidentally the leading element of the advancing forces is known as the "point" and troops are fully aware of the danger of this position. Consequently a commander must rotate the "point" units regularly so the risk is shared throughout his command and failure to do this fairly will seriously affect the morale and effectiveness of his unit.

Strictly speaking, therefore, ambushes are short, small scale battles which can be part of a general conflict or a guerrilla campaign.

In a conventional conflict both sides use patrols to probe each other's positions and to limit this activity each side will ambush opposing patrols to scare them off. The prime purpose here is intimidation and the killing is almost coincidental. No one pretends they are inflicting significant loss on the enemy, as the actions are a very small part of a much bigger battle.

This is not the case in a guerrilla war. As in conventional war, the ambushers are trying to dominate ground but according to Maoist doctrine the purpose of the guerrillas is to gain control of an area to allow a conventional army to be trained and equipped for the next stage, which is full-scale battle between regular forces. Again the killing is more or less coincidental but the guerrillas know that if caught, they and anyone who assists them can expect little mercy.

Where there is no possibility of organising and training a conventional force as such in Western Europe, one gets the "political" type of guerrilla campaign.

The main purpose of a "political" campaign is to gain publicity and through it create the impression of the invincibility and ubiquitous nature of the guerrillas. As the best way to grab headlines is to kill people and blow things up, the killing has a much higher priority. Paradoxically, it is also essential that the guerrillas are protected from the retribution of their opponents by the legal and political system they are seeking to destroy otherwise they are doomed.

So we can say that regardless of the type of campaign, an ambush is a group of armed men lying in wait to overwhelm and kill a weaker group of enemies at a place they are expected to pass. Therefore, to describe a surprise question to a politician or even an individual sniping at a military column from a hillside as an ambush is simply poetic use of language.

Ambushing has only come into its own as a military tactic in modern times. The same advances in military technology that caused armies to hide in the landscape, gave small groups of soldiers the necessary firepower for an ambush.

That firepower is provided by efficient explosives, machine guns and automatic rifles that allow them to annihilate their opponents in the ten second "shock window". Consequently, the modern ambush has moved a good way from the age-old practice of irregular forces, be they bandits, patriots fighting to preserve their culture or guerrillas fighting for freedom.

Ambushes now come in several variations, but the most simple and common is the linear ambush.

In this the ambush party lies in three groups along the road or track used by the enemy. The size of the ambush party will depend on the anticipated strength of the victims but it will have to be superior in numbers and firepower. The main body is known with brutal candor as the killing group and this is positioned overlooking what is described with equal logic as the killing ground.

At a suitable distance on either side of the main killer group are the stop groups. These may be only two riflemen and, as the name implies, their purpose is to stop (kill) those who escape the killing group. Their other purpose is to give advanced warning of the enemy's approach, which is vital when they may have been lying in wait for days.

The sophistication of this basic ambush will depend on the available weapons and the time the ambushers have to set it up, but for all but the smallest ambush at least one light machine gun would be considered essential. If time and resources allow, remote detonated mines and grenade traps, together with landmines are laid around the killing ground and on the victims' likely escape routes.

When the victims are caught in the killing ground they are for all practical purposes on the bullseye of a target with every weapon aimed at them at point-blank range.

The only option the survivors of the first devastating burst of fire have is to get out of the killing ground as fast as possible. They must leave their wounded and dying and run while they still can. If they can see the enemy and the ground permits they will attack the killer group, as this offers a better chance of survival than just running into the stops or mines while being shot at. If a counter attack is not possible, the rule is still to run - as fast as they can and as far as they need to.

These are the essentials of ambushing, but it is also standard procedure that ambushes are set at natural obstacles which can be expected to distract the victim's attention, for example a bridge or a bend in the road.

It should be said this is not always the case. In Vietnam the incredibly industrious Vietnamese would dig carefully concealed trenches along the length of a clear and open road. A passing convoy would naturally consider such a road fairly safe until the leading vehicle was blown up by a remote controlled mine. Then the Vietcong would literally come out of the ground blazing away with everything they had.

In the case of vehicle ambushes, which usually take place on roads, it is essential to disable the first and last vehicle to close the trap. The middle vehicles can then be systematically destroyed. It follows from this that the most basic anti-ambush technique is to keep the maximum distance between men or vehicles at risk so that as few as possible are caught in a killing ground.

In the 1920s ambushes had not reached this level of development. The ambush of which the British Army had most experience was on the North West of India and technically these were not really in ambushes at all.

What usually happened was that tribesman in the hills on either side of a road would fire down on columns of troops moving along the valley bottom. Rather like shooting at fish in a barrel, and an officer of the time noted that the tribesmen had no great political or social objectives but did it for sport as much as anything else.

The British counter to this was to have troops hold the high ground until their column had passed in exactly the manner of the Roman legions 2,000 years earlier. But this particular British experience could be considered when studying what happened at Kilmichael.

We may summarise by saying that the linear ambush is the most basic type, but all ambushes require surprise.

Whatever variations and developments there may be in layout and weapons, the enemy must enter the killing ground so the ambusher can subject him to concentrated fire from a concealed and protected position. This must allow him almost complete safety, not only from his victim's weapons but crucially from his own side's weapons. The intention is to completely destroy his opponent in under a minute or if not destroy, inflict such casualties as will allow the ambusher to escape unscathed before the victims can come out of shock and react. This is the only action that can truly be called an ambush.

Chapter 3

THE MEDICAL & PSYCHOLOGICAL ASPECTS OF KILLING

Killing is an almost coincidental part of warfare as for immediate purposes a soldier's task is usually achieved by incapacitating his opponent.

The extinction of life itself is a consequence of his actions rather than the objective. A seriously injured man's first priority is to ensure his own survival so most immediately lose interest in any further fighting. Once his will and capacity to injure his opponent is removed he is no threat and can usually be ignored in the face of the greater threat of his uninjured comrades. Indeed Western Society requires that in these circumstances he must not be subjected to further injury and actually helped. Illogical it may be, but it is to our credit that we are expected to help wounded enemies as soon as reasonably practicable.

Until very recent times most weapons provided crude and unscientific ways of killing. This has been understood in the last 50 years and modem weapons are required principally to produce an incapacitating wound. The cruel logic behind this is that a modem soldier does not expect to be left to die on the battlefield and it is calculated the evacuation of one wounded soldier requires 2-4 other men and it is therefore another way to tie up your opponent's resources.

The only soldiers who are trained to kill scientifically are the Special Forces who need to dispatch sentries or other unlucky people as quickly as possible. One could include in this group the elite of political killers, the assassins, and the snipers who are trained to lie in wait for specific victims and shoot accurately at the most vulnerable parts of the body, the head and chest.

Just how little professional soldiers can know about killing is illustrated by the tragic case of the German General von Stulpnagel. In 1944 he was summoned to Berlin for questioning about his involvement in the plot to assassinate Hitler and, aware of the fate in store, he decided to commit suicide and therefore travelled back through the Somme battlefield where so many of his friends had died in 1916.

At an appropriate place he ordered his driver to stop, made his way alone into a small wood and shot himself in the head with his pistol. Tragically he had fired the weapon into his right temple and only succeeded in shooting his eyes out. Consequently he was hanged by piano wire with the other conspirators. The point of this sad tale is that having fought in one of the worst battles in Europe for centuries and spending his whole life as a professional soldier he still did not know how to kill people efficiently, even himself.

The weapons and the methods used to kill people by the military have always been wasteful. From the club and the flint spear to artillery firing nuclear shells, the economic and technical input in every age far exceeds that actually needed for the task. Killing can be achieved at little cost and effort by anyone prepared to get close to the victim and strangle them with a piece of cord or stab them with a knife, or fire a couple of pistol shots into a vital area.

Compared to these, every other method of killing is incredibly expensive and wasteful. The rule is that the greater the distance between the killer and the victim the greater the financial cost and technical effort needed to kill. A good example of cheap close-quarter killings is strangulation with a fine cord or cheese wire. As this requires close personal contact with the victim during their death agonies there are understandably few people who care to do it. But as always there are a few who will not only do it but enjoy doing it.

In the brutal business of killing, the bullet, bomb and shell are no more than the industrial equivalent of the club and spear, all are intended to smash the body using physical energy to disable or kill.

It was not until the development of gas, chemical and germ weapons in the 20th century that practical alternatives were available. These attack the respiratory and nervous systems to incapacitate the body by suffocation or use bacteria or chemicals to destroy it. As such they are the main means of mass killing other than the age-old method of tearing bodies apart using physical forces. However even these were not new because poisoning wells and catapulting decaying horses or even human corpses in to a besieged fortress has been done for centuries and were respectively chemical and germ warfare.

What we may call traditional weapons kill in two ways, the first and quickest is by causing loss of blood because when a major artery is cut death can occur in under a minute. The second way is by inflicting irreparable damage to major organs such as lungs, brain and heart. Here the effect is just as deadly but it takes a lot longer. General Hackett, commander of a British Parachute brigade at Arnhem was asked for his opinion of war films. Among the points he made was that the most harrowing thing about real battle was that one's comrades did not die quickly and there was very little one could do for them in the middle of the battle. It usually takes hours, days or even years to die from wounds. This fact was recognised in British Civil Law for hundreds of years, because it allowed a prosecution for murder if the victim died within a year and a day of the fatal injury.

Indeed, it is only late in the 20th century that the advances in medicine have been taken into account and there is no longer a legal time limit between the injury being inflicted and the resulting death.

The French army was the first to understand this in the First World War when they devised a system for casualty management known as triage - thirds. All armies adopted this and it is still used as a means of concentrating medical resources on those casualties who are likely to survive.

Quite simply wounded were divided into three categories. The first were those who needed only immediate first aid and could be sent back to hospital without much risk. These were usually described as the walking wounded.

The second category were those who would benefit from immediate medical attention to stabilise their condition and these were treated at once, while the third category were the unfortunates who were so severely wounded that they were simply made comfortable and left to die quietly. Or even quietly helped on their way.

However, a healthy young body is programmed to survive to the extent that one veteran of Normandy in 1944 recalled his horror at seeing a "thing" on a stretcher. It was a body so mangled it was like badly butchered meat but worst of all, it was still alive.

Compared to cutting and stabbing weapons such as swords, bayonets, knives etc, bullets and shells are more effective in terms of damage inflicted. The bullets or shell fragments not only damage every body part in their direct path i.e. tearing apart organs and a shattering bones, but they have an accompanying shockwave that crushes the flesh and destroys the blood supply that keeps the flesh alive.

Also, used unscientifically, edged weapons are very poor killing mechanisms although highly cost-effective, as they do not become obsolete and need very simple maintenance.

The Romans understood how ineffective slashing and hacking weapons were, requiring a great deal of physical effort in relation to the wound inflicted. This was why their main close combat weapon was a short stabbing sword, broad bladed and aimed at the opponent's vital parts. A quick 50 mm deep wound can be fatal and requires much less effort than hacking at a body.

Again there are qualifications and one would be the heavy cavalry swords of the 17-19th centuries which were designed to cleave the heads of foot soldiers. Here the height of the cavalryman allowed gravity and the sabers' own weight to increase the energy in the blow.

One would also make passing reference to the double-handed battle-axes used in the Dark Ages. As one Saxon noted, they needed a lot of practice to handle properly but they were good weapons, as no second blow was needed.

The Romans were arguably the last people to scientifically study weapons before the modern era and to combine their use in a logical sequence. First a javelin was aimed at the enemies' shields not to kill them but to embed itself in the shields, making them so heavy and unwieldy that the enemy was obliged to throw them away. Then they were exposed to the legionnaires' swords.

The design of stabbing weapons is crucial, as the location of the wound and the body's capacity to survive wounds from edged weapons can be remarkable. An officer at Waterloo survived with his arm and half his face hacked off, while a British infantryman in the same battle survived 18 stab wounds from Napoleon's Polish lancers. However, much depends on the design of the lance, as survivors of Cromwell's unsuccessful expedition to the West Indies were impressed by the performance of the broad bladed Spanish lance that "let the life out of a man very quickly".

But to conclude, the purpose of this section is to make clear two things:

1. Killing people is rarely quick or easy - unless you have practical experience.
2. More importantly, even with a mortal wound it takes time - and often a long time - for someone to die.

The mutilated state of the bodies at Kilmichael is quite simply explained by reference to the memoirs of a British Medical Officer in WW1. Required to attend the execution of a deserter by firing squad, one of his first duties was to fasten a white card over the victim's heart.

He then related: "I wondered what on earth will happen if they miss him and they don't kill him completely and I was very anxious about that. But when they fired he fell to the ground writhing as all people do - even if they have been killed they have this reflex action of writhing about which goes on for some minutes." Not knowing this the IRA assumed the writhing of the bodies after the victims were shot meant they were still alive. So wanting to make sure they were all dead they just kept hacking and stabbing at them until all movement stopped.

As people become more civilised the desire to use stabbing, hacking and cutting weapons diminishes and mercifully few people are able to enjoy the agony of another. This is why the trend has been to separate the killer from the victim as far as possible, which leads us to the psychology of killing.

Killing psychological - What makes men kill?

The great secret of what draws young men to killing is never stated. This is, in simple terms, it is exciting and they have no real concept of the morality involved and even less of danger to themselves, because when you are young you believe you are immortal.

George Macdonald Fraser's excellent "Quartered Safe Out Here" about his war service in Burma relates that having survived the initial attack on a small town, his unit took up firing positions in railway wagons and began picking off retreating Japanese. He is honest enough to admit that it was one of the most exciting experiences of his life. He is also honest enough to express regret at killing a wounded Japanese who had tried to kill him shortly afterwards.

Ordered to take two men and check that a small building near their position was empty, he was tired after the excitement of the attack, fed up and just wanted to get something to eat. As he entered the building the Japanese who was sitting against the wall with a leg wound reached for his rifle but Fraser fired first, killing him. It is easy to understand his remorse but he accepted his quick reaction had saved his life, which otherwise would have ended like his victim's, in a dusty little hut outside a Burmese town. He consoled himself with the thought that if he had died the Japanese soldier would have been killed by his friends anyway.

Young men make the best killers as they have little property and no serious emotional relationships; their families are, of course, taken for granted and, being young, they believe they are invincible. They wish to prove themselves and what better way than in the cult of the warrior? This phenomenon is common to all cultures, but even young men cannot be fooled for long. One of the earliest Greek historians noted that army recruiting at the start of the Peloponnesian War in 431BC was not a problem "as there had been no war in the Peloponnes for some time". Consequently, young men joined up in complete ignorance of what they were really getting into and this is common at the beginning of wars the world over.

Ideas do not matter much to young men, be they teenage freedom fighters or patriotic teenage soldiers. Depending on one's politics they can be pitied as dupes, or honoured as patriots, dismissed as thugs or praised as heroes. The truth would be they are better-educated versions of the vandal or thug but have been sanctioned to kill for a political programme, which is supported by an adequately large section of their society.

This primitive urge to kill for the pleasure of it still exists and 2,000 years of Christianity have reduced but not eradicated it.

Also, the rewards of any successful killer are considerable, be it as a member of a street gang, a freedom fighter or a soldier in an army. He gets the respect of other members of his caste and commensurate material rewards.

Societies will condemn the motivation of the former group and praise the latter but the results for the individual are the same. Whatever the cause or reason, killing is a mean and squalid thing and the truth is that few victims have anything like a fair chance, as giving someone a fair chance to kill or maim you is quite foolish. Having said that, unlike freedom fighters very few soldiers ever do any killing on a one-to-one basis.

In the Second World War the Russian army used woman snipers and in her old age one of them told of her first killing. She and another girl got into a position where they could see some German soldiers loading a truck and as usual the priority target was the officer in charge. Trained to recognise him by his rank badges, she said to her companion that they should shoot him, but they could not decide who was to do it and he went out of sight into the building. When he came out again they were still discussing which of them should shoot him and they decided they must do all the preliminary checks on their weapons and check the wind speed etc before they fired. When they had finally done all this their target had been in and out of that house several times before they killed him. This is quite a tragic story and a tribute to their humanity that despite everything their country had suffered they still shrank from the cold-blooded killing of their enemy.

A humane reaction is perfectly normal and after the Falklands War a Royal Marine said that the worst experiences he seemed to keep in little boxes in his mind that he took out and looked at now and again.

Many good people are haunted by their experiences for the rest of their lives, as is the case of a very old Russian whose horror at his first killing in Stalingrad was still obvious in 2002. He was only 14 at the time and fired his sub-machine gun at close range by reflex action, hardly bothering to aim, only to see a German falling with bits of blood, flesh and overcoat flying out of his back. He vomited for the rest of the day, despite the fact that his friends cheered him up by slapping him on the back saying "Don't worry it's only a German". But 60 years later, one could see the horror of the memory still undiminished.

This is not of course a universal reaction, as another Russian in the same documentary said that a sharpened shovel was a very useful weapon in close-quarter fighting and the effect on a body was rather like chopping up tomatoes. He had always used one and said with unpleasant satisfaction that he had "Chopped quite a few of them (Germans) up with it".

It is perhaps worth recording that even Dan Breen, who started the whole bloody Kilmichael business by shooting down two village policeman in 1919 eventually felt guilt at least for them.

He gives the most fantastic false account of the incident at Solbeghead in his book in 1924 telling among other things that they wondered if the RIC would throw grenades at them as "it was a skill they had recently been learning". He later wounded an army Captain he chanced on who was having a quiet picnic outside Dublin in 1920 and forced his lady companion to load the wounded man into the car, then drove out into the country where he finished him off. Even towards the end of his life he expressed regret at killing the Constables at Solbeghead declaring the RIC were "as good Irishmen as any and should not have been killed".

The problem is, of course, that we Irish are better at killing than most and always have been. In 1825 Sir Walter Scott declared that the Irish "will murder you on the slightest suspicion and find out the next day that it was all a mistake and that it was not yourself they meant to kill at all".

The French, of course, have a lot to answer for, because they marketed the first people's revolution offering to all a brave new world promising heaven on earth.

Thanks to them we know that wherever we are in the world "The Revolution" is a very good thing and certain to end all want and injustice! Therefore it follows that those who oppose "The Revolution" have usurped their position and have ill-gotten and undeserved wealth that they want to keep. Consequently, they are probably evil, certainly greedy, selfish and unjust, quite simply heretics of a secular kind and so deserve the normal and just punishment for heresy.

However, there is a psychological element in some Irish minds in the 1920s which few appreciate existed, and Englishmen could not understand. That was the belief that it was a holy war, what we now call a Jihad.

This was raised on a BBC radio phone-in following a major IRA attack in the early 1970s. As always the motivation was incomprehensible to all in Britain except the intelligencia but an elderly Englishwoman offered a simple explanation. She was a Catholic and had been educated by Irish nuns at a Convent in Sussex in the 1920s. She told listeners that with cheerful disregard for where they were or whom they were teaching the nuns had assured their charges that "If you (they?) died for Ireland they went straight to heaven".

Given the Irish enthusiasm for matters sexual the English should just be thankful no Christian denomination promises virgins to its martyrs or the slaughter would be incalculable.

It is perhaps worse that most men lose any sensitivity about killing not because they are bad but because day-to-day exposure to violence has numbed their senses.

An example of this numbing of senses is given by Alex Bowlby. One morning he met two artillerymen in an observation post that overlooked a stretch of road behind German lines. He had seen them before but this particular morning they seemed excited about something so he naturally asked what was happening. They explained that a German dispatch rider came down the road on the dot of 7.30 every day and they had got permission to fire one round per gun to try and kill him. No great purpose would be served by his death, it would not make any difference to the war or the cause of freedom, and they were just bored. They had done nothing for days and it would be a bit of fun. Bowlby was absolutely appalled at the entirely pointless and casual way they were going to kill a man but could do nothing to stop them. He did however pray for the German dispatch rider and his prayer was answered; he got away, to the disappointment of the artillerymen and he would certainly break his routine in future.

It is not so much the brutalising effect of war that is most horrifying, but the general indifference that men acquire killing. One could cite the experience of an English boy settled with a German family by his eccentric mother in 1938. He saw a woman and her two children killed by an Allied fighter-bomber in the last week of the war. She was picking potatoes in a field when a free roving aircraft came down and used her and her children for target practice. On the first pass he killed one child and as she ran for her life with the other he came round again made a second pass and killed them both. This shows how casually cruel even intelligent, educated men can become without the experience of close combat numbing their senses.

But killing is a mean and squalid thing and the truth is that few victims have anything like a fair chance and few servicemen do any killing on a one-to-one basis. Even veterans can have an adverse reaction. A British commando, Alan White, described in his novel *The Long Days Dying* the appalling business of killing a man:

He was not dead but starting to scream in agony. The airline in his windpipe was severed and no actual sound could come out. A stream of bubbles came from his throat, blowing the welling blood into red iridescent bubbles. His mouth was open so I put the barrel of my rifle and fired three more shots to end his agony

Then dazed I started to walk back to the barn. I hadn't gone five steps when I started heave, bitter bilious vomit jerking spasmodically from my throat, wrenching its way up my entire body. I staggered and sat in the hedge with my knees open and my head down and still vomited. Then a great convulsion shook me and it was as if all my orifices had opened at once. Tears streamed from my eyes and there was a roaring sound in my ears and my bowels and bladder opened together. Great heaving sobs racked me, great tortured gasps of horror, hatred, pain and remorse.

I sat there in my own stink drawing the back of my hand across my lips wiping the streaming tears from my cheek with the cough of my jumping jacket smelling of my own stinking sweat.

The young men at Kilmichael (after only one week's training) had to watch this process carried out on over a dozen men. It was not a trained man cutting their throat or putting a bullet in each of their heads but a handful of killers, blasting men with shotguns, firing revolvers into heads, hacking, bludgeoning and stabbing victims. Victims who spoke the same language, mostly of the same class and similar culture to themselves. They had to listen while they pleaded for their lives and screamed with pain as they were being butchered.

No wonder they were shaken afterwards

Chapter 4

WEAPONS

The purpose of weapons has always been to mechanise the task of killing, thereby reducing the physical effort required. Men have also worked to increase the distance between killer and victim which serves both to lessen the psychological strain of killing, while increasing a killer's sense of safety

As noted in the earlier chapter on the details of killing, the business of extinguishing life in a healthy body requires both a strong arm and a stronger stomach.

One can imagine that cavemen quickly realised that the most effective use of the club was to strike an opponent on the skull and that one blow was seldom enough.

One can assume that the spear was a first attempt to reduce the physical effort of killing and increase the distance between killer and victim. It also had the advantage of inflicting penetrating wounds with the mass of the body as its main target, which made inflicting a disabling and distracting injury easier. In addition a spear was comparatively cheap. The only technical input was the head, the shaft was cheap and easy to produce.

The next major step in weapon development was probably the sword and this required a quantum leap in technology as swords not only require much more metal than a spear but that metal has to be of a far higher quality. They also require a great deal of skill to manufacture. To produce good quality swords in any quantity requires a sound industrial base and knowledge of basic metallurgy, so only the most developed empires could afford to equip ordinary soldiers with them.

Until the modern age, the height of industrial technology was the production of body armour which offered a good degree of protection from the weapons used by the majority of foot soldiers.

The greatest risk to the wealthy armoured warrior came from his own class who had the weapons to defeat his armour, however this unpleasant reality was overcome by the development of the code of chivalry. This decreed that a nobleman who had been clearly defeated and was willing to surrender should be made a prisoner and in return for his life he was required to pay a substantial ransom to his captor. Consequently in one 12th century battle there were a 1,000 dead, of which only three were knights. One must assume that much of the mythology of heroic warfare stems from this time when there was very little risk to the most wealthy - and consequently best protected - people taking part. As usual, the people on both sides with the money looked out for each other

This happy state of affairs for the wealthy came to an end in the Middle Ages when the weapons that used mechanical rather than physical force to defeat armoured knights came into use. Armour could reduce the injury caused by most battlefield weapons except those of another knight who could in any case be expected to spare anyone who surrendered. What it could not resist was concentrated mechanical force of an arrow or a crossbow bolt and ordinary soldiers who were quite indifferent to the social status of the victim could use both. One of the best examples of this would be the English archers whose longbows were cheap mass produced weapons that required only a small amount of expensive iron for arrowheads.

Trained to shoot either in mass formation several hundred strong or individually, they could pick off an armoured knight from his horse at 200 paces, however longbow men required years of training and a great deal of regular practice if they were to be effective.

Consequently, armourers developed the crossbow that required a higher level of technology but a much lower level of training. This trend of increasing technology and reducing skill has continued up to the present day. It is a matter of record that the users of early firearms were so hated by the aristocracy that they considered it perfectly reasonable to hang any prisoner whose equipment showed them to be Musketeers. This was not so much because muskets alone were un-chivalrous, as they had a very similar attitude to captured bowmen and often cut off the first two fingers from the right hand. Musketeers were however a different matter. Armour as finally developed in the 15th century offered a high degree of protection from arrows and crossbow bolts. By then to kill or disable a knight any type of bowman needed a great deal of skill to get an arrow into a chink in the amour. By contrast a bullet would just go straight through.

As a suit or more properly "harness" of plate armour required the ultimate in metallurgy and metalworking skills the cost was enormous. It is quite understandable that having spent a fortune on ensuring his security a knight would resent a common musketeer rendering his investment useless with a cheap and simple weapon requiring little skill.

Until very recent times men always used their weapons in massed bodies; either pikemen or musketeers or spearman working together. For the commander this had many advantages, the first being that they were easier to control and the second being the sheer mass movement is sufficient to intimidate an enemy to the point that they may run away before battle is actually joined.

In the Napoleonic wars having first selected the ground with care the French commanders would subject the enemy to carefully worked out artillery and sniping attacks until they judged the moment right. Then they would send forward massed columns up to 20,000 strong who would so overawe the opposition that they would not need to take the weapons from their shoulders before the enemy broke and fled. This tactic was not in fact new, like most military ideas it had just been rediscovered and it seldom worked against the British whose commander the Duke of Wellington could rely on steady infantry which he was careful to protect from the worst of the cannonade and sniping.

It was the development of mass produced firearms of a standard quality in the 19th century, which made the deployment of large bodies of men suicidal. From then until the mid-20th century the development of firearms went down the route of precision in manufacture and high training to allow individuals to make the most effective use of them and make each individual soldier a marksman. In theory there is nothing wrong with this but in practice, as had been discovered in the 15th century, you get far more effective results from thousands of men discharging muskets simultaneously than a few hundred skilled men aiming at specific targets. So now the practice is again massed volume fire and weapons which can be used by soldiers who have the minimum amount of training.

This 'volume fire' is vital, as operational research into ambushes has shown that 90 % of casualties occur in the first 10 seconds and it takes an average of 50 rounds fired to secure a fatal hit.

If we know that in 1920 the rate of aimed rifle fire for the trained British regular soldier was 15 rounds per minute that would be 2.5 rounds in 10 seconds. In theory it would require 450 rounds to be fired in ten seconds to kill the nine men in the first tender which would have required the rapid fire of 180 men. However that is the theory. In practice, because they were in a group in the back of the tender it would take a lot less than that; let us say 50 would be sufficient.

If we believe Barry's claim that only half his men fired and there is no reason not to, because he constantly stressed their lack of experience and half of those who did fire were not in a position to fire effectively, we are to believe that nine inexperienced teenagers got off six rounds apiece in 10 seconds. Not only that, they achieved the same accuracy in semi-darkness as was normally achieved by trained professionals in clear daylight?

Whatever one says about Michael Collins it cannot be denied that he had a considerable natural intelligence and he carried out operational research to ensure he could kill people effectively and quickly. Richard Abbott tells us that his men had been waiting to kill Detective Sergeant Smith of the Dublin Metropolitan Police near his home for several nights. When they eventually saw him, they opened fire with 0.38 revolvers hitting him several times and were amazed to see that he could still keep running for his home.

With his clear analytical mind Collins studied the incident and in future made sure that his assassins were armed with 0.45 revolvers. He also had them work in pairs and divided the task of killing between them, with one man detailed to hit the victim in the body where the heavy 0.45 bullets would knock him off his feet. The second man was to fire into the target's head while he was on the ground to make sure he died. He also employed up to eight men for each killing, including backup to lookouts. This is operational research of a very high order.

But weapons can be *too* powerful and the value of a full bore military rifle at close quarters is limited. Here it is a truism that the most dangerous weapons are those of one's friends. Nobody in his right mind would consider using a rifle in confused hand-to-hand fighting except when he had a very clear shot. A bullet will go through several men before it stops and there is no guarantee that they are all enemies. This total indifference of weapons to the cause, nobility or wickedness of the victim is seldom understood by the public and comes as a considerable surprise to green troops,

These problems led to the invention of the sub-machine gun in the First World War. Armies discovered to their cost that in close fighting the trenches were too restricted to allow them use of rifles and the rifle bullets were far too powerful anyway. Consequently sub-machine guns were developed to fire low-powered pistol calibre bullets that would not pass through much more than one man at close range. Also being shorter, they were easier to use in the restricted spaces of trenches, dugouts, or in later years, vehicles.

The lack of weapon training would have been a problem with any weapon in 1920 but it has of course been overcome by Sergeant Kalashnikov's cheap and simple AK47 assault rifle. Requiring little training and little or no maintenance it is said the people in Africa can bury it for a year, then dig it up to find it still works. Light and small enough to be used by children it has killed millions by just spraying bullets in the general direction of the target.

The conclusion is that while weapons have mechanised killing and reduced the physical effort required, until very recently the main factor in any weapon's effectiveness has been a highly trained and practised soldier.

As atrocities go - and Kilmichael is nothing much - in the First World War the Australians bayoneted 18 German prisoners and thought nothing of it. The British Army to its disgrace used snipers to pick off German medical orderlies before Dunkirk and in 1940 a German unit was so incensed by the resistance of some elderly French reservists that it stood them against the wall of their pillbox and shot them when they surrendered. At Suez in 1956 a French paratrooper machine-gunned a group of helpless Egyptian dockworkers hiding in the water and in 1943 an American sergeant machine-gunned 40 German and Italian prisoners on the way to the prisoner of war cage for no reason, except perhaps personal revenge.

THE WEAPONS AT KILMICHEAL

What can we learn by examining in detail the weapons used at Kilmichael?

Well, quite a lot if you know anything about weapons and the principal weapon on both sides was the standard British Army Lee Enfield Mk 3 rifle. The Webley revolver was also used, most likely .45 calibre, and according to some reports several IRA men only had shotguns. How and when these were used is a crucial piece of evidence in building a picture of what happened, so let us examine the two close range weapons first, beginning with

The shotgun

Until quite recently shotguns were mainly designed to kill small animals for sport as with pheasant and partridge shooting or as a means of clearing farm vermin such as foxes and rabbits. This is the type of shotgun that would have been available to the IRA at Kilmichael. To be blunt about it, for killing a man the normal agricultural shotgun is only effective up to 20 yards. Certainly, to be hit by shotgun pellets at any range is unpleasant and below 15 yards you're almost certainly going to be dead because at close range a shotgun blast will take off a limb or most of the head. Beyond that, say between 15 and 20 yards you have a better chance of survival and this increases considerably after 20 yards.

As with anything else this has to be qualified and lethality depends on the size of the shot and type of restrictor or "choke" in the shotgun barrel but we are probably talking about the most common agricultural shot, a number six, that has 280 small pellets.

These are not very effective against men at a distance because the pellets (shot) are small and at a comparatively low velocity. A few yards after leaving the barrel the shot spreads out over a radius of about three to four inches to increase the chances of one of the pellets hitting the bird or animal. Naturally, for a small animal or bird one pellet is sufficient to seriously injure or kill. This is not so when a shotgun is used on people and while it can inflict terrible wounds at close range, at longer ranges the small shot and its low velocity are unlikely to produce a fatal wound. At close range the shotgun is one of the most deadly weapons available and far more effective than most pistols as the shot still has a considerable velocity and the mass is concentrated into a much smaller area, probably not more than 25 mm diameter.

At close range the main disadvantage of the shotgun is its overall length, which is why criminals normally saw off at least half of the barrel and most of the stock. They then have an extremely effective close-range weapon that is much easier to handle, the only disadvantage of course being that they normally only have two barrels with one cartridge in each and quick loading and reloading is difficult. Criminals are seldom faced with the need to reload, so this is not problem for them. However, for anyone using a shotgun for military purposes, two shots can never be enough.

The military has long realised the value of shotguns for close-range fighting and therefore developed specialised types. These have magazines containing up to a dozen rounds and both cartridges and shot used are more powerful than available to civilians. Instead of the 280 pellets in a normal No 6 cartridge, a military shotgun cartridge might have only six to eight pellets of 9 mm diameter. In certain circumstances military shotguns will literally tear a body into pieces but while such heavy cartridges were used in the trenches in the First World War they are unlikely to have been available to the IRA in 1920 who would only have had normal agricultural shot.

The Webley 0.45 revolver

The second weapon used at Kilmichael was the Webley 0.45 revolver which held six rounds of ammunition. It was, and is still, an extremely effective weapon at close range but the maximum range for accurate shooting is about 15 yards. It will of course kill at several times this range but to be hit by a revolver bullet at extreme range one has to be particularly unlucky. It is possible to fire all six cartridges in less than two seconds but then one has the problem of reloading because the rounds often have to be hand loaded one at a time. It is frequently stated that one of the police did fire a revolver at Kilmichael and the circumstances of this are considered later.

The Mills Hand Grenade

In 1914 the British Army had no hand grenades, even though grenades or granadaos had been used for almost 400 years. This was because the type of warfare most armies engaged in did not require grenades and in any case in the pre-industrial age grenades were so unreliable they were reckoned to be almost as dangerous to the user as to the enemy. Unless handled carefully, they still are.

Trench warfare changed all this and the British Army had to improvise grenades from empty jam tins filled with small stones and explosives. Something better was obviously required and an army officer named Dewandre chanced to meet Mr Mills, an engineer and manufacturer who specialised in foundry work and metal casting. Between them they developed a small hand-thrown bomb that became the British Army's standard grenade for over 50 years. In time they came to be referred to as the No. 36 hand-grenade but for the first 30 years they were usually referred to in the British army as "Mills bombs" or this was just shortened to bombs. So when writers of this period speak of "bombs" being thrown we can be reasonably certain they mean Mills bombs i.e. hand grenades.

The first bombs, or Mills Hand Grenades, were issued in early 1915 and as with any new weapon there were initial problems with defective components and handling accidents. It was quickly realised that such a dangerous weapon required proper training and intensive practical courses in both handling and combat use were held for specialist bombers.

One of the first things learned from combat was that the time delay between releasing the hand lever and the explosion was often too long. So bombers were taught to count to three <u>after</u> releasing the lever, and before throwing, so the enemy could not take avoiding action or even throw the grenade back.

The standard method of throwing a Mills bomb (grenade) became the cricket-ball bowling action with a high lob which gave a maximum optimum range of 22-yards which is the length of a cricket pitch. The high trajectory was to drop the Bombs into a 4 -feet wide trench, but for other targets, 30 yards range was normal. As in any area of activity, specialist bombers developed their skills and could exceed these range limits considerably and with a high level of accuracy.

As most people know, the Mills Bomb had deep grooves along its surface to allow it to break up into large fragments to be dispersed on detonation but as with many other fragmentation grenades of its time the fragmentation pattern was erratic. The critical thing to remember about the Mills bomb is that the blast radius was so large and powerful that the thrower had to immediately take cover to avoid injury and in enclosed spaces the Mills grenade amounted to "overkill".

18 inch sword bayonet

That a bayonet charge incites and stimulates aggression in its participants is well proven by evidence from battlefield and military studies. British and Empire soldiers of this period, including even the auxiliary and service units, had bayonet fighting as part of their basic training.

The British 1907 Pattern, 42cm, (16.5-inch), bayonet of the period was a modification of the Japanese sword bayonet and chosen to extend the length of the Lee Enfield rifle to make it long enough overall for bayonet fighting. This sword bayonet was standard equipment for every British infantryman and aggressive bayonet drill was a regularly practised skill.

However it is usually said that bayonets were more useful for chopping wood, opening tin cans, digging and a 1001 other tasks, than they were in combat. Two hundred years ago a book, *Advice to officers of the British Army* informed them "the bayonet was an excellent instrument for digging potatoes and onions and turnips".

But as the Great War progressed, the bayonet became a combat weapon of opportunity and was used when a suitable situation presented itself.

The professed ideal target areas of the body for a bayonet were the throat, the groin and the chest, the first two being the site of major arteries and cutting these caused rapid death. Most people understand that a bayonet thrust to the chest of the enemy could present problems in withdrawing the blade, whilst a stab to the groin meant the victim tended to grab the weapon and refused to let go. Obviously in hand-to-hand fighting this made the bayonet user vulnerable and so some claimed slashing at the face and the hands was more useful in disabling an enemy.

Why use the bayonet at all in close quarter fighting? Why not just shoot the enemy?

There were occasions when ammunition was low or had run out or the rifle had jammed. But one reason was that firing in close quarter fighting was putting one's comrades at risk, as a bullet could pass through several bodies.

As with all bayonets, its principal effect was psychological. As a veteran of the Monte Casino fighting in 1944 wrote, "It is the threat of the bayonet and the sight of the point that usually does the work. The man invariably surrenders before the point is stuck into him." Many enemies are prompted to surrender when faced by cold steel and in the Second World War it was noted that Australian infantryman in particular were willing and proficient users of the bayonet. In the battle for Crete in 1941 an Australian veteran thought the bayonet was a "pretty handy weapon" and noted that victory usually went to the side that decided to charge first. In these circumstances a military historian wrote that those on the receiving end usually remembered an urgent appointment elsewhere.

The number of casualties inflicted by bayonets on the enemy in the First World War was comparatively small. Apparently the total was never systematically recorded, but including injuries and deaths due to accidents etc. it was put at 1%. However the British official casualty record is 0.3% of the total casualties. Some accounts state of that 0.3% the percentage mortality was high due to shock and heavy loss of blood.

Anyone who reads military history can clearly see that bayonet fighting is very rare indeed. That is not to say that bayonets are not used, but as one historian wrote, "For most of the Great War bayonets were an anachronism, useful as a toasting fork, biscuit slicer or an intimidator of prisoners".

However all this conceals the value of the bayonet for one unspoken combat practice. The bayoneting of apparently unconscious enemy casualties to "make sure", which is one of the areas where the rules of warfare and the reality of war part company.

The rules make it quite clear that provided they have ceased fighting, wounded enemy must not be injured and must be helped and anything else constitutes a war crime. However individuals may "play dead" to avoid injury and decide to start fighting again when the immediate danger is past.

In the First World War, a British unit pinned down in a forward position was losing a man a day to a sniper and being experienced they realised he had to be behind them. The only place he could be was in a group of German dead lying in the open between them and the main British line. After two days they had a marksman watch them and sure enough one of the "dead" came to life, albeit for the last time. Which is why soldiers do bayonet wounded; not out of malice, or brutality, but as a simple precaution.

But with the exception of the shotgun, the weapons described are peripheral to any account of Kilmicheal.

The main weapon that is supposed to have been used is the Lee Enfield Mk 4 rifle, the British Army's standard weapon from the early 1900s to the 1960s. The reason I say *supposed* to be used will be explained later but sufficient to say that this rifle was in British service for over 60 years. Which most soldiers and weapons specialists would say was at least 20 years too long.

The first thing that needs to be understood with any rifle is that the sights have to be adjusted or "zeroed" to suit every soldier.

This is because every man holds a rifle in a particular way every time and looks through the sights in the same unique way every time. Therefore the sights have to be adjusted to his individual line of vision if any kind of accuracy is to be achieved. This zeroing is normally done on the range at 200 yards from the target. The soldier fires five rounds at the centre of the target which is then inspected to see where the rounds actually hit and this might be anywhere but the centre.

The important thing is that all five rounds are grouped together and ideally they will all be in a 50 mm radius if the man is a consistently good shot. It is then a matter of mechanically adjusting the sights on the rifle to bring the fall shot onto the centre of target.

A well-trained riflemen can correct the sights of his weapon using as little as 15 rounds, five to see where it is firing, five after he has made his adjustments and the final five to check that both his aim and the sights are consistent. However with a recruit, even a natural marksman, this can take several hours because the adjustment has to be done by an experienced man or NCO and the average soldier can use 30 or more rounds simply correcting his sights.

It is also important to understand the sights on the Enfield Mk 4 in 1920 were quite different from those used 20 years later. The foresight remained pretty much the same, with a small flat blade over the muzzle and prominent site protectors on either side. The rear sight, on the other hand, was about halfway down the barrel and consisted of a 'V" shaped notch, the height of which could be adjusted by a slide to allow for ranges up to about 800 meters.

This was a disadvantage as the back, or rear, sight was actually about 300 mm away from the rifleman's eye while the blade foresight was about another 450 mm forward of this. In the final modification of the rifle introduced in the Second World War this was corrected and a circular aperture sight provided at the rear of the rifle 30mm or so from the firer's eye. One should not need to spell out the difficulty of aligning two objects 300 mm and 750 mm from one's eye as compared to two objects 30mm and 750 mm from the eye, particularly in the poor light conditions that existed at Kilmichael on that late November afternoon.

Another feature of the Enfield rifle, which is very important, is the way the cartridges were loaded. The rounds were issued fitted into clips of five and the magazine held 10 rounds. The bolt that loaded and emptied the chamber was held open, while a clip of five was placed on top of the magazine. The rounds were pressed down with the thumb and the process repeated with the second clip. The bolt was then pushed forward to load the first round and locked down.

A small but vital detail is that each cartridge case had a projecting rim on the base to allow it to be extracted after firing and because of this they had to be positioned in the clip in a certain manner. If this was not done the cartridges would not load smoothly into the magazine, and if they were forced in they were likely to jam at some point when being pushed into the chamber. All these things were overcome by training and the highly professional British Army of 1914 had no problems, nor indeed did the well-trained volunteer armies later in the First World War.

But overcoming these difficulties, even the simple matter of ensuring the cartridges were in the clip in the correct order, took a lot of practice before it became instinctive. It might be of interest to point out that this problem would have been completely eliminated had the rifle used a cartridge with a groove around the base instead of a projecting rim, but when it was introduced the British government had several million rimmed cartridges in its depots and had no wish to throw them away. One could speculate on the number of British soldiers who died in the panic and confusion of battle because they did not check that their cartridges were correctly placed in the loading clip. However, the consolation is that the British taxpayers must have saved a few pounds by not having to throw away millions of cartridges in 1900.

Having said all this, it is accepted that the British regulars in 1914 were probably the best trained riflemen in the world. Regardless of the difficulties in loading their weapons every man was required to fire 15 aimed rounds per minute which is quite remarkable when you consider that in this time they would have to completely reload their magazines with 10 fresh rounds. One does not have to be a mathematician to appreciate that this gives a rate of fire of at least one round every four seconds.

It is worth mentioning that in Oliver Stone's movie *JFK*, he has the two leading characters explain to each other how Lee Harvey Oswald could not have got off the three fatal rounds in eight seconds. Even though Lee Harvey Oswald had served in the Marine Corps and was a consistently good marksman they informed the world that it was not possible for him to achieve the rate of fire required of every single British regular soldier in 1914. Furthermore in tests, a highly trained man could fire at twice the standard rate, getting off 30-aimed shots a minute. The British soldiers' test was actually called the "Mad Minute", in which the firer had to put the required 15 rounds into a target at 300 yards, but many could actually exceed this and achieve 25 hits.

Finally we must consider another technical detail, the combined length of the British Army rifle with a fixed bayonet. The Lee Enfield was 50 inches long and with

18-inch bayonet this would increase to 68 inches long. Except at a military parade you will never see troops riding in vehicles with rifles and fixed bayonets. In the restricted space of a lurching vehicle the chance of the men bayoneting each other is very high. In the rush to escape from a vehicle under attack, soldiers carrying a 68 inch-long (1.5M) bayoneted rifle would not only find it difficult to get out, they would be almost certain to impale each other in the process.

CHAPTER 5

ONE WEEK'S TRAINING

Great play is made in Republican accounts of the fact that Barry's column had only a week's training before going into action.

As Dr Hart discovered this was at best half true, but anyway we are expected to believe that his ability as a soldier was so great that he could take 36 ordinary Irishmen, few of whom were no more than 20, and in just one week transform them into soldiers. Not just soldiers but soldiers who could defeat a group of British officers with years of combat experience in Europe's bloodiest war for centuries. To anyone who knows anything about military training such an assertion is absurd.

So far as skills, weapons and abilities are concerned, the military are the most unprejudiced people in the world and there are no boundaries, political, scientific or social they will not cross to learn new techniques.

Much is made in Irish accounts of the fact that Barry's book is in the library of the Britain's Royal Military College at Sandhurst and this alone is cited as proof of his military skill. We are to believe the British were so impressed by his achievements that they studied his methods!

It is quite possible his book or books are held there but it is a quantum leap from having a book in a library to claiming it is a standard textbook. The most interesting things about the memoirs of many IRA and Sinn Fein leaders is not their motivation or methods, which are admittedly of interest, but what they reveal about themselves. Anyone who reads these memoirs would have to agree with the British officer who observed that the IRA are not noted for their modesty or reticence and one can therefore learn a lot from them.

Consequently if Barry had achieved such spectacular results in just a week, every army on earth would study his training methods. Basic military training requires an absolute minimum of six weeks to produce a soldier and it is then reckoned it needs another three months at his unit to bring him to a useful level of proficiency.

As Reinfret tells us, even basic training in handling a rifle safely and efficiently took many hours. This confirms my statement that the Lee Enfield rifle used at Kilmichael was simple and effective but required a level of skill that it would be impossible to teach in a week.

Thorough basic training is the bedrock of an army and allied commanders up to and including Winston Churchill had a tremendous respect for the German army. This respect was earned by its combat efficiency and this in turn was based on what was possibly the most thorough training programme in the world. Not for the German Army Churchill's lamentable practice of throwing green, semi-trained troops into battle for political purposes.

Every army has a comprehensive set of manuals collectively referred to as "the book". The difference between the German army and any other is that every German soldier is expected to learn the book by heart. Pierre Reinfret observed that the American army had a manual for everything but its manuals were nothing like as thorough as those of the Germans whose officers at the height of the war still had to learn a drill for presenting flowers to their commanding officer's wife.

Nevertheless Reinfret put his survival down to the fact that in the two years before he went into combat he read every single manual he could get his hands on, regardless of whether it was directly combat related or not. He learned that even field hygiene was important, but considered that the standard of basic combat training among many American replacements in the last year of the war was not just bad, but absolutely criminal. It was so poor he described them as nothing more than meat being sent to the grinder and his experience is not unique. In other American units the veterans were appalled to find that casualty replacements did not even know how to handle their personal weapons let alone understand the capabilities of tanks and artillery.

In my opinion those responsible for sending them into action so ill-trained should have been prosecuted for manslaughter, or in the case of the United States, second-degree murder.

By contrast, while the Germans may have had a manual for presenting flowers they also carried out thorough field training. This included the use of live ammunition on a scale that caused casualties that would be unacceptable in any other army. A senior German officer observed that these casualties were unfortunate but unavoidable and looked at in the cold light of military reality he was correct. If casualties suffered in training with live ammunition produced greater confidence and proficiency in the use of weapons you will almost certainly suffer a lot fewer casualties in the real thing. Their training methods allowed the Germans to produce the best-trained and most effective soldiers in the world and by having learned their trade the auxiliaries who died at Kilmichael were in every sense their equal.

I have mentioned ammunition requirements and we are constantly reminded that the IRA were short of ammunition and would often go into action with as little as 50 rounds per man. As pointed out, the British Army used an absolute minimum of 35 rounds for the most basic range practice and this was just to check that a soldier was proficient and to set his sights. Barry had nothing like the amount of ammunition required for the most basic sighting of their weapons, never mind the time or skill to do it.

I purposely avoided direct reference to other writers in the text but in the matter of the amount of ammunition available to the IRA at Kilmichael there are references of particular interest. In his book, Dr Hart quotes from Barry's report to his superiors on the ambush in which he mentioned he had a hundred rounds per man.

This has been seized on by one of Hart's most ferocious critics, Meda Ryan, a native of county Cork, the niece of one of the participants at Kilmichael and author of a biography of Barry. In her book to quote one patriotic writer she was "driven by a genuine heuristic urge" - to put it philosophically - by a desire to find out.

Her search for the truth about Barry's career and Kilmichael led her to conclude that he was indeed a mighty warrior, the auxiliaries were treacherous men and everything the IRA side said about the affair was true. It is hardly surprising that since then she has been asked to address the annual commemoration ceremony on the ambush site. By contrast the same writer who praised her work concluded that Dr Hart was just an apologist.

The interesting thing she challenges Dr Hart on is his quote from Barry's report to his superiors that they had a hundred rounds per man. This cannot be true, therefore the report is British forgery. I would say that this is quite usual as I know of no instance of documents which challenge patriotic accounts or reflect badly on the IRA which are not held to be British forgeries.

She asserts that if Barry had had a hundred rounds per man he could have stormed the Auxiliaries' base at Macroom Castle, not just ambushed an 18 strong patrol. As it happens she confirms most accounts of the IRA's ammunition availability and therefore unwittingly supports my assertion that they were insufficiently practiced or equipped to carry out a proper ambush at Kilmichael. I have also no doubt that Barry was such a great commander that with a hundred rounds per man he could have stormed Macroom Castle. Therefore Ireland should be extremely grateful that he did not have 200 rounds per man or he would probably have marched on Moscow. Such is his standing in County Cork that people there would have no doubt that he could have taken Moscow too, but as with the Anglo-Irish treaty the victory would have been thrown away by weak politicians and traitors.

Arguments about important details like ammunition aside, it has never occurred to anyone to ask why they were sent into action after only a week's training.

As the IRA frequently say, they had been observing the movements of the auxiliaries for some time and they were using fixed routes. Logically they could easily have waited until their men had at least a month's training before ambushing them. Of course the usual reason given is the need to protect the civil population of the area from the depredations of the brutal British.

It has been pointed out that however many times the IRA cite this as justification for the ambush, no evidence has ever been presented of just where these assaults on the civil population occurred. Bearing in mind that Collins boasted that he had a direct line to independent newspaper columnists in London who would print pretty much anything he gave them this is more than surprising.

Nevertheless we are repeatedly told that Tom Barry, Ireland's legendary guerrilla leader could produce soldiers to beat the best in the world in just a week. All professional soldiers would consider this assertion to be too absurd to be worth considering even if Barry was a military genius - which despite all assertions he was not - and even accepting that Irishmen are natural soldiers, which to some degree they are.

No, I think the fact that they were used after only a week's training was driven by something else,

THAT THERE WAS A TIME IMPERATIVE DRIVEN BY AN EVENT FAR AWAY FROM COUNTY CORK.

CHAPTER 6

MILITARY ORGANISATION
& RANK STRUCTURE

The majority of Irish historians, as opposed to patriotic praise singers, comment on the IRA's capacity to scale up its actions in this period. As the English historian Edward Norman wrote in his very unpopular history of Ireland 20 years ago, "A shot fired at a police station constituted an attack and if a couple of shots were returned it was a gun battle". I would add that if they repeated the exercise a couple of hours later it would become a "two-hour gun battle".

This is nowhere more apparent than in the description of the IRA's military organisation that appears in all published work. This is particularly apparent at Kilmichael where the unfortunate 16-year-old boy who was killed with the IRA is described as the column's "Signals Lieutenant". This would suggest that he was a specialist trained in the vital task of unit communications, whereas any normal commander with a unit of this size would have said he was the "platoon runner". To use the civilian term of "messenger boy" would be nearer the truth but it sounds unnecessarily dismissive and that is not my intention. As it happens in the military the runner or messenger is usually a good soldier of higher than average intelligence, such as one Adolf Hitler. He was still just a messenger.

Unlike 50 years ago, most people today simply do not understand the military organisation or the armed services rank structure. It always puzzled me as a schoolboy in Britain why the cheap diaries we got always included details of the rank insignia of the three armed services.

I later realised that this was very useful at a time when boys were likely to be conscripted into one of the services at the age of 18. Nevertheless, in the interest of general education it is worthwhile setting down a guide to the rank structure among armies in 1920. This has not changed much, but the numbers in each unit have, as infantry battalions in 1920 were about a 1,000 strong. Today they seldom exceed 600.

Starting from the bottom then:

Lieutenant or Second Lieutenant – Commands a platoon of 50 men
Captain - Second in command of a company
Major - Commands a company of four platoons, total 200 men
Lieutenant Colonel - Commands a battalion of five companies with a total of 1,000 men.
Colonel - Can command a battalion but his rank may be a staff or administrative appointment.
Brigadier-General - In the British Army usually described simply as Brigadier, in the American army one-star General. In the infantry he commands a brigade of four infantry battalions with specialist units for transport, signals, artillery, engineering and medical services normally totalling about 5,000 men.

Major General - in the American army two-star General. Commands a corps of three or four brigades of the total of up to 20,000 men.

Lieutenant General - in the American army three-star general, commands the three or four corps described as an "army" with up to 80,000 men.

General - in the American army four-star general, commands any number of corps usually described as an army

Field Marshall - In the American army five-star general, commands several armies or a very senior staff appointment.

The organisation of the rank structure in the IRA at this time defies analysis in conventional military terms. Barry expressed rage because British officers did not treat IRA generals with the respect due to their rank, particularly as they were generals in an army that had defeated them. I cannot see the British were unduly arrogant in this respect as an officer in any regular army can be excused a little incredulity if not amusement when meeting a 25 year-old general whose command would only be appropriate to a captain.

Reference is made in Irish history books to the Bandon battalion of the IRA and the "Skibberen battalion" as though each of these was a conventional formation a thousand strong.

Even British official documents refer to these formations as battalions, but the population of Bandon in 2005 was just 1,500 and if you include the surrounding area you would get up to a total of 4,500. To put this in context, in the patriotic rush to join up in

1914 British towns and cities tried to raise their own battalions of "Pals". The Lancashire town of Accrington and the surrounding area had a population of little over 40,000 and just managed to produce 1,000 fit men required. They were known as the "Accrington pals" and tragically most of them were killed on the first day of the Somme. But nevertheless writers glibly talk about Irish villages with less than one 10th of Accrington's population having their own IRA battalions. Statistically the Bandon battalion would not be more than 110 strong or little more than one 10th the size of a normal battalion. In fact given that every fit man in Bandon had joined the IRA they would only have had enough for half a company, not a battalion.

We might put this whole thing into context by referring to Barry's file at the Public Record Office in Kew. This shows the extent to which the British, by simply recording the IRA's descriptive terms for its military structure can actually mislead historians about its actual strength. Barry's file records that he was an "officer commanding dispatch riders and scouts, the IRA's Bandon battalion before being appointed Commandant of the Skibbreen Battalion". British records therefore implied that the Bandon district with only 4,500 people today and Skibberen with a similar size population, raised 1,000 strong battalions for the IRA. This is too ridiculous to require detailed dismissal.

From reading the various patriotic accounts it is apparent that while most armies have about 14 non-commissioned and officer ranks below General the IRA only has five ranks and in ascending order these are,

Volunteer
Lieutenant*
Captain
Commandant
General

* There is also a rank of "First Lieutenant", it seems this is an automatic honorary promotion for any IRA man below the rank of Captain who gets killed.

A village would have anything from 10-30 men to form a "company" and there could be any number of companies in a "battalion" and any number of battalions in a "Brigade". One assumes every "company" had a "captain" and if there were say 30 men he would have a "lieutenant". A battalion would have a "Commandant" while the next step up was full General who commanded two or more battalions in a "brigade". So by using no more than language one or at most two hundred men less than quarter of who had weapons let alone service rifles acquire the status of a regular formation 5000 strong with artillery, cavalry, engineers, signallers and other sub-units. No one then or now bothers to look past the language to see what was in fact a paper army. This is understandable because tragic as it was for the victims it was mostly a paper war as Collins himself acknowledged.

The value of using military ranks and terms cannot be underestimated when describing IRA attacks. Elsewhere in the book I refer to an ambush at Rineen and what happened there is simply told. An IRA man had been killed in an attack on the police some time previously and they wanted revenge. The local RIC happened to make a regular journey at much the same time every week and IRA had noted this. Consequently they decided to ambush them and one day at the appropriate time up to 50 of them lay in wait for the single lorry and 6 men.

The attack opened with two grenades being thrown by a former American soldier both of which missed. This did not matter because the rest of the IRA opened up at once firing at point blank range with six to eight rifles using exploding bullets. The 4 police in the back of the truck were wounded or killed immediately while the sergeant in the front seat was severely wounded and died the following day. The sixth man initially escaped but was tracked across the bog and killed.

The ambush would have taken less than five minutes if one excludes following and killing the escapee. However before the IRA had cleared the scene a military party who were looking for a kidnapped magistrate chanced along. There then followed a gun battle in which a great number of rounds were expended by both the army and the IRA without casualties to either side. This is actually not uncommon with inexperienced troops let alone freedom fighters particularly when the weapons have not been zeroed (calibrated).

One can look at the whole business rationally and say that 50 countrymen were determined to avenge the death of one of their number who had been killed by the RIC. Presumably this occurred when the RIC had shot back on being ambushed but in the IRA lexicon when one of their people is killed it is always a "murder". This raises their subsequent killings above the sordid business of revenge onto the plane of "justice".

It is worth mentioning that of the six RIC Constable's killed only one was a British. The other five were all ordinary members of the RIC most with 8 or more years' service so only one of the dead was a "Black and Tan"

Quite simply 50 murderous countrymen were out for revenge but that is not the way it is told.

The patriotic account is in the appendix but it describes how men from seven of the 9 IRA companies in the battalion area took part in the ambush. As noted a normal battalion would only have five companies with a total of 1000 men. That about 200 countrymen with less than 20 rifles between them should make up 9 companies and style themselves as a battalion doesn't strike anyone in Ireland as preposterous. On the contrary it shows how heroic they were because in the Irish mind 200 men with 20 rifles are taking on the might of the British Empire. That "Taking on the might of the British Empire" consists of killing 6 policemen, five of them Irishmen, in a couple of minutes is just a boring detail and does not diminish their heroism.

That they were largely protected from military reprisals by the legal system upheld by the men they killed would not be of any consequence to them either. Neither would it be of any consequence that the same legal system would continue to be enforced after "freedom was won" by very much the same men they were heroically killing. Unless it was to claim that their "glorious victory" had been thrown away and demand further killing so their "heroism" was not wasted.

However there are reports that in the aftermath of the attack police and troops smashed up and burned property in surrounding villages. This might well be true or it might be a result of another rather sordid blow struck by the freedom fighters in the same area at the time. The troops who stumbled on the aftermath of the ambush were actually looking for a magistrate who had been wounded and kidnapped by the same IRA. It is reported that he was buried on a local beach up to his neck and left to drown on the incoming tide. However when the IRA returned they were surprised to find that due to changes in the tide pattern they had buried him above the high-water mark. Nothing daunted they dug the wretched man up and buried him further down the beach so he would be certain to drown in the next tide.

Whether the troops and police took it out on the nearby villages in the aftermath of the killing of the police at Rineen or after finding the drowned magistrate is difficult to say. My guess is it would be the latter because many of the accounts of the heroic men of the East Clare Brigade do not mention these attacks by the troops. If these were in retaliation for the sadistic killing of the magistrate it would not do to draw anyone's attention to them.

There are of course memorials to the heroic men of East Clare and the committee has been set up to see that the centenary of Rineen is properly commemorated. I doubt they will commemorate burying the magistrate alive below high-tide mark. While they would probably see no shame in commemorating this it would be difficult to make speeches over a hole in a beach. Also accurate re-enactment would involve some interesting problems. Should they dig the hole in the wrong place and return the following day to dig the second hole? Should the re-enactors dig the hole or holes by hand or save time by bringing in a mechanical digger?

CHAPTER 7

THE BLACK & TANS

Who were the Black and Tans and why do they inspire not just hatred but real loathing to this day? Not only in Ireland, but from the intelligentsia and academics in Britain and America. Sir Roy Strong in his *History of Britain* refers to the fact that the government sent them to Ireland as part of Britain's "irredeemable shame".

One could cynically say that they committed the greatest crime anyone connected with the British government can commit in Ireland. That was to shoot back. Accurately.

My father was immensely proud of his connections with the British Army and attended The Royal Hibernian School for the sons of soldiers. While he regularly reminded us that our grandfather served as a Sergeant in the 11th Hussars and they were an elite cavalry regiment, he was just as virulent in his hatred of the Black and Tans as anyone else and just as ill informed about the reality.

When we first moved to England, an elderly neighbour had been a Black and Tan and on discovering this I referred to him contemptuously as only a 12-year-old can, as "The Black and Tan".

However my parents were conscious that living in England we could hardly insult the host population and responded to me by telling me, "Shut up you!" This aggressive and outraged attitude has carried on through later generations. In the early 1990s my daughter and her then boyfriend - second-generation Irish father and English mother - were watching the film *Michael Collins*. I remarked that there was more to the Black and Tans than most people knew. I am not sure that the young man had ever been to Ireland but his response was amazing, his face contorted with rage as he spat out, "They were rapists and murderers they sent over there!"

Of course they get the universally bad showing in plays and films. In the 1950s a British film *Shake Hands With the Devil* set in the 1920 Troubles has a scene where senior British officers are meeting to decide tactics against the IRA. At one point they turn to an officer who has the attitude of a gangster whom they clearly dislike and we find he is the commander of the Black and Tans. This was probably a fair statement of the attitude of regular army officers towards the Black and Tans but as we shall see it does not reflect anything like the credit on them that is implied.

About the only man who comes anywhere near the truth is the Reverend Norman who says that the Black and Tans were men "eternally damaged by the war". While being true it is too simple and smacks of an excuse.

So let us begin by saying that wars totally change the perspective of every man who serves in them. How this change affects their later life depends very much on the nature of their experience and the character of the individual but there will be a very small number of men who can never recover their former way of life.

They can be found in every war and in Michael Heller's famous book on the Vietnam War, *Dispatches* he tells of meeting a soldier of the elite reconnaissance Force, the "Lurps". This man had done one tour of duty in a regular infantry battalion which suffered heavy casualties before joining the elite Green Berets. During his first tour with them he was the sole survivor of a patrol having managed to conceal himself while the Vietcong finished off his comrades with knives "just to make sure". After that there is nothing left for him but the even more exclusive "long-range patrol force" the "Lurps" and he has ceased to have any life or purpose other than the war. Such men are an exception but generally combat veterans are not people to mess with and some are very dangerous men indeed.

Sensible people, even their own officers, leave veterans alone. During the First World War a young officer noticed that the Military Police ever-present at the major London railway stations generally made a nuisance of themselves with the soldiers. However men who were obviously veterans, men with "the smell of death and the trenches about them, men fresh from the killing" they carefully avoided. The Military Police were having a soft war in London and they knew better than to mess with the men who were not.

In the Second World War it was not much different and in 1943 Alex Bowlby was undergoing basic training at a camp in England with a battalion that was being sent to Italy having been rested and reinforced. He was surprised one day when there were no officers or NCOs to be seen anywhere on the camp and found it was because the veterans of the Western Desert were rejoining that day. They had already survived three years of desert warfare and made it clear they thought that was enough, they had done their share and now it was someone else's turn. They marched into the camp like a mob, uniforms in every state of disarray shouting 'Where's the f******g Sergeant Major!" so it was hardly surprising that authority stayed out of sight until they had settled down.

Of course the liberals who run British television have never had any sympathy for the Black and Tans and in the early 1960s the BBC showed a play, *The Iron Harp* which was about the Irish Troubles. Such plays were part of a political program as we now know that the British government had been warned that the IRA was preparing a new campaign against Northern Ireland. The 1950s campaign had failed under pressure from the British and Irish governments but Britain's "New men" of the 1960s decided that a "modem" approach was the order of the day. Consequently, the IRA and Ireland were now getting sympathetic treatment in the British media which was a considerable change from 10 years earlier when the IRA were always portrayed as villains.

The plot of *The Iron Harp* involved an IRA veteran, blinded in an ambush and a British officer held in his house as a prisoner and of course, a pretty girl with whom both IRA man and the officer are in love. The officer's feelings for the girl are returned and when he is freed he promises to marry her in "the little Catholic Church" near his home village in England. The drama is provided when the IRA decide to shoot three of the prisoners as a reprisal for the execution of three of their men. The executions formed the opening scene of the play and were made worse by the fact that the IRA men were not allowed to see a priest before being shot. The victims of the IRA's reprisal are to be selected by the blind IRA man drawing names out of a hat and of course the last name drawn is the officer whom he personally likes and the girl loves.

Early on in the play the blind IRA man asks the officer, now that he has seen for himself what decent fellows the IRA are, "Whose side are you on now?" He confirms that he is a decent fellow himself by saying forcefully "Well I'm not on the side of the Tans!" The Black and Tans' awfulness is confirmed when a couple of coarse brutes burst into the house having survived an ambush nearby. They find the blind IRA man alone, recognise him, and are about to carve him up with knives when in the nick of time the IRA arrive to save him. The Tans' demeanor then changes to one of abject terror and they are led away as prisoners.

So why did the British Army hold them in such contempt to the satisfaction of the IRA and the righteous approval of the British intelligentsia? Also, why does the officer's attitude in the play - which may have been based on the truth - reflect such little credit on the British officer corps?

Essentially the much reported contempt of regular army officers for the Black and Tans was rooted, not for what they were, or even much what they did, but in *who* they were.

If one looks at the background details of ex-officers recruited into the Auxiliaries Division of the RIC, including many of those who died at Kilmichael one thing springs out at you. They may have formerly been officers but their home addresses were not given as "Courts", "Halls", "Villas", "Houses" or even "Avenues" but as just house numbers in "Streets", "Roads" and "Terraces".

The Officer class at that time might just have their homes on "Roads" but never in "Streets" and "certainly not in "Terraces" which were about as poor and common as you could get. This social detail tells you many Auxiliaries were working class men who had been promoted to the commissioned ranks during the war, something absolutely unthinkable before 1916. Some of the Auxiliaries had even been officers in non-combat formations such as the Chinese Labour Corps but most seem to have served with distinction in front line units of all three services.

Prior to the war the British and German Armies' recruitment of officers was restricted to a very narrow social class and selection had nothing to do with the level of education but was based on where you were educated, your class and particularly whether you had a good private income.

R C Sherriff, who wrote probably the best British play about the First World War, *Journey's End* was initially turned down for a commission. Regardless of his background and education, the school he attended was not on the official lists of schools considered suitable for potential officers so he was rejected. When he protested, "It was a 400-year-old Grammar School and had been founded by Queen Elizabeth!" he was cheerfully told, "Sorry old chap, it's not on my list."

The appalling casualties among young officers rapidly changed this attitude and men were often promoted to commissioned ranks on the recommendation of their colonel alone and commissions were open to almost all who survived and could show their ability as leaders. At the end of the war, to the disgust of regular officers, many of the war promoted officers continued to serve because the war had allowed them to rise far up the social scale and they wished to stay there.

There appears to have been nothing the army could do to get rid of them other than make their lives in the peacetime regular regiments as unpleasant as possible. One of the Irish/German poet Robert Graves' fellow officers in The Royal Welsh Fusiliers was a captain who had been an escapologist performing on various seafronts before war - quite simply a busker. As such he would frankly have been socially unacceptable to the respectable working class, let alone to upper-class army officers. The colonel made his feelings about such officers clear by having two messes, an open mess for the unacceptable war commissioned hoi polloi and a mess to which access was by his personal invitation for himself and the "gentry" officers. This attitude, however disgraceful it seems to us today, appears to have been common throughout the army.

Cadet Hooper-Jones, one of the auxiliaries killed at Kilmichael is an example of a working class man commissioned as a matter of necessity during the war.

He was as far from being a product of the slum and criminal classes as it was possible for a working class man to be, being born and living in the Lancashire hamlet of Hawkshaw, near Bury, which was built near a small cotton mill. Even today when it has become a village and a quiet dormitory area there is little or no public transport to it and the nearest town of any size is six miles away. Six miles may not be much today but in the early 20th century when travel any distance could only be done by railway it might as well have been 60 miles, so he lived well off the beaten track.

In civilian life Hooper-Jones had been valet to the mill owner and then a grocer's assistant. This was far from making him a gentleman but both occupations were very respectable at the time and considered a cut above the average mill worker. He would have had to be intelligent, courteous as a matter of routine and would naturally have learned how to dress and act like a gentleman.

Like many young men at the time he joined the local Territorial Army unit, partly out of Patriotism but probably for a chance to break the monotony of village life and the adventure of attending the annual training camps. The Scots comedian Billy Connolly scoffed at his own service in the Territorial Army singing, "The way to see the world my boys I've been to Edinburgh twice". But it would have been quite something for a young man in the early 1900s to go to a camp 30 miles from home and spend a week with young men, let alone go to Edinburgh. This was still true until the 1960s when as a matter of interest Billy Connolly himself attended a training camp in Cyprus long before package holidays made "lads' holidays" and Mediterranean destinations commonplace for everyone . . . so much for his having been to Edinburgh twice.

Hooper-Jones was called up with his battalion of the Lancashire Fusiliers in 1914 and, along with many other Territorials, he was sent to Egypt and there promoted to Lance-corporal, one grade below Tom Barry. He must have had military ability because unlike Barry he was then commissioned into the Northumberland Fusiliers.

His experience as a valet would have been invaluable as he would be familiar with the dress, manners and attitudes of the middle class, so as an intelligent man all he would have needed to do to fit in would be to adjust his accent. It would have been be quite normal for him to transfer out of the Lancashire Fusiliers as it was rare for a man promoted from the ranks to remain in his own regiment. He was fortunate enough to survive the war as most young officers did not, and he would have gained considerable combat experience in France.

With the end of the war and the running down of the army he had not only survived four years of bloody combat, he had enjoyed the incredible privileges of an army officer at that time. For a grocer's assistant living in a terraced cottage in Lancashire to have become an officer would have been beyond his wildest dreams when he joined the TA. Not only had he experienced the social status of an officer but also the very practical benefits, good living quarters, good food with his own servant or batman as a matter of right and these were things few men would want to lose.

The fact that he and others like him had no private income to support their new position would not be a problem during the war because officers would spend so much time on active service they would not need money. Even when they were out of the line opportunities for expensive living would have been few and far between and when they existed he would have accumulated enough back pay to allow him to afford it.

This all changed with peacetime when officers were expected to maintain an expensive social life and that would have been quite beyond his means. It was therefore a choice of going back to being a grocer's assistant in Hawkshaw or, if he could, remaining in the services. Like many young men in the same position joining the auxiliaries, the risks of serving in Ireland would have been considered acceptable after surviving several years on the front line in France and much preferable to returning to life in the village grocery store.

The future Field Marshal Sir William Slim found himself in the same position but solved it in another way. Slim had been a teacher in a poor - one hesitates to say slum - school and then a factory clerk in Birmingham before the war. Like many war commissioned officers he understood that without a private income he could not hope to stay in the post war regular army, but he had no intention of going back to a clerk's stool in a

Birmingham factory. During the war a colleague from his office whom he kept in touch with all his life asked him, "Are you coming back to sit on the stool next to me after this is all over Bill?" His quiet answer spoke for many men, "I'm never going back to that!"

His solution was to apply for a commission in the West India Regiment where the soldiers were black and consequently the regiment was prepared to accept officers who were to quote Slim, "Chaps who had no money". Fortunately for the army and country he was able to transfer to the Indian Army where officers could live on their pay and while they were still looked down on by the British Army they were nevertheless some way above the officers of black infantry.

That is why many regular army officers despised the Black and Tans. Not because of their brutality but because they were working class and lower middle class men who had risen well above their social position.

Consequently, when the government wished to recruit experienced men to clean up the mess its inaction had created in Ireland it had no shortage of volunteers. Fighting the IRA was a lot less dangerous than anything they had done in the war and it allowed them to maintain their newly acquired social position without the financial cost or having to face daily humiliation from their upper class "brother" officers.

It should be made clear that much as people rant about the British class system and its unpleasant aspects, this attitude is not exclusive to Britain or the British Army. Scott Fitzgerald made passing reference to it in a number of his writings. The leading character in his major novel, *The Great Gatsby*, is a working-class American who has risen to be a major in the war and taken advantage of a post war programme to study at Oxford University. Thus he had gained entry into the upper class twice over and he is determined to stay there. Likewise in the French Army, war promoted lower class officers were referred to as "brawlers" or perhaps a closer English translation would be "roughnecks". The German army had the same problem but solved it in a different way. They did not make their NCOs officers as the British, French and for that matter the Americans did, they did the logical thing and simply "appointed" senior NCOs to officers' commands. Therefore suitably experienced sergeants and sergeant-majors would be appointed to the command of companies and battalions as necessary, thus avoiding accepting them into the officer corps.

The Black and Tans provide yet another example of the historian's need to collate disparate pieces of information which may be centuries apart. We can find an almost exact parallel of the situation in Ireland in 1920 and the way the government dealt with it, in Machiavelli's classic treatise The Prince. Machiavelli was secretary to the Florentine Republic in the 15th century and analysed the politics of Renaissance Italy in such an acute manner his book is an anathema to politicians to this day. But English politicians 400 years ago had a greater grasp of harsh political truths and praised him for showing what men actually did and not what they said they did.

Essentially the British Government was faced with much the same situation the Borgia Duke faced in central Italy in the 15th century. Following a long period of political unrest the region of the Romagna had fallen under the control of powerful warlords fighting between themselves and answering to no authority other than their own. The Duke therefore appointed as governor one Don Romiro d'Orco with the authority to do whatever was necessary to establish control of the area. This he proceeded to do by employing a level of cruelty, which exceeded that of the warlords and thereby reduced them to submission. A consequence of the pacification was that the governor became one of the most hated men in Italy and by association so did his master.

Duke Valentino Borgia then showed his ruthlessness by sending a respected lawyer to investigate and report on his governor's actions. As a result of this he had his own governor executed and Don Romiro was hacked in two and his body left on display in a town square with a proclamation that the Duke had punished him for exceeding his authority and for the harm he had done to the people.

In Ireland the government had allowed the political and administrative system to fall into chaos and order had to be restored somehow. As with Duke Valentino they proceeded to send in men who could be expected to do what it was necessary but who were not part of the normal political, police and military apparatus. When the dirty job was done they did not actually repudiate them or punish them - they just let them take all the blame.

Nobody since Machiavelli has ever thought about how to deal with a ruthless political organisation that refuses to join in the normal political process, considers it normal to rig elections, refuses to negotiate and was allowed to shoot not only the police, the army but anyone deemed spies and traitors. In Ireland, and particularly in the IRA, the classification "spies and traitors" is wide enough to include just about anyone but the penalty was not always death.

Two women who had contributed a few pence to a wreath for the local police constable who had been killed by the IRA were given seven days to leave Ireland for this act of treason and they did.

Men who had served in the British Army were a particularly "legitimate target" to the extent that the IRA went into hospitals to shoot any they had only wounded in their beds. Some IRA were however more sensitive about this sort of thing and took the trouble to carry the wounded men into the streets on stretchers before shooting them again. One assumes that because the target was immobile on the second occasion they would have made sure they got it right and would not need to go back a third time.

Of course this did not only happen in Ireland. At the fall of Singapore in 1942 the Japanese bayoneted British wounded in the hospitals, and when the doctors tried to stop them bayoneting patients on operating tables they were bayoneted too. This was put down to oriental barbarism and considered an atrocity but to be fair one should say that the Japanese General visited the hospital in person to apologise on behalf of the Emperor and ordered the summary execution of several of the soldiers responsible. However, when the IRA calmly walked into Irish hospitals to shoot men in cold blood in 1920/22 nobody in Ireland then or since has thought anything of it. One assumes that unlike the Japanese who were just barbarians running amok, the Irish were motivated by military necessity and, unpleasant though it may have been, they had no option and as they usually say, "It was war, we were fighting for our freedom, it had to be done".

Much is made of the occasions when the IRA released prisoners and even helped wounded having simply taken their weapons for future use. But it would be interesting to quantify these cases against the cases of wounded men being pursued and finished off with rifle butts, the unarmed servicemen shot down in the street and most of all the civilians taken from their homes at night to be found shot with a card around their necks reading "Tried sentenced and executed by the IRA, spies and traitors beware". There were an estimated 70-80 men found in this manner and as the only paperwork found seems to have been the notice/card on the body the trial procedure is unknown.

One must also assume that those bodies found without such notices were not what the IRA Leader Joseph Sweeny called "official jobs" just the work of enthusiastic local patriots trying to help.

Time and again historians explain that the behavior of the Black and Tans was a result of their experiences on the Western Front - the war had brutalised them and they should never have been sent to Ireland. The

Western Front explanation/excuse is not wrong but misinterpreted.

By November 1918 the British Army was a thoroughly professional force and many of its soldiers had long since ceased to kill Germans just because they could and were within sight and rifle range. General Crozier told how in the final months they were following so closely behind the Germans that they could see them evacuating the trenches, but nobody bothered firing at them; except, of all people, his Welsh non-conformist chaplain who had got hold of a rifle and was blazing away. Cozier took the rifle off him and unloaded it without saying a word and said that no one could understand why the man took such pleasure in doing something they were all tired of doing. The chaplain later resigned his vocation to join an infantry battalion as a private soldier so he could shoot Germans as much as he wished.

The reality of their experience was that the war had not turned them into psychotic killers but rather into men who were indifferent to killing. They had become thoroughly professional soldiers and like all good soldiers did not exert themselves unnecessarily. If an enemy posed no threat to them they often let him go about his business because they knew killing him wasn't going to make any significant difference. But if a position had to be taken where serious fighting needed to be done, they would kill as and when necessary without a moment's hesitation or remorse.

Writing 45 years later, A E Coppard said that by two years into the war, "The men had an ingrained sense of duty and obedience in keeping with the times. They were wholly loyal to their own officers and that was as far as their confidence went. It was trust and comradeship founded on the actual sharing of dangers." Later he observed, "Though only kids (he was a veteran by the time he was 18) dealing out death was our business — whatever the rights and wrongs of the war, and we didn't know too much about that, we were in it up to our necks for better or worse."

Like the Black and Tans he had learned to soldier by instinct. To cite poet Robert Graves again, he realised how instinctive soldiering had become when on leave in North Wales. Walking in the peaceful countryside he found he was automatically looking for the most likely location of enemy machine guns, deciding where he would position his own guns and planning the best route for a counter-attack.

Men who have reached this level of professionalism are not unduly bothered about the cause, that has sunk well into the background and soldiering on its own has become a way of life. When a fully professional soldier is killed, or even attacked, it is natural for them to try and kill the attacker. If a man is shot dead in any war his friends have neither the time nor resources to investigate exactly which enemy soldier fired the fatal shot and to expect them to do so is ridiculous.

Quite apart from the simple revenge for a dead comrade, if someone has tried to kill you and failed, commonsense says you do not wait to give him a second chance. For the soldier, revenge is not a dish served cold or even to the people who deserve it, it is served in whatever portion they feel necessary regardless of the guilt or innocence of the recipient.

This applies to all front line servicemen. In the Second World War, British airmen were outraged when one of their friends was machine-gunned in his parachute after bailing out. Shortly afterwards, the squadron brought down a German aircraft in the sea and each pilot made a machine gun pass over the stricken aircraft as the crew tried to escape into their dinghy. Tragically the victims of this act of revenge were not only entirely innocent of the original killing but were certainly ignorant of it and that is the nature of war. It should be made clear that the Germans occasionally did the same thing e.g. the original commander of the 8th Army was to be General Gott but he was killed when his aircraft was shot down and the German pilot strafed the wreck setting it on fire. It is worth adding that the British pilot survived and was to meet the German 50 years later who asked, "How many were in your plane four, five?" On being told there were 18 men, many of whom were evacuated wounded he understandably broke down.

I have previously referred to Vietnam, but imagine taking a group of men who had done multiple tours there killing and seeing friends killed in the casual and indifferent nature of war. Then put a company of such men on the streets of what we euphemistically call a high-crime area where gangs have been operating without hindrance, openly killing anyone whom they thought posed the slightest threat.

The civil police have been driven out and the veterans are the first government presence for two years. The response of the gangs is to carry on as before and when they meet the first two "veterans" they question them, then put them against a wall and shoot them through the head. They then scream foul when the legal system that they have not only treated with contempt, but have actively tried to destroy fails to protect their lives.

What the Black and Tans possessed, apart from being accustomed to killing, was exceptional military skills born of the hardest experience. In every occupation and profession, regardless of theoretical education, most people naturally develop a range of skills that can never be taught in a training course or in a classroom. Everyone from a sweeper-up to a managing director gains priceless experience that allows them to deal instinctively with any situation.

The foundry man who knows by the colour of molten metal when it is right to pour, the joiner who knows by the look, weight and even the smell of a piece of timber how it will cut, the family doctor who can tell from a patient's appearance whether they are ill or not.

The Black and Tans were not criminals and rapists and the IRA's task would have been much easier if they had been.

Criminals and rapists do not have the fine honed military skills that only come with experience, the skills necessary to fight in town and country.

Criminals and rapists do not know how to move across broken ground without looking to see where they're putting their feet whilst all the time keeping their eyes on the enemy.

Criminals and rapists could not simultaneously observe where they might take cover while returning fire and keeping a mental note of the number of rounds they had fired themselves.

Criminals and rapists could not reload their weapons by a reflex action, carrying out half a dozen essential tasks, including checking the position of the rounds in the clip, positioning the cartridges, fastening ammunition pouches. All without one moment of conscious thought while simultaneously watching the enemy and assessing his firepower.

Criminals and rapists could not identify the type of weapon firing at them by its sound alone and pinpoint the location of the firer in the same way.

Criminals and rapists could not tell from the noise of a passing bullet whether it was close enough to be dangerous and they should take cover or whether the enemy was firing wildly.

As veterans they had a range of skills that a peacetime soldier could never acquire and that is what made them so formidable. Not their brutality as broadcast around the world by the Sinn Fein propaganda machine, but their cold-blooded military professionalism.

On the other hand, one can understand the indignation of the IRA on meeting the Black and Tans and this is not being sarcastic.

A BBC correspondent who took part in the airborne crossing of the Rhine in March 1945 said that no sooner had the wood and canvas glider he was travelling in come to rest than a burst of machine gun fire cut through it killing two soldiers before they had time to even open the doors. His instant reaction was to think, "That's not fair!" then he collected himself and realised that in this war there was no such thing as being fair. Despite the romantic imagery, the IRA was not the much-trumpeted secret army. Everybody knew who they were and what they were doing. They had been getting away with it unhindered for over a year, so for that reason alone it was perfectly natural for them to think not letting them carry on as before was not playing fair.

To the delight of many later Irish writers, foreign journalists told how the reputation of the Black and Tans often preceded them to towns and villages and there would be real fear in the civilian population at news of their approach. There is however a document in the British Public Record Office which tells with perhaps understandable satisfaction how this fear was transformed into surprise when the infamous "Tans" arrived. Far from wrecking the town, beating up and murdering the inhabitants, raping children and old women, they exercised perfect discipline, behaving with courtesy in a quiet and businesslike manner. The same paper noted there was no trouble from the local IRA as they had very wisely left town. This is understandable. As I have said, it is not the nature of veterans to waste energy on gratuitous violence. If left alone they will do no harm to anyone but if they are assaulted, attacked or injured their attacker can expect no mercy.

All history is a collection of lies and half-truths, but of all the lies and half-truths perpetuated by Irish historians, the reputation of the Black and Tans is unquestionably the most vicious.

It has long been known that they were not recruited from the criminal classes or the worst parts of British cities, but were ordinary men from every class whom the war had turned into professional fighting machines. It was not that they were unemployed or unemployable it was just that they went young into war and consequently soldiering was the only job they knew. Again this is best expressed by George Coppard. He was never a Black and Tan and probably never went to Ireland in his life but he wrote, "Glossing over my childhood I was an ordinary boy of elementary education and slender prospects". When he joined up in 1914 he was just 16 and leaving the army four years later he was an expert machine gunner but "an absolute numbskull in all the skills necessary to earn a living".

The dispassionate and professional outlook of the Black and Tans was best illustrated by one who was interviewed on British television in the early 1960s, along with *a* former member of the IRA from The Troubles. As I have noted at the time, the British approach to the IRA had undergone a fundamental change to being seen as quite ordinary chaps having previously been portrayed as out and out villains.

The Black and Tan who appeared on television looked as I remember him very much like the Major from Fawlty Towers, well turned out with a fine clipped moustache and very military attitude. There the resemblance to the bumbling Major in Fawlty Towers ended because this man was nobody's fool and he retained a straight-talking attitude about his experience in Ireland. He told the interviewer they didn't mind the IRA who attacked them in the countryside; that was what soldiering was about and they accepted it. But they weren't going to mess about with anyone who thought he could just go out and shoot the village policeman and get away with it. While he did not say so he would have the same approach to anyone who thought it was reasonable to shoot police and soldiers in bars when they were having a quiet drink. This sums up professional soldiers rather well, they are prepared to take their chances in any sort of regular fight or shoot-out but they have no time at all for gun happy amateur patriots.

Why the Black and Tans were called police when they were in fact soldiers is a remarkable indication of the way the functions of the police and army have become separate in the public mind. It is also a tribute to the political skill of the founder of British (and Irish) policing, Sir Robert Peel and is precisely what he intended. In the police he created a uniformed and disciplined organisation to enforce the day-to-day administration of the law but under direct civilian control.

In heavily populated mainland Britain, control of the police was originally delegated to quite small towns and counties, unlike the army which is always a national organisation firmly under central government control

The public would be surprised to know that the distinction between police and army is not as sharp as they imagine and the duties of a police force depends entirely on the action needed to enforce the law. When the Canadians had to establish some rule of law in the wild North West provinces in the 19th century they recruited mostly former British soldiers into a force that was originally to be called the North West Mounted Rifles.

It was a shrewd political move by the Prime Minister of Canada that at the last moment he crossed out the word "Rifles" in the legislation which unquestionably made them a military unit and substituted "Police". This may have been with an eye to the reaction of the United States to the Canadians sending a regular military unit into a border area where none had been before. Nevertheless, the Northwest Mounted Police faced a situation that would require more than the normal duties of civilian police so whatever they were called or later became they started as a paramilitary force.

In Ireland in 1920, matters had deteriorated far beyond anything that could be dealt with by a civil police force and if anything was to be achieved a paramilitary force was required. This was entirely new to Ireland, as for all republican propagandists claiming the RIC was a paramilitary force it was not, the main difference between it and British police forces was that it was responsible for the entire country, with the exception of the City of Dublin and was centrally organised. It is worth recording that in common with British practice, large Irish Cities were originally allowed to form and manage their own police. Apart from Dublin, Belfast and Londonderry had their own independent forces. But the two Ulster forces were disbanded when they failed to act effectively against Protestant rioters in the 1860s. It is a measure of the quality and professionalism of the mainly Catholic Royal Irish Constabulary that it replaced them both.

The government could not expect the RIC to take on ruthless armed organisation, nor did it wish to retrain them because the truth was they just wanted to get out of Ireland and would have no use for such a force in the long term. It should also be said that they were genuinely concerned for the long term future of the men of the RIC and did not wish to create a situation where its members might be driven en-masse out of Ireland when the government had gone. Sending in a separate force made up mostly of Englishmen to do the job was a sound political move, if rather dirty on the individuals concerned.

Essentially the Black and Tans were the true face of war, they were very hard men indeed and when the Irish freedom fighters saw them didn't like what they saw. All the IRA's experience at killing and bombing under the general protection of the Civil Law told them the Tans were just not playing fair. They were not just professional soldiers but very experienced professional soldiers, veterans and seasoned campaigners working with the highest degree of efficiency. They were a world away from the disorientated men of the RIC trying to carry on as civil police as they had for almost 80 years and a universe away from the half trained often-teenage soldiers of the regular army.

It is a quite extraordinary comment on the state of affairs that had been allowed to develop in Ireland that had the

IRA killing as and when they pleased and yet they were outraged by the behaviour of the Black and Tans. But they were only being repaid in their own coin, as George Coppard related when they found the Germans were using soft nosed bullets, "As the opportunity offered when they got hold of German rifles they had a grim satisfaction of firing them back. This was probably against international conventions but they knew nothing of such things, simple justice demanded that whatever was used against us it was meet and proper for him to get back."

Consequently, while the IRA considered it perfectly normal to shoot an auxiliary when he was quietly having tea with his wife in a Dublin hotel, they were absolutely outraged when the auxiliaries went round to one of their own volunteers and killed him. Such an appalling lack of discipline was beyond their comprehension and it is a tacit admission that in their experience the British just did not do that.

In the Black and Tans and auxiliaries the IRA were faced for the first time with men who were simply not prepared to be killed or have their friends killed without striking back. The IRA had virtually had the whole of Southern Ireland as "fire free zone" for over a year killing police, army and anyone else they cared to classify as "spies and traitors" with little or no risk to themselves. So their indignation at meeting such men is understandable. It just wasn't fair - it wasn't in the script.

People do not understand that the population then was nothing like as mobile as it today and the only means of fast travel was by railway. Outside the towns, the main roads were little more than tracks of crushed stone and 12 miles an hour was considered a fast speed for a car or lorry. This meant that neither side could move quickly and they operated in restricted areas and having killed someone the IRA could not run far or fast they could only hide. To talk of the IRA as a "Secret Army" is utter nonsense. They had been openly organising for years and there is ample evidence that everyone knew who they were. One can have no better witness than Dan Breen, who with a price of £1,000 on his head boasted that anyone who talked "would not be serving their families' interest" and this included the RIC.

With this in mind the Black and Tans, who were used to the rules of a real war, not the patriot freedom fighter version, had no compunction about pursuing and killing outright anyone who attacked them, or failing that, their known associates. This was unlike the Regular Police and army who were expected to carry on as if nothing had happened and given neither the encouragement nor leadership to take coordinated counteraction.

Almost the only response the IRA had previously faced was when soldiers outraged by the killing of their comrades would smash a few windows. Wrong of course, but compared with what most armies would do in this situation quite moderate and not at all unhelpful to Sinn Fein. The forces of law and order are not supposed to do that sort of thing and Sinn Fein would see such acts got full publicity. They would naturally make great play of the fact that the culprits were not punished but not mention that the government usually paid adequate compensation for the damage.

The lot of the regular Royal Irish Constabulary was worse. They were as decent and honourable a group of men as you would find anywhere and were smeared and sneered at as hirelings in the service of a foreign power. But just how good they were is shown by another incident described by Barry. He told how during the truce preceding the treaty of 1921, the RIC, in contravention of the terms of the ceasefire, arrested the driver of his official car. He cited this as yet another example of British duplicity and told how he kidnapped two policemen and held them until the man was released. What he fails to mention is that his "official car" was not actually his or even provided by the IRA. He said it was captured, but as far as civil police were concerned it was stolen. When the RIC found "his" driver in possession of what was as far as they were concerned a stolen car they arrested him.

To those who care to think about it, that they did not realise he was the driver of the IRA General Commanding the Cork Brigade is extremely interesting. It suggests that Barry's grip on the countryside was nothing like as great as people believe otherwise the mere mention of his name would have caused police to release the driver. It is also a great tribute to the Royal Irish Constabulary that after two years as the target of a vicious campaign of murder and propaganda they were still carrying on the normal duties as civil police by arresting a man found in possession of a stolen car.

There are those who would see this as an attempt to justify, defend or reclaim the name of the Black and Tans. Such words are inappropriate as they carry moral implications and while to say I wish to "explain them" would be closer but even "explain" hints at an apology. It should be understood that moral outrage at their actions is utterly pointless and akin to rage because a guard-dog bites you when you walk up to it and give it a good hard kick.

As to why the individuals joined the auxiliaries or Black and Tans some may have had reasons beyond unemployment or maintaining their newly-acquired social status. One Irish writer bitterly claimed that their pay of £1 a day plus expenses made him the highest paid coercive force in the world. It would be interesting to know where he did his research. By the standards of the time, a pound a day was quite good money but a highly significant detail that everyone overlooks is that they were recruited on a one-year contract. This confirms yet again that the government had no long-term plans to reconstruct its administration in Ireland, but only wished to fight the IRA to a standstill. They were expected do this within one year but in fact they managed to achieve the result in a little over six months.

A year would have been enough for Cadet Pallister, formerly Captain Pallister who died at Kilmichael. He came from Sheffield and married his childhood sweetheart in April 1920 and they had a baby daughter born just three days after he left for Ireland.

It does not require a genius to calculate that his wife was about three months pregnant when they got married and as they were living with her parents his employment and family situation must have been less than ideal. With a new wife and baby it is very unlikely he intended to go back to soldiering as a career but had he survived the year in Ireland he would probably have been able to save over £300. That would have been enough to buy a house so one can assume he just needed the money to get out from under his in-laws roof.

One IRA propaganda song about the Black and Tans claims,

"They sent them all over to pillage and loot
To burn down the houses the inmates to shoot."

Poor William Pallister; he didn't want to loot, pillage or terrorise anyone, all he wanted was to survive the year and get a decent house for his wife and baby daughter. What he got after five weeks was an expanding bullet over the heart and his skull smashed in with a "heavy instrument" to make sure he was dead.

All in all the Black and Tans are regarded by the world as the ultimate in human brutality and the object of universal condemnation. Most Englishmen feel the need to apologise for them while pointing out as mitigating circumstances that they were the product of their terrible experiences during the war. This is of course true because the war had not only turned killing and dying into a daily routine, it had taught them how to kill efficiently as the IRA deaths at Balbriggan and Dublin Castle discussed later will show.

One ardent patriot recently declared that they were the blueprint for the Nazi "Einsatzgruppen" and the difference was only the colour of their uniforms and the degree of killing they carried out there was no difference in kind.

My only comment on this piece of nonsense would be to quote Professor Lee, an Irish historian, who considered the IRA were fortunate that they were not facing the Germans (never mind the Nazi Einsatzgruppen) "who had ways of dealing with recalcitrant populations that made the Black and Tans look like a Boy Scout Brigade".

What is quite remarkable is that the IRA were a good deal more casual in their selection of victims than the Black and Tans.

Also lack of experience meant they were considerably more inept and therefore brutal in the way they killed them. While the IRA usually shot their victims, even when shooting trussed up prisoners they tended to use a lot of bullets and more than once they finished them off by beating their skulls in, which is an inefficient and messy way to kill someone. This is of course because they had not had years of experience on the Western Front to teach them how to inflict death in two minutes or less. The critical point that everyone misses is that they had both the inclination and stomach for this kind of savagery and it is savagery whoever does it in whatever cause, without the brutalising experience of the Western Front.

The unfortunate conclusion is that it took years of war to turn an Englishman into a brutal killer but it is natural for an Irishman. Nevertheless, no one has ever dreamed of condemning them for it, let alone accused them of brutality or barbarism because the triple explanation of, "It was war, we were fighting for our freedom, it had to be done" excuses everything.

For my part I do not attempt to excuse the Black and Tans, I wish only to explain that people should understand.

Ireland had not experienced a real war for over 100 years and when the Tans brought home to the IRA what war was really like they cried "Foul!"

If you think about it, this is a tribute to the restraint of the government, police and military up to their arrival.

The truth is that the IRA had been operating the law of the jungle but had forgotten the rule best expressed by the Welsh Socialist Aneurin Bevan 20 years later, "If you want to use the law of the jungle you should remember you are not the strongest animal in it."

CHAPTER 8

THE SACK OF BALBRIGGAN

Any account of the Black and Tans behavior includes a mention of the most notorious incident they were accused of, or more correctly involved in, apart of course from the burning of Cork which is discussed later.

This is the "The Sack of Balbriggan" a small village of Balbriggan just north of Dublin. When a town is "sacked" in war it usually refers to up to three days of looting, pillage and rape after a prolonged siege, together with the murder of a large part of the civilian population. Until the 17th, and perhaps the 18th, century the right of sacking a town was the reward given to the storming troops in return for their casualties in the final and inevitably bloody assault. As we shall see the "sack" of Balbriggan did not last three hours. It is a prime example of one of the most fascinating things about history, an event which is always taken on its own without any reference to many circumstances that caused it, not least pure chance.

Historians usually quote sources on a pick and mix basis without detailed research. Sometimes this is a consequence of their political background, but usually they need to condense information and, lacking the breadth of knowledge to carry out a detailed analysis, they miss apparently insignificant details, which are in fact crucial.

To understand what happened at Balbriggan that night in 1920 we have to look at the political situation and the long-term policy of the government. We also need to take into account the attitudes, what we now call perspective, of each group involved, the government Sinn Fein, the RIC, the people of Balbriggan – specifically of one street in Balbriggan - and the newly-arrived Black and Tans. We also need to consider what appeared to be quite banal details which, when linked to others, are absolutely crucial.

The first thing to understand is that in Balbriggan, as in other places in Ireland at the time, some people got carried away with the events they thought were taking place and wished to be part of them. Much of the country had degenerated into a state of violent temporary insanity as playwright Sean O'Casey observed, "The whole of Ireland has gone mad".

Accounts of The Sack of Balbriggan usually start off with the killing of Head Constable Burke on the 20th September 1920. But five months earlier on 14th April another police officer was killed in Balbriggan, Sergeant Finnerty, a man with 25 years' service. He was one of three RIC monitoring a Sinn Fein demonstration when he was shot several times at a range of four to five feet and died from his wounds the following day. Sadly, some of the crowd are reported to have cheered when he fell, shouting, "That's the stuff to give them!".

This seems appalling to us, but throughout history crowds have cheered in these situations. After all, if you see someone being killed and do not want to be killed yourself, possibly the best and only defence you have is to applaud the killers.

The thing to remember is that the shooting of Sergeant Finnerty has all the hallmarks of the hysteria killing when someone was carried away by the mood of the crowd; "psyched up" in modern terms. He had a pistol and impulsively decided to use it and was showing off to the mob, nothing more.

In theory, Sinn Fein had a non-violent policy to take over government by setting up a parallel administration that would function through popular support. In practice this is utter nonsense but explaining why is not the purpose of this paper. As part of this policy they set up a "police force" and it is reasonable to assume that Sergeant Finnerty was shot by one of the Sinn Fein "police" who must have been present at the demonstration. The hundred or more people present would know this so we can assume that within hours the whole town knew. We can also assume that not long afterwards the authorities would know, but for political reasons they did nothing.

Sergeant Finnerty and his colleagues had not been expecting trouble and the shooting of a fellow officer was completely outside their experience. They would have no reaction but to go into shock and on recovering get what medical help they could before reporting to their superiors and requesting assistance. That is how a civil police force is trained to react, investigation is the work of specialists and retribution is a matter for the legal system.

Regarding the second shooting even Sinn Fein admit it was two of their "police" who killed a head Constable

Burke and seriously wounded his brother in November. Richard Abbot's book "Police casualties in Ireland" notes their claim that two of these police fired on in self-defence when Burke drew his gun during an altercation after being refused out of hour's service in the public house. But if we were to assume that these men had already killed Sergeant Finnerty in a fit of patriotic hysteria then the self-defence claim is very doubtful. If they had killed one policeman when "psyched up" by the crowd and got away with it, the chances they would do so again when they were psyched up during the altercation, are quite high. This is surely a reasonable assumption as they can only be a limited number of trigger-happy patriots in any town.

This brings me to the apparently mundane but crucial detail that I see as a key to the whole affair. A contemporary report in the press headed "Barbarous reprisals at Balbriggan" informed readers that the trouble began when the soldiers who had been spending the night in the town's public houses got the train back to Gormanstown Camp and told their comrades what had happened.

Therefore following the murder of Sergeant Finnerty, the army and later the Black and Tans continued to use the public houses in Balbriggan as normal. So, in common with everyone else, they would have known who had killed him but the town's RIC Constables, having told their superiors, would not expect to do anything further about it. Because Sergeant Finnerty was a policeman it was a civil matter, so the army as an organisation and as individuals would have considered it none of their business.

Sinn Fein would, of course, justify the killing of Sergeant Finnerty with the usual line, "It was war. We were fighting for our freedom, it had to be done". For months they had killed policemen "spies" and "traitors" almost at will and then expected to revert to civilian status with the full protection of the legal system of the state they were trying to destroy.

But in war soldiers would consider this attitude ridiculous because in war if you kill someone you must expect his comrades to arrive shortly afterwards to kill you. That is what war means to soldiers and they do not complain.

The mistake Sinn Fein police made this time was to get carried away again and kill someone actually known to what the government described as the "new police" i.e. the Black and Tans. These men were a totally different prospect than Sergeant Finnerty and the regular RIC and indeed different from the regular army which only wanted to settle back into peacetime routine. They had been soldiers in an incredibly brutal war and with only a brief training in police work they had none of the restraint expected of a regular police officer. With a life of war in the trenches behind them the idea that the killer of a comrade should be allowed to retire to his bed under the protection of the civil law was beyond their comprehension. After years of real war it was instinctive for them to make an effort kill the enemy in revenge and preferably, but not essentially, the enemy who was responsible

This is not what anyone in the British Isles expects of normal policing, but normal policing in Ireland ended when Dan Breen killed two Constables at Solbeghead and in doing so decreed that "all witnesses were now informers" who could and would be killed. By failing to react vigorously to this and later incidents the government lost the authority and this led to a total breakdown of civil policing. A different kind of policing was required. While Black and Tans may have been called police by virtue of their experience they were not inclined to leave the business of retribution to the legal system, particularly when it had clearly failed to do its duty by someone they considered a comrade.

Let us then consider a few reasonable propositions that added together might bring us to that elusive conclusion we call the truth

We can take it for granted that the authorities and most of Balbriggen would know the killers in April and September were the same men but as noted for political reasons they did nothing. That I think is why there were no court marshals or official punishments; only the promise of an inquiry. The press response of the British "Daily News" is probably typical when it declared:

"The only inquiry needed is the identity of the police who took part so they may be instantly and severely punished!"

But if there had been prosecutions suppose that the defence was: "Everyone in Balbriggan knew the same local Sinn Feiners had just killed a policeman for the second time, "How many police were they to be allowed to kill, before anyone did anything to stop them?"

This is no defence in law it is true but very embarrassing for the government.

But the press would certainly have taken a close interest in any court-martials. If in the process they discovered it was well known in Balbriggan that the two men killed by the Black and Tans not only killed Head Constable Burke but also Sergeant Finnerty? That might have made even the lazy British press ask why they had not been arrested six months earlier.

The truthful answer, which the government could never have given, would be, "We are trying to come to terms with Sinn Fein and in these circumstances had we arrested them in due course we would have been obliged to hang them. This would have aggravated an already difficult political situation. So we pretended we didn't know."

Whatever the embarrassment caused by the behaviour of the Black and Tans that night in Balbriggan it would have been nothing compared to the outcry that would have resulted and the political fall-out would have been incalculable.

Before anyone dismisses this as conjecture I would point out that it is a good deal more objective an analysis than found in most histories.

I have read accounts of "The Sack of Balbriggan" and time and time again they contradict each other. Indeed they seem to owe more to poetic imagination than objective analysis. Damage is quoted as "12 houses burned", "40 houses burned" with various other buildings, from public houses to a small factory added in for good measure. In one otherwise objective history, that is Robert Kee's account, he declares, "the Black and Tans ran through the streets firing rifles and throwing hand grenades indiscriminately".

To anyone who knows anything about rifles and hand grenades this is ludicrous, not least because if true the casualties would have been considerably higher than "two citizens shot and bayoneted in their nightshirts". He may well have genuinely overlooked the detail that the two citizens were at least "closely connected with the killers".

One might of course make passing mention of the account by an Irish army officer and former member of the IRA who declares as a fact that a girl of 11 and a woman of 70 were raped that night. Not content with informing everyone that the Tans were thugs, they were also branded paedophiles and perverts. Interestingly, he does not accuse them of raping anyone between 18 and 50; perhaps because he assumes soldiers raping women of this age group is normal and not worth a mention.

Even T P Coogan's most recent book informs readers that the town was burned and two civilians were killed after the RIC were fired on. Having written millions of words about the IRA he seems unaware that the two civilians are generally acknowledged to have been Sinn Fein police or IRA volunteers - the terms being interchangeable depending on the situation. Nor does he seem to be aware that one of the RIC was killed and the other severely wounded with exploding bullets. However his comment that the reprisal "probably did not have official sanction" is interesting as it suggests he is aware of the circumstances but does not think it necessary to mention them.

Of course they did not have official sanction. The time between the killing and the reprisal was too short for it to be anything but the reaction of very angry men.

As to the actual damage done at Balbriggan, the accounts vary so much because everyone writing about it seems to read everyone else's book so they can then decide on an aggregate. It never occurs to anyone to plot the area of damage on a map or even look at some of the photographs taken at the time. If they took the trouble to do this and consider the physical factors such as the nature of fire and the construction of the houses in Balbriggan at the time they would have been faced with some interesting questions.

Everyone accepts that the majority of the damage was done in Clonnard Street, which was then known locally as "Sinn Fein Alley" and the home of the two IRA men who were killed. A photograph of the damage shows that Clonnard Street, in common with much of Balbriggan at the time, consisted of traditional Irish cottages with thick straw thatched roofs.

So if one was to catch light it is inevitable that the fire would spread and burn out the whole terrace. There are no indications where the rest of the damage occurred but the nature of fire in thatched roofs is such that burning material is carried into the air and when it comes down again it would almost certainly start a fire in any thatched roof it landed on. The amount of damage done would depend not on the malice of the Black and Tans, but on the number of houses in the terrace where the fire started and the speed and direction of the wind at the time. I would guess that away from Clonnard Street it was a case of incidental damage as a result of burning material drifting on to nearby thatched roofs downwind of the main fire.

As to the damage to public houses, many accounts claim that four public houses were destroyed. However, a dissertation given by one publican to an American Commission investigation makes no mention of damage at any public houses apart from the one he owned.

Most interesting of all is the burning of the hosiery mill owned by an English company which is mentioned in almost every account. The implication is always that the Black and Tans were so out of control that not content with destroying Irish property they actually destroyed the property of an Englishman.

It has never occurred to anyone to enquire where the English-owned hosiery mill was located. The map of Balbriggan included in the illustrations is dated 1906 shows it standing on an open site in the shape of an inverted triangle and the only other building close by is the coastguard station. The main Dublin/Belfast railway line forms the western boundary of the site, with cliffs and the seashore forming the eastern boundary. A road closes the top of the triangle to the north with the coastguard station and brickworks the only other buildings nearby. At the time Balbriggan was very small and while no one can say the mill was outside the town it was not actually part of it either. The distance from the town was not great therefore the allegation that it was deliberately burned down is probably true and not as a result of what we now call collateral damage as probably happened around Clonnard Street. Not only was the mill about as far from Clonnard Street as it is possible to get without actually leaving Balbriggan it almost certainly did not have a thatched roof to catch fire.

The isolated site could only be reached by heading north out of Balbriggan on Droheda Street and just as you're leaving the town, turning right down a side road with no residential buildings and only a clay pit on the southern side. Three hundred yards further along this road was a level crossing over the rail line and after this you had to turn right again and go for about 150 yards down what looks like an unmade lane to reach the hosiery mill.

So by implication, all accounts allege that having killed the two Sinn Feiners and setting fire to Clonnard Street, the Black and Tans - instead of going straight back to camp - stopped to collect some petrol and went out of their way to burn a hosiery mill owned by an English company. If the purpose of this was to punish the people of Balbriggan by depriving them of work why did they not burn other buildings and the town centre that were much closer and much easier to access than the mill? More to the point, these were Irish owned and if they were in the business of punishing the Irish they were a much better target.

Drawing all the strands together, we can accept that the mill by its location and construction was deliberately burned down, unlike most of the houses in the town. This is not to defend the action, it is simply saying that much of the damage in Balbriggan that night was a consequence of one fire spreading rather than a series of fires being started. It has been accepted without question that because the Black and Tans were responsible for the depredations in "Sinn Fein Alley" and the adjacent streets they must also have burned down the mill. Nobody ever asks why they would have made a detour specifically to burn down an English-owned property. Why would they do this particularly when there are plenty of Irish properties much closer at hand? We must ask ourselves is it likely?

I think a commonsense answer would be no. Then we must ask ourselves if the Black and Tans did not burn down the English-owned mill who did? This is where a really interesting proposition comes to the fore.

Is it not just as reasonable to ask if the residents of Cllonnard Street, "Sinn Fein Alley", having had their homes burned by Black and Tans decided to take their revenge by burning down the only English-owned property in the town? Why not? The Black and Tans would almost certainly all be Englishmen and in the "logic" of the moment they would wish to destroy English property, regardless of the fact that it was a major employer in the town. After all, cutting off the nose to spite the face does seem to be an Irish national obsession.

Let us try and reconstruct the events that night with reference to the political and physical background as well as the various people involved.

Local members of Sinn Fein had killed one of the local policeman six months earlier in a fit of patriotic fervour and to put it quite simply - got away with it.

Clonnard Street and quite possibly the nearest public house were well known centres of Sinn Fein activity in the town and almost certainly the home of the killers of the police sergeant in the previous April.

The RIC party, not knowing the area, stopped for a drink and by misfortune happened to go to a Sinn Fein pub. The landlady, partly to demonstrate her patriotism and partly for fear of her regular clients, refused to serve them.

The Sinn Fein police arrived on a scene and an argument developed. The regular local RIC arrived, saw who was involved and remembering the fate of Sergeant Finnerty they quietly left.

As the two RIC men left, no doubt shouting in anger, a Sinn Feiner got carried away for the second time and shot the two policemen. Some accounts say the fatal shots were fired from inside the pub as the men were in, or getting into, their car.

The word went around town and soldiers returning to Gormanstown Camp told some Black and Tans who happened to know Head Constable Burke well. They probably also knew of the death of Sergeant Finnerty six months earlier and were determined not to let Sinn Fein get away with it this time.

They went down to Sinn Fein Alley, dragged out the two best known Shinners, then quickly and professionally bayoneted them and set fire to their homes for good measure.

In the dissertation to the American inquiry only one public house is mentioned as destroyed. Could this be the Sinn Fein public house where the landlady started the trouble by refusing service in the first place? If they were going to smash up any pub that would be the one to choose. Why smash up any more? They used the other pubs in town and they had no trouble getting served in them.

The fire spread along Clonnard Street and burning debris carried on the wind set fire to houses nearby.

Outraged at the destruction, the residents of Sinn Fein Alley obtained petrol and proceeded to the only English-owned property in town, the mill, and burned it down.

Consider also this detail. It is accepted that the Black and Tans had not been in Balbriggan very long. Yet without any guidance and certainly without the help from police or military intelligence they went straight to the main area of Sinn Fein activity to punish those they thought responsible. Therefore, far from being a secret and undercover organisation, the members and homes of Sinn Fein/IRA members was public knowledge in the town, even to newly arrived Black and Tans.

Let us go back again to the murder of Sergeant Finnerty in April as described to in Abbot's book:

An RIC patrol of one Head Constable, one Sergeant and three Constables have followed a crowd of approximately 150 Sinn Fein supporters to a bonfire at Clonnard Hill, which was three-quarters a mile outside. The town police cautioned a man that the procession was illegal but did not take any other action.

On their return the police again followed the crowd, with 20 to 25 people and a smaller group following behind police. On reaching Clonnard Street a flash was seen behind the Sergeant about three or four feet from him. He called out "I am shot". The police did not anticipate trouble and in the confusion the smaller crowd behind them got into the larger one in front with a person in a larger crowd calling out "That's the stuff to give them"

Given that historians do not have the time to delve into apparently minute details prior to an event it is not surprising that they are ignorant of the time and place of Sergeant Finnerty's murder.

Nor would they be able to consider the effect that it went unpunished would have on the attitude of everyone from the hysterical and murderous residents of Clonnard Street, to the local RIC.

Regardless of the incident soldiers continued to routinely use the town's public houses - no doubt taking good care to stay away from the ones in or near Clonnard Street.

The true Irish patriot would not consider his killing to be relevant because he has a right to kill anyone, particularly policeman to further the glorious clause.

The lawyer would not consider it relevant in the absence of any detailed investigation to firmly establish their guilt. The Sinn Feiner's of Clonnard Street were innocent.

The politician would not consider it relevant because it complicates his long-term political aims and might reveal the extent of his duplicity.

However the Black and Tans would not consider it in such terms. Knowing two men – in effect comrades - had been killed in the same place and almost certainly by the same people in six months they would want to make sure there were no more. To let them get away with it twice would be asking just too much of veterans of the trenches and however much this might outrage legal and liberal opinion, lawyers and liberals were not doing the dying.

Balbriggan Final analysis

Having mentioned Robert Kee's account of Balbriggan, it is worth quoting it in full. An experienced journalist of the highest integrity, Kee presented a television series on Irish history in 1972. The intention was to explain to the British public as honestly as possible the roots of the Troubles in Northern Ireland that were then at their height. The accompanying book was called *The Green Flag* and in Volume 3, *Ourselves Alone,* he gives this account of Balbriggan. Like all his work on the subject he made a considerable effort to be scrupulously fair and he tells how:

"On 21st September a head Constable Burke was shot down in daylight in the streets. Burke had been popular as an instructor at the nearby Black and Tans recruits' depot at Gormanstown and lorry loads of Black and Tans arrived in Ballbriggan during the night and again the following day, setting fire to shops and houses, firing rifles and throwing hand-grenades indiscriminately, generally terrorising the inhabitants under cover of a search for the culprits and shooting and bayoneting citizens to death in their night shirts. Their corpses, declared an eyewitness, looked as if they'd been killed not by human beings but by animals. A sight hitherto associated with the flight to Belgium of French refugees before the German invaders was thus seen within 20 miles of the Irish capital as women and children fled from the blackened ruins of their homes with belongings on perambulators and handcarts in anticipation of another visit from the Black and Tans during the night."

But, of course, Constable Burke was not shot down in broad daylight. He was shot in the evening from inside a pub from which he had been refused service, probably because he was a policeman. Some Irish accounts being nearer to the facts even go so far as to claim the Sinn Fein people only shot him in self-defence. It was the unfortunate Sergeant Finnerty who was shot in broad daylight in front of a cheering crowd. The Black and Tans certainly came to town but they were by no means indiscriminate, going straight to the centre of Sinn Fein activity and dragging out two well-known 'Sinn Feiners'. If these men had not actually shot Head Constable Burke a couple of hours earlier they would certainly know who had. It is a detail that does not interest historians, but as I have explained, the Black and Tans did not set fire to shops and houses indiscriminately but only those in the part of town known then as 'Sinn Fein Alley'.

Again as I have already pointed out, had they *"fired rifles and thrown hand grenades indiscriminately"* casualties would have been a great deal higher than two citizens bayoneted in their nightshirts. They could not have thrown grenades without considerable risk to themselves and may well have fired rifles, but the fact that as veterans they did not hit anyone proves they were very discriminating indeed.

And, of course, they did not set fire to houses or terrorise the entire town out of simple brutality or use the excuse of setting up a search for the culprits to cover their actions. They went straight to the known heart of Sinn Fein in the town and took it out on them.

As to the eyewitness saying the corpses of the citizens bayoneted in their night shirts looked as though they had been killed by animals and not human beings. All we can say was well he would say that, wouldn't he? What method would this person quoted suggest to kill men quickly and efficiently?

As to the people taking refuge in the countryside at night, this is certainly true. But it seems to have been confined to known Sinn Fein activists from Clonnard Street . This was out of shock as much as necessity because when they had murdered Sergeant Finnerty six months earlier there had been no "come back" whatever. The Black and Tans' action told them in the most brutal way possible that there was a new game in town. No wonder they were shocked.

It is worth mentioning that there are memorial plaques on Clonnard Street commemorating the murder of the two Sinn Feiners by the Black and Tans. It is reasonable to assume there are no plaques recording the murders of Sergeant Finnerty and Head Constable Burke in pretty much the same place. History is very selective.

The point is that even a scrupulously fair and honest writer like Robert Kee has probably relied on assessments of other writers' accounts to produce what he considers to be a balanced conclusion. Unfortunately, due to a lack of research into the detail, it is very misleading indeed. It presents a picture of indiscriminate revenge on a whole population who are assumed to be innocent.

I accept that my conclusions on Balbriggan are not based on hard evidence, rather on a logical analysis of the events, attitudes and interests of all those involved. But I would argue this is better than poetic imagination any day.

For that reason I believe my conclusions are probably closer to that final elusive conclusion called "the truth" than anything else I have read.

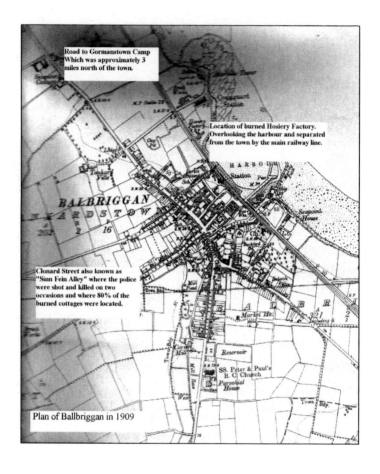

Road to Gormanstown Camp
Which was approximately 3
miles north of the town.

Location of burned Hosiery Factory.
Overlooking the harbour and separated
from the town by the main railway line.

Clonard Street also known as
"Sinn Fein Alley" where the police
were shot and killed on two
occasions and where 80% of the
burned cottages were located.

Plan of Ballbriggan in 1909

CHAPTER 9

SEAN O'CALLAGHAN'S
"THE EASTER LILY"

It is worth considering a book by Sean O'Callaghan, *The Easter Lily: The Story of the IRA* which was published in 1956. O'Callaghan was an officer in the Irish regular army and his father and uncle were active in the IRA from The Troubles and on into the 1930s when he joined it.

His account of the burning of Balbriggan might be more lurid than most and as his allegations of paedophile and geriatric rapes do not appear anywhere else we can assume they are a product of his imagination.

Nevertheless, his book does give a fascinating insight into the mind of the average IRA member, the class of small farmers from which they were drawn and their moral code.

The most interesting part of his book is his categorical statement that the behavior of the Black and Tans at Ballbriggan "bore close resemblance to the behavior of the Nazis at Lidice in 1942." When I read this at the age of 15 I had never heard of Lidice and accepted this glorious piece of nonsense as confirming still further the horrors England had inflicted on my country. For those few who have not heard of Lidice I will describe what happened there so you can make your own comparisons.

Free Czech agents parachuted into the country by the British had assassinated Heydrich, the German governor of Czechoslovakia. At the time, and for many years afterwards, it was believed that the villagers of Lidice, just outside Prague, had provided food, shelter and general assistance to the assassins. Even Churchill's *History of the Second World War* states there was "irrefutable proof" that they had.

Subsequent accounts suggest the Germans had in fact got the wrong village and it was a village with a similar name and not too far away that was actually responsible. Whoever was or was not responsible, Hitler's first instruction was that 30,000 Czechs should be killed as a reprisal. He was dissuaded from this on the practical grounds that it would seriously impact on the productivity of the Czech munitions industry that was working flat out for the Germans. So Hitler settled for punishing Lidice.

This started when early one morning the village was surrounded by the SS and all males over the age of 16 were separated from the woman and children. These men and boys, 172 in total, were then shot in batches of 10 and the women and children, with the exception of a few "Aryan" children who were sent to German families, were shipped off to concentration camps where most of them died. The village was then destroyed building by building with explosives, completely leveled until not a trace remained, and grain was planted over the site. The name was then removed from all German maps, while the whole exercise was filmed and the film circulated through Czechoslovakia as a warning to the population.

Elsewhere, the Gestapo and SS also hunted down Czech agents, resistance members, and anyone suspected of being involved in the attack on Heydrich. In total 1,000 people were killed. In addition, 3,000 Jews were deported from the ghetto at Theresienstadt for extermination and in Berlin 500 Jews were arrested, with 152 executed as a reprisal on the day Heydrich died.

At Balbriggan, two members of Sinn Fein who had probably killed a policeman - if not them then certainly one of their associates and someone known to them - in a fit of patriotic hysteria were themselves bayoneted to death and two cottages were set on fire.

According to the American Commission Report on Conditions in Ireland, as a result, 25 adjacent properties were burnt, 17 of them on Clonnard Street. Several local men who might have been well known Shinners were beaten up and others thought it wise to sleep in the surrounding fields for a few nights.

There were, of course, several other atrocities which are not generally reported but included in the statement given to an Independent American commission of inquiry and these are listed later.

So, to compare Lidice and Balbriggen as O'Callaghan does we must list the damage as follows:

Lidice: 400 men women and children either shot or died in concentration camps, because a few of them were wrongly believed to have aided assassins. Up to 100 houses destroyed and the whole village bulldozed flat and planted as farmland.

The whole bloody affair filmed and broadcast as an example to others.

Balbriggan: Two men who may have just have shot two policemen in, or from, a bar were professionally bayoneted to death. Among the further atrocities recorded by the independent American Commission were that the Black and Tans drove through the town in a dangerous and reckless manner. Some time later (days?) they fired into a crowd of young women - without hitting any of them. They threw a Mills bomb (grenade) into the local butcher's and a piece (of shrapnel) went through an apple in a lad's pocket.

They fired into a grocer's shop and broke some scales. They fired at a child and the bullet went through the pocket of his jacket. They drank their fill then smashed all the bottles in a public house. They looted and wrecked two grocery stores until the floor became waist-deep in tea, sugar, soap and candles. They cut the tails off three pullets (young chickens) as a result of which one of the pullets died. Oh yes - and they used bad language. Burned down a Hosiery Mill? As I have said, I believe this to be extremely unlikely.

Most people would expect a professional soldier like O'Callaghan to be more objective but the problem is that most people in Ireland will accept every word he wrote without question. How can anyone for even one-second compare the two actions and retain any claim to reason?

Regarding his membership of the IRA and his account of his first parade in a country field watching his friends performing parade drills "to compare with the finest military forces in the world" some of his stories are quite positive.

His father's reluctance to kill the local policemen and the way he manipulated an attack on the RIC Barracks to avoid doing so is very commendable. He also relates how, after initial unwillingness, his father encouraged his membership of the IRA and presented him with his own .22 training rifle. As to his own "operations" in the IRA, these are interesting. They include his participation in a raid for arms on the home of a British officer living in Ireland during the1930s. Much more serious is his description of his part as an accessory to two political murders.

As I remember the first victim was a government spy who was enticed into what he thought was an assignation with an IRA girl he had been making "sheep's eyes" at for some time. What he found was an IRA squad who questioned him by knocking him about a bit, found him guilty, tied him to a fence post and shot him.

The second killing was, if not a hysteria killing, certainly an impromptu and quite unprovoked murder. The IRA had decided to protect the people from the fascist Blueshirts and they would wait for groups of Blueshirts coming from meetings and order them to remove their shirts at gunpoint. This included the Blueshirt women and he says that as few Irish girls then wore brassieres before they were 30 he found it embarrassing.

Much more seriously, on a particular occasion the leader of the IRA, who I think he called Bill, shot the Blueshirts' young leader. The Blueshirts were unarmed and I do not remember the reason the man was shot. Maybe "Bill" was provoked by insulting language which, after all, is all a patriot and idealist needs to shoot somebody. Bill was well known as an atheist and as the man lay dying he begged the IRA to get him a priest. Despite his increasingly urgent pleadings Bill refused this until finally a Blueshirt girl ran forward and whispered the act of contrition in the dying man's ear. O'Callaghan, in common with the other members of the IRA present, was disgusted by Bill's action and noted that "Bill lost a lot of friends that night".

For reasons I forget O'Callaghan subsequently joined the Irish regular army as an officer. To his friends and neighbours in the IRA this constituted an act of treason and, while his life was not threatened, several of them refused to speak to him when he went home on leave.

What is really interesting is that he could write quite freely about his complicity in two political murders just 20+ years before without fear of prosecution, even though one of the victims was by implication a government officer. It is also worth noting that he expresses no regret whatsoever about what was unquestionably a cold-blooded - and one may say unprovoked -political killing because to his mind no moral question arises. As a patriot he and his comrades had the unquestioned right to kill anyone opposed to the great cause of Irish freedom.

Consider the unique or rather strange set of values these people have.

Tying a man to a fence post and shooting him? No problem.

The casual murder of an unarmed political opponent? No problem so long as he is allowed to see a priest.

Ordering young women to take off their blouses and go topless? Dreadfully embarrassing!

One should not be too judgmental about this sort of thing because the truth is everybody has in their head a list of people whose deaths would not cause them to protest overmuch. Gilbert and Sullivan expressed this in their satirical opera the Mikado. The Lord High executioner is a tailor who has no wish to execute anybody but should the day ever come when he needs to he has a little list of society offenders who might well be done without.

So we should not be too indignant about O'Callaghan and his comrades shooting men tied to fence posts and murdering right wing opponents just because his little list is different to ours. The real difference is that we confine ourselves to thinking about it, while he went out, did it, and got away with it without expressing the slightest regret - as long as the victim saw a priest first.

THE KILMICHAEL AMBUSH SITE

1. The first tender was found burned out where the car is parked. The "tombstone" to the right commemorates the location of the IRA "command post" at the corner of the main road and a track. The mutilated bodies of the 8 Auxiliaries who were traveling in this first tender were found grouped a short distance up the track.

2. The crew of the second tender formed a skirmish line just before here and had reached this point when the IRA opened fire killing 3 of them.

Although more wooded now, this is the view they would have had of the first tender whose crew were prisoners and completely hidden by the rocky hillock in the center and left. Two members of the skirmish line were about to climb the hillock that was already occupied by the IRA when they were killed.

3. A view of where the 3 bodies of the skirmish line were found. This is taken from the road and they were moving in line abreast from left to right across the picture. The body of the man on the extreme left of their line was just past the barrier in the center of the picture. As noted the IRA were on the hillock to the right and also behind them on the now overgrown hillock seen on the left. Again, the 2 men furthest from the road were about to walk onto the IRA position when they were killed.

This confirms that there had been no firing and certainly no grenade thrown up to this point. Had there been, they would not have got this far let alone formed up in a line between two enemy positions.

Not knowing the IRA were on the hillock (to the left) overlooking their own tender, they moved down the road before forming up here to continue their advance. They took up the infantry formation known as "Extended line advance to contact" which is adopted when enemy presence is possible. The IRA were in fact on the hillock to their front - the right of picture - and their rear – the left of picture. More IRA were positioned along a 300 yard stretch on "this" side of the road and at a distance of between 50-75 yards from it.

This was the logical place to organize their line as it was about 200 meters from where the first tender was stopped and the practical range for a rifle shot given the terrain and daylight in late November. A small party of their comrades had gone ahead to investigate the reason for the stop and as a precaution they were following on in tactical formation as support.

4. The advance party of 3 men from the second tender had just passed this point when 2 of them were killed. The third was shot as he tried to escape into what he thought was open country out of the picture to the right. This was Cadet Hooper-Jones whom one IRA man claimed died in a suicide charge against their positions 50 plus metres southwest. In fact he was doing the only sensible thing and trying to escape the killing ground when the IRA near the "command post" hit him several times in the back.

Again the location of the first tender is shown by the parked car and its crew were prisoners and hidden behind the hillock where their bodies were subsequently found.

5. The parked car again shows the location of the first tender looking down the road from the second main IRA position. This position is on another rocky hillock and completely overlooks the location of the second tender which was out of the picture to the right.

The crew of this tender moved down the road in two parties leaving only the driver and a bodyguard with their vehicle. The first party went forward to investigate the reason for the stop. The main body formed a skirmish line in the open area in the center and left of the picture before continuing their advance. The bushes now obscure this forming up area. This was taken on a wet dull day in October so consider the view that existed at dusk in November when the ambush took place.

6. The last to die were the 8-crew members of the first tender. Their mutilated bodies were found a short way up this track having initially been shot at close range in the head or body. Their vehicle was stopped at this point and the marker of the IRA "command post" is in the right foreground. The trees were not planted in 1920 nevertheless one only needs to go a very short distance down the track before being completely hidden from the second tender by the hillock taking up most of the picture.

Chapter 10

BARRY'S COMBAT EXPERIENCE.

All accounts make a great deal of Barry's combat experience in the First World War, portraying him as a veteran of much heavy fighting. He may have seen action, but that does not make him a veteran of the type of close infantry combat that is supposed to have taken place at Kilmichael.

Anyone looking at the disposition of his men there can see that by failing to concentrate his force, he not only had no effective command and control, he also wasted his already limited firepower. In truth, if it was his intention to mount a conventional ambush, it is crude and amateurish, although it has been pointed out to me with justification that this is being pedantic. The most basic yardstick for anything is to ask whether it succeeded or not and at Kilmichael he unquestionably succeeded, regardless of whether a military purist thought disposition of his force was good or bad.

Few people realise that only a minority of soldiers actually see any close combat and get even near the frontline. There are many technical and service units that are not expected to fight and are actually incapable of fighting. In 1943, a British battalion was in a convoy moving up to the front when they were ordered to deploy because it was thought the Germans had dropped paratroopers close by. The infantrymen were much amused by a frantic sergeant of the Mechanical Engineers running up to them with his Thompson sub-machine gun asking them to show him how it worked. Fortunately it was a false alarm and he did not need it.

Barry said he joined up because he wanted to see what war was like and enlisted in the Royal Field Artillery because he was assured that they would be at the front of the action. This is only half true, because artillerymen are basically technicians and are usually positioned miles behind the front. Because artillery is such a vital part of any army it is generally well protected in gun pits and even crews for the largest guns seldom number more than a dozen men. Add to that the fact that for tactical and technical reasons the gun batteries are dispersed over an area in such a way that a single shell hit is unlikely to affect more than one crew.

Briefly there are three principal kinds of artillery - field, medium and heavy.

As this suggests, as the calibre increases with each category so does the distance from the frontline.

Consequently, medium and heavy field regiments are usually well back and in the First World War their main threat was from the enemy artillery. They were also sometimes at risk from aircraft, but not to the extent they became later. If one takes the experience of two British medium regiments in the Second World War, the 77th Regiment suffered 12 combat deaths during 11 months in North West Europe, while its sister regiment, the 88th, lost 27 men during two years in Italy. Half of the 88th's loss was suffered in a single unlucky direct hit, so we can see that, compared to the infantry, service in the artillery is comparatively safe. By contrast, an infantry unit in the two world wars could lose 20 dead on a bad day. In the 1944-45 North West Europe campaign less than 10% of the infantrymen who landed on D Day were still in the line 11 months later.

But this is where the half truth comes in, because of all the types of artillery, apart from the specialist anti-tank regiments that appeared in later wars, field artillery is the one most likely to see close combat. But frankly, even then they have to be unlucky and get too close to the front or be overrun during an infantry attack before they suffer anything like the infantry's scale of casualties.

There is also a detail about warfare which gets very little publicity in memoirs and that is that soldiers on either side often adopt a 'live and let live' approach to each other. An old lady who served as a nurse in the First World War told me that British soldiers generally liked the Saxons. On one occasion a notice appeared over the German front line that read, "You are Anglo-Saxons, we are Saxons, you aim high, we aim high". The British naturally complied so it was understandable that they preferred facing Saxon regiments to the Prussians who would never have considered such private truces.

Similar cosy arrangements were also found in the field artillery. Before the battle of the Somme in 1916, a British artillery officer said both he and the opposing German Field Artillery unit knew where each other's billets were and they avoided shelling each other's living quarters. They cheerfully shelled everything and everyone else but not each other. However, on the outbreak of the main battle on 1st July, when all deals were off, he had no compunction about putting five rounds rapid-fire into the German billets. Nevertheless, such incidents apart, his regiment served in the worst battles on the Western Front from 1916 to the end of the war, including a spell on the Italian front, and in his memoir he does not mention casualties. This is not to say there were none, but it does suggest that even in fully engaged field artillery the casualties were neither frequent enough or numerous enough to be worthy of mention.

If this was the case in a highly mechanised and industrialised war in Europe then the casualty rate cannot have been worse in Mesopotamia (Iraq) where Barry saw most of his service. Indeed it is probable that the majority of casualties his unit suffered would have been the result of sickness and fever, which is probably why in five years service he did not get beyond the second step of the promotion ladder - Bombardier (Corporal). When one considers that in infantry regiments men from every kind of background were rising to the rank of Major and commanding 200 strong companies we have to ask why such a keen soldier did not get any further.

One reason might be because he could not grasp the high level of mathematics required even of NCOs for promotion in the artillery. But it is more likely that casualties were so few there were simply no vacancies for him to be promoted into. If there were no casualties there was no combat experience and certainly no infantry combat experience as evidenced by his apparently amateurish layout of the force at Kilmichael.

Unless his artillery unit was used as infantry as a temporary measure - which does happen from time to time as infantry casualties cannot always be replaced quickly - Barry would have had no man-to-man combat experience whatsoever. In normal circumstances artillerymen do not engage in any infantry combat; their job is to operate what is a highly complex and dangerous piece of equipment. They are first and foremost technicians and if they are endangered they must rely on their infantry for protection because they cannot serve the guns and fight as infantry at the same time. They and their guns are far too valuable an asset for the army to put them in machine gun range let alone to get within the 600 yards of the front that is normal maximum rifle range. If they did get within machine gun and rifle range they would be a prime target and dead within minutes.

Therefore it would be reasonable to assume that while Barry may have seen death and destruction aplenty it would be the aftermath of battle. In all probability he had never had the opportunity or indeed the need, to kill anyone at close quarters before Kilmicheal.

As to why he offered his services to the IRA, in many of his accounts he gives the conventional patriotic reasons and claims that they approached him because of his military experience. There is reason to believe that this is the opposite of the truth and he approached them, but because of his background - son of a policeman and five years' regular service in the British Army - they were understandably suspicious of him and took him on probation. I believe he actually left the British Army out of a sense of frustration at his lack of promotion.

His account of his reasons as given in *Curious Journey* is classic Barry. He claims that while serving in Mesopotamia at the time of the 1916 rising he could do nothing but was enraged by the executions of the leaders. For good measure he informs us that he could have cut their plan of campaign to pieces, which is not bad for a 20-year-old gunner with less than a year's service in the field artillery at the time. To quote him directly:

I got indignant with the idea of Dublin being shelled and I said to myself, "what the hell am I doing in the British Army? It's with the Irish I should be". From that time on then, although I went on all fronts and wasn't demobbed until January 1919 in Oswestry in Wales I was never happy until I could get home.

Actually, his file says he only served in Mesopotamia but this is not necessarily a complete record of his service. What is significant is that it notes he was discharged over a year later than he claims, on 31st March 1920 under Kings Regulations 392 (xxvi) which, when I checked, allowed for "discharge at own request". This would not have been difficult at the time as many army units were cutting back to peacetime levels but it suggests strongly that contrary to his declared patriotic rage and *"I was never happy until I could get home"*, he continued to serve as a regular soldier for almost 18 months after the end of the war.

So in all probability he left the army because he was frustrated by his lack of promotion. If in five years' service in a world war he did not get beyond Bombardier, his chance of advancement in the peacetime army must have been poorer still. At this point it is interesting to compare his army career to that of DI Craike, commander of the Auxiliaries, whom he killed. At just 27, Craike was two years older than Barry and from a working class background in Newcastle-upon-Tyne, yet he had won the Military Cross and risen to the rank of Captain in the Hampshire Regiment. Then he would have commanded a company of up to 200 men, twice the number General Barry had under command in his greatest "battle" at Crossbarry.

One must therefore accept that in every sense Barry was the inexperienced new man as Dr Hart states:

"Nine (of the IRA) had taken part in the great hunger strike in Wormwood Scrubs prison.... They were experienced local leaders and activists - hard men - with years of organising experience behind them and many battles ahead of them. Two had been wounded in previous fights another one died and seven more interned in 1921. Five were still with the column (later that year) at Crossbarry It was Barry who was the new man, the outsider.

The fact that Barry was new to close quarter killing is actually suggested by another obscure detail. Shortly after the affair he was hospitalised with what would now be called post-traumatic stress, which is only to be expected of an artilleryman witnessing slow butchery for the first time.

This is in contrast to the "hard men", who by all accounts were quite unaffected by the whole affair, although there are reports that one of the other "new" men's hair turned white and he never recovered from the shock of what he had witnessed. This unfortunate man was probably recycled as a victim of British terror as we shall see later.

To sum up Barry's close combat experience briefly, in practical terms - until he joined the IRA he didn't have any.

CHAPTER 11

PUBLISHED ACCOUNTS
OF KILMICHAEL

The absolute refusal of almost every Irishman and woman to consider Kilmicheal anything other than a glorious victory, despite typical British treachery reminds one of the story of the Sorcerer's Apprentice. Having used a spell to get a broom to carry buckets of water from the well, the apprentice finds he cannot stop it and the house is becoming flooded. In desperation he chops the broom in pieces only to find the pieces become brooms each carrying more buckets and he is worse off than before.

This is why it is impossible to discover the truth by analysing the hundreds, perhaps thousands, of written and oral accounts.

Any challenge to a detail produces at least two alternative explanations or excuses to justify it as a great patriotic feat of arms and when these are challenged, in turn even more improbable justifications are presented. The process continues until finally, as happened to Dr Peter Hart in 1998, patriots who were enraged at the mere idea that one of their great freedom fighters could be a liar never mind a vicious killer, threaten physical violence.

Nevertheless we need to compare some of the accounts written by various historians and of course the most "standard" of the many accounts given by Barry himself and these are as follows:

1. As described by Dr J Boyer Bell in his Book *The Secret Army, The IRA*

Dr J Boyer Bell is an American who has virtually made it his life's work to record "the determination of the Irish people to resist Saxon arrogance and brutality".

Which naturally means he is well thought of by Irish Republicans who cite his work as an example of how foreign academics see their history. They therefore present him as offering an independent, wholly impartial, view and his description of Kilmichael is as follows:

A typical round (of the fighting) occurred at the end of November when Tom Barry C/0 Cork No. 3 Brigade, carried out a most successful ambush at Kilmichael. 18 auxiliaries were killed, two armoured lorries were burned, and the British arms and ammunition captured for a loss of three IRA men.

There is little to say about his description of Kilmichael and one cannot criticise his statement that 18 auxiliaries were killed, as most writers quote between 16 and 18. However his praise of *"the determination of the Irish people to resist Saxon arrogance and brutality"* is neither independent nor academic and worthy of comment.

While they do have the occasional brainstorm, a less arrogant and brutal people would be difficult to find. Two quite different Irishmen noted their dislike of brutality. The first is the future Field Marshal Montgomery, when serving as a staff officer in County Cork during the "War of Independence" wrote, "We cannot win a war like this, but the Germans could". The second is Professor Lee, of the National University, who noted in his1997 book *Ireland Since 1900*, that the IRA were very fortunate they were not up against the Germans who had methods of dealing with recalcitrant populations *"which made the Black and Tans look like a Boy Scout Brigade."*

2. As described by F C L Lyons in his 1971 book *Ireland Since the Famine*.

At Kilmichael near Macroom Castle in County Cork, Tom Barry - Commandant of Cork No 3 Brigade of the IRA and unquestionably one of the most ruthless and successful of all the guerrilla leaders - placed his flying column of less than 40 men in ambush to await the return to their barracks of two lorry loads of auxiliaries. The lorries were slowed down by a ruse and as the police climbed down from them, they came under heavy fire; only one man survived and he had been left for dead

A fair, if incomplete, account and very unusually he notes that they were tricked into stopping (*"the lorries were slowed down by a ruse"*) and then shot down. Given the poor light, the inexperience of the IRA, the disposition of the IRA and of course, the location of the bodies (which he would probably not have known) this account does not fit.

They could not have been mown down in a blaze of gunfire, as half the IRA (about 20 men) were too far away to see and shoot and if Barry's own account is to be believed half of those who could shoot did not.

Interestingly there is no mention of a "false surrender" or any bayonet fighting - just that they were tricked into stopping - true - and then mown down. Which is essentially a sanitised version of what happened, so perhaps he learned what had actually happened from oral accounts but did not care to give the details?

3. From Townsend's *The British Campaign in Ireland 1920* written in the 1970s.

Somewhat different was the final dramatic event of November - the ambushing and annihilation of an A.D.R.I.C. patrol near Kilmichael, County Cork, a week after Bloody Sunday. It owed a good deal to their operational slackness, because the Macroom company had taken to sending patrols on almost fixed routes. The slaughter of 16 cadets in any area which had been quiet for some time, and which had come to look on the A.D.R.I.C. as in Tom Barry's words "super fighters and all but invincible" was a notable triumph for Barry's West Cork flying column, and a comment on the inefficiency of the measures taken so far against the rebels. ......the shock of Kilmichael numbed the police...

Maybe they *had* used fixed routes, but their reaction to the ambush was not slack. Their initial reaction was correct in every detail, they just did not calculate at being duped by a man posing as a British officer and possibly some men in something passing for British uniforms.

The slaughter of 16 cadets in any area which had been quiet for some time, and which had come to look on the A.D.R.I. C. as in Tom Barry's words "super fighters and all but invincible" was a notable triumph for Barry's West Cork flying column, and a comment on the inefficiency of the measures taken so far against the rebels."

Note no mention of "Tan Terror". The area had been *"quiet for some time"* and until then no effective action had been taken against the IRA.

"The shock of Kilmichael numbed the police…"

It didn't, it motivated them. He claims that the government suffered more casualties in the next six months than it had in the previous year and a half - but it had been trying to avoid fighting during the previous year and a half.

4. From *An illustrated History of Ireland* by Dr J Renlagh

A week after bloody Sunday, Tom Barry's Flying Column successfully ambushed a convoy of 18 auxiliaries at Kilmichael near Macroom in Cork, killing 17 of them. Two weeks later, auxiliaries and Black and Tans went on another rampage, burning the centre of Cork city to the ground. Damage was estimated at £3 million.

A fairly standard account, but earlier in the book he makes the following ill-considered comment which I shall return to later:

The story of Ireland is fundamentally one of a conquered people who suffered the worst of all possible fates; they were made first to feel and then believe themselves inferior. Tom Barry the legendary 1919-23 IRA guerrilla leader once told me that only half his men could bring themselves to fire at the British auxiliaries during the famous ambush at Kilmichael, because, when they actually faced naked British authority, they were frightened by their own temerity.

This is sadly quite the wrong conclusion as will be shown later.

5. British journalist Robert Kee in his book *The Green Flag* published in the 1980s:

The deadlock was made all more grim and complete when........ the authorities received from a different quarter another shattering blow to their prestige. Two lorry loads of auxiliaries stationed at Macroom Castle ran into a well-laid ambush position prepared by Tom Barry and the West Cork Flying Column on a lonely site of bog land and rocks near Kilmichael. It was the auxiliaries' first major engagement and a terrible one. After a savage fight at close quarters in which three IRA were killed and, according to Barry, the auxiliaries made use of notorious false surrender tactics, the entire convoy was wiped out, and 17 of the 18 auxiliaries were killed. The 18th was so severely wounded that he was in hospital for a long time afterwards. Some of the auxiliaries' bodies were afterwards found to have wounds inflicted after death and the first British officer on the scene after the fight said that although he had seen thousands of men lying dead in the course of the war, he had never before seen such an appalling sight as met his eyes there. The doctor at the inquest, an Irishman, said that there was no doubt that some injuries had been inflicted after death.

The government made full propaganda use of the injuries, even going so far as to state that the corpses of the cadets had been mutilated with axes. Bayonets were certainly used in the fight and they may well have accounted for some of the mutilation on both counts and that some bayoneting may even have taken place deliberately after death is not impossible, since irregulars in action often have to make up with primitive emotion for the steadier nerve required by professionals in long training. Barry concedes that the morale of the column was so disturbed by the fight that to reassert discipline he had to drill them in the road for five minutes among the corpses and the blazing lorries.

He makes the following notes

Survivors of an ambush in County Clare two months later said that the wounded had been bayoneted in the road by the IRA (Irish Times 25* January, 1921)

Summary

We can see all these writers think Kilmichael is worthy of mention, but none of them go into any detail. Robert Kee appears to be the only one to go beyond setting down the bare details and suggest the killing of wounded may have happened as the IRA were said to have done it elsewhere.

To me the most interesting account is that by F C L Lyons. He tells us that the lorries were slowed down by a ruse and the police were then mown by heavy fire as they dismounted. Setting aside the details of timing and the course of the action it could be said that this is a pretty accurate statement of what happened. One wonders if he did some original research and knew precisely what happened but did not think appropriate or perhaps wise/safe to publish his findings.

However, it is with regret that I must take particular exception to a reference to Kilmichael in Dr John Renlagh's book. His description of the ambush in the main body of his book is straightforward:

A week after Bloody Sunday Tom Barry's Flying Column successfully ambushed a convoy of 18 auxiliaries at Kilmichael near Macroom in Cork, killing 17 of them.

This is of course beyond dispute and he totally accepts Barry's account, which he recorded first hand. However when combined with his complete ignorance of military practice, military technology and, not least, reality of ordinary men's behavior in war, it results in him making the following quite appalling presumption:

Half his men could not bring themselves to fire at the British Auxiliaries during the famous ambush at Kilmichael, because, when they actually faced naked British authority, they were frightened by their own temerity.

It is unfortunate that a man as honest as Dr Renlagh could write this, but when it comes down to it, Irishman of all classes fall back on standard perceptions to explain our history. In this case the Irish being so degraded that they could not bring themselves to fight for freedom. Thus he does not understand that getting ordinary people to kill each other is not as easy as one would think. A thousand years of Christian teaching and a couple of centuries or so of reasonable civil government means that most Western Europeans have a distinct aversion to killing - particularly if they lack the intensive indoctrination given during military training with no motivation beyond a desire for adventure fired by a patriotic fantasy.

Dr Renlagh would not consider it possible that they were for the most part just a group of decent young men thrust into a violent action who were at the last moment too shocked to break the ultimate taboo of killing. They were expected to act in a manner that was outside anything they had experienced in their lives.

This is more common than one would think. The Welsh author Leslie Thomas recorded that when his hotchpotch patrol composed of army pay clerks and depot staff met with a crowd of rioters in Singapore he obeyed orders as if in a dream and kept asking himself if he was really there and what he was doing. When THE moment arrives intelligent men in these situations ask themselves the question,

"What the hell am I doing here?"

Consider the words "*When they actually faced naked British authority, they were frightened by their own temerity.*

No! In any battle only a minority of men fire their personal weapons and American studies in 1944-45 put the figure at only 25% until they introduced a more intensive training programme that managed to raise the average to 50%. The truth is that the overwhelming majority of men finding themselves in combat just want to be somewhere else, not only on the first occasion but on many subsequent occasions.

It has nothing whatever to do with belonging to an emotionally crushed race and everything to do with disorientation and natural fear when faced with the possibility not just of imminent death but a very unpleasant death indeed.

One could give no better reference to the feelings of men in combat anywhere than is found in Shakespeare's *Henry V*. The heroic speeches are well known, "*Once more into the breach dear friends!*" and "*We are but warriors for the working day.*"

Few quote the quiet observation by a soldier the night before the battle, "*There are few die well that die in war.*"

It is the custom in Ireland that when we wish to attack someone we begin by praising them, before sadly saying, "How could such a decent fellow/person like you get it so wrong?" I should therefore make it clear that I consider Dr Renlagh an honest historian. His book *An Illustrated History of Ireland* from which this quote is taken is generally a very objective short history. Furthermore I shall always be grateful to him for an observation he made on the suppression of rebellion in Ireland in the 16th century: "the suppression of rebellions in England was no less brutal".

This made me ask, "What rebellions in England? They never told us about any English rebellions at school!"

I was interested enough to check this and found to my surprise that Queen Elizabeth I, "Good Queen Bess", ordered 700 men be hanged in Yorkshire. They had taken part in a rebellion that was little more than a protest march with some minor violence. A rather embarrassed English historian wrote that due to the difficulty identifying the "rebels" - they had all gone home - "probably only 300-350 were actually hanged". Others guess at between 600 and 900 and most were hanged outside their own homes as an example to their neighbours.

But let us look finally at Barry's own account from *Curious Journey:*

The auxiliaries first arrived in Cork late in the summer of 1920 and from that day on they spent their time driving into villages and terrorising everybody. They'd beat up people and strip them and shoot the place up, and then go back to the barracks drunk on the stuff they'd looted. We knew we had to stop them, that was what the fight at Kilmichael was all about

We nearly had to call it off before it happened. I'd selected a spot near Macroom - the only spot we were sure they'd pass - and we had a long march there all night through the rain. We didn't know when they'd come, and we had to wait lying low in the ditches all day without food. By 4 o'clock - it was 28th November - it was getting dark, and I nearly called it off then. But then we heard two lorries of them coming.

There was a bend in the road there and we had to make sure they'd slow up. So I had an IRA officer's tunic, and the idea was that when they came along the road they'd see an officer standing in the ditch facing the, they'd see this man in a trench coat and leggings, and they'd slow down to see who it was. They might even think it was one of themselves. There were going round in all sorts of dress at that time. And that's what they did, they slowed down about 50 yards away and kept coming very slow until they got about 20 yards away and a Mills bomb was thrown from our side. It landed right in the driver's seat and killed him.

Fire was opened up then and it became a hand-to-hand fight. It was so close that one of our fellows caught a spurt of blood full in the mouth from a severed artery of one of the auxiliaries. We had the better of them there because they were screaming, yelling and our fellows just kept quiet and wiped them all out. There were nine of them dead on the road and all of our men were still alive.

In the meantime the second lorry had come along, and a section of our men up the road giving battle to them. So I went along the side of the road with some of the men from the command post and as we got up behind them - they didn't see us - they threw away their rifles and we heard them shouting "We surrender!" We surrender! Three of our men stood out from their positions to take the surrender, but the minute they did the others open fire on them and killed two of them. So we continued up behind them and I gave the order to keep firing until I said to stop, and then after we killed a couple more of them they saw they were sandwiched between two lines of fire. They started shouting "We surrender!" again. But having seen the false surrender I told the men to keep *firing and we did until last of them was dead. I blame myself, of course, for our own losses because I should have seen through the false surrender trick.*

After that some of our men were shaken by the whole thing and I had to drill them in the road, march them up and down, to preserve discipline. I've written about this and I don't want to go into all the details, but it was a strange sight, with the lorries burning in the night and these men marching along, back and forth between the blood and the corpses. They'd gone through a terrifying experience and proved themselves to be the better men in close combat. Their clothes were soaking and by the time they marched off they'd gone 36 hours without food. But if they didn't keep their discipline we might lose everything. Discipline was all we had.

This is probably Barry's definitive account and worth detailed examination

The auxiliaries first arrived in Cork late in the summer of 1920 and from that day on they spent their time driving into villages and terrorising everybody. They'd beat up people and strip them and shoot the place up, and then go back to the barracks drunk on the stuff they'd looted. We knew we had to stop them, that was what the fight at Kilmichael was all about.

But no details of the time, place and extent of these assaults on the population have ever been given. There is a report that a prominent member of the IRA, Liam Deasy, had met the commander of the auxiliaries DI Crake, who was killed at Kilmichael and thought him a very decent fellow. There is also a statement by a one of Crake's company who was not at Kilmichael that DI Crake kept them on very tight discipline. Also Professor Townsend states categorically, *"The area had been quiet for some time."*

We nearly had to call it off before it happened. I'd selected a spot near Macroom - the only spot we were sure they'd pass - and we had a long march there all night through the rain. We didn't know when they'd come, and we had to wait lying low in the ditches all day without food. By 4 o'clock - it was 28th November- it was getting dark, and I nearly called it off then. But then we heard two lorries of them coming.

So he heard TWO lorries!

There was a bend in the road there and we had to make sure they'd slow up. So I had an IRA officer's tunic, and the idea was that when they came along the road they see an officer standing in the ditch facing them, they'd see this man in a trench coat and leggings, and they'd slow down to see who it was. They might even think it was one of themselves.

In *Curious Journey* he tells how he captured a uniform belonging to a Colonel of the Kings Regiment with the mess bill in the pocket that he courteously returned. Would this be the same uniform? If so it was deliberate deception. "They might even think it was one of themselves" had nothing to do with it.

There were going round in all sorts of dress at that time. And that's what they did, they slowed down about

50 yards away and kept coming very slow until they got about 20 yards away and a Mills bomb was thrown from our side. It landed right in the driver's seat and killed him.

So why was the lorry found pulled up on the correct side of the road by his "command post" if the driver had been killed outright by a grenade while the lorry was "20 yards away" and still "coming very slow" towards him?

Fire was opened up then and it became a hand-to-hand fight.

Hand-to-hand with men in the back of a lorry out of control because the driver was dead and most of Barry's own men in the immediate area were on a rocky hillock 4-5 metres high overlooking the road?

It was so close that one of our fellows caught a spurt of blood full in the mouth from a severed artery of one of the auxiliaries. We had a better than them there because they were screaming, yelling and our fellows just kept quiet and wiped them all out. There were nine of them dead on the road and all of our men were still alive.

Teenagers with a total of one week's training and they could outfight nine men with up to four years' combat experience each? The spurt of blood appears in several of his accounts and will be covered later.

In the meantime the second lorry had come along, and a section of our men up the road giving battle to them.

But Barry said he heard TWO lorries coming and even with the noise of a grenade, gunfire, screams and yells 300 yards away the second lorry had just "come along"?

So I went along the side of the road with some of the men from the command post and as we got up behind them - they didn't see us - they threw away their rifles and we heard them shouting "We surrender!" We surrender!

So why were three bodies found lying out in the open as if advancing in extended line formation if they were firing at men on high ground to their front and rear?

Three of our men stood out from their positions to take the surrender, but the minute they did the others open fire on them and killed two of them.

Just does not make sense given the relative locations where the auxiliaries' bodies were found and the known IRA positions.

So we continued up behind them and I gave the order to keep firing until I said to stop, and then after we killed a couple more of them they saw they were sandwiched between two lines of fire they started shouting "We surrender!" again.

They were in a trap from the moment the shooting started. If Barry moved as he says and they were sandwiched between two lines of fire it means his men would have been shooting at each other.

But having seen the false surrender I told the men to keep firing and we did until last of them was dead I blame myself of course for our own losses because I should have seen through the false surrender trick.

How did he pass the order to 30 men scattered across several hillocks up to 300 metres away over rough boggy ground and in semi darkness?

After that some of our men were shaken by the whole thing and I had to drill them in the road, march them up and down, to preserve discipline.

This is generally accepted to have happened and as I shall show, is the only creditable thing in the whole bloody business.

I've written about this and I don't want to go into all the details...

Too true he doesn't want to go into details.

CHAPTER 12

KILMICHEAL COURSE OF THE ACTION BASED ON STANDARD OPERATIONAL PROCEDURES (SOP)

Few people understand that every army, and Western armies in particular, operate according to a series of standard procedures usually referred to as "The Book".

The experience that is gained in every conceivable type of operation and military situation is analysed and the best procedure for dealing with them is written into "The Book". The use that is made of the book depends very much on the national characteristics of the army writing it.

Pierre Reinfret put his survival down to two things, firstly luck and secondly in the two years the US Army spent teaching him to march on parade and scrub kitchens he took the trouble to read every single manual he could get his hands on.

By contrast the German army had a book for every conceivable situation and made sure the contents were drummed into every soldier. That way they could all be relied on to act in the same way and apply the best solution to a situation when the need arose.

The Germans went to the ultimate as far as best procedures were concerned even requiring a corporal to march his section to the latrine to empty their bowels every day. Had George Coppard known this he might have understood the photograph he found on a dead German. This showed the man and his comrades sitting in a row looking over their shoulders at the camera with their bare backsides exposed. Soldiers' humour.

Those who sneer at this as bone-headed Prussian militarism might consider that by common consent the German army was unquestionably the most efficient army in the Second World War. Churchill considered its performance to be quite remarkable and more than one British officer openly stated that man for man the Germans were better soldiers. There are a number of reasons for this, but not least of them is the fact that everybody knew "The Book" by heart and when to apply it.

This was explained to me in the 1960s by a man who had been a lance corporal in Britain's Royal Corps of Signals who told me, "The trouble the Americans have in Vietnam is that they are fighting by the book and every army reads the same book. When a conventional unit is fired on the book tells the commander where the enemy should be and it is usually right because the enemy army uses the same book. The problem with the Vietcong is that they are guerrillas who make it up as they go along because they have not read the book." Several other men who had more direct experience of fighting guerrillas have since confirmed this to me. As they put it, they simply "don't work to the book".

Bearing in mind there is a standard military response or what is now called Standard Operational Procedure for

EDWARD BROWNING

every situation, we can look at the map of Kilmichael and see what would have happened had it been a regular ambush and started as Barry and his champions insist.

When fighting erupted around the first vehicle the commander of the second would have immediately halted, dismounted his troops and taken up a defended position on the hill to the north of the road. He would then have assessed the situation and done one of two things. His first objective would be to go to the aid of the crew of the first vehicle, if this was tactically possible he would have left a party on the hill to provide covering fire while leading the remainder forward to help. If on the other hand he considered the crew of the first vehicle completely lost he would order his own vehicle to turn round, pull back and covered its retreat until they got to a position where they could remount and go for help.

Of course, he could not have moved on to the hill and set up what is now called a firebase because it was already occupied by the IRA. We know he did not do this because if he had, fighting would have erupted on the occupied hill and there would have been more bodies there and by the second vehicle. Instead the dead were found in the open, half way between the two lorries in an advancing skirmish line. There is another reason why he would not have occupied the hill before moving forward, because there had been no grenade and no firing when the first vehicle stopped. He did not realise he was inside an ambush and saw no reason to occupy a position so far back.

Therefore he took what was a reasonable tactical decision at that time. He left two men to defend his vehicle and

184

moved forward himself with a couple of men to investigate why the first vehicle had stopped. He also instructed the remainder to follow him at a reasonable distance, moving into a tactical formation as soon as they were within a couple of hundred yards of the first vehicle. Allowing for failing light at that time of day that would have been the distance for a reasonable rifle shot to and from the area where the first vehicle had inexplicably halted.

This is why three bodies from the second vehicle's crew were found formed in a line, the end man of which was about to scale a second hillock and walk unto an IRA position. At that point there was a burst of fire, which immediately brought down the three men on the left hand end of the extended line.

In this situation the only course of action for the crew of the second vehicle to take was to fall back to their vehicle as quickly as possible. But they were completely surrounded and with riflemen at close range on the side of the road they were brought down quickly and only the driver of the second vehicle, Cadet Guthrie, was able to escape in the darkness

COURSE OF THE ACTION

So what *actually* happened at Kilmichael on that dark winter afternoon - and just as important, why?

To understand, we need to remember the boring details of ambushing, weapons, psychology etc. we have just read and refer to the plan of the ambush made by the Auxiliaries when they recovered the bodies.

We can take it for granted that Barry stood by the road and flagged down the first vehicle and that he was wearing a British officer's uniform, because he said as much ("They may have mistaken me for one of themselves"). From Kenneth Griffith's book, Barry tells how they "captured" the uniform from the Colonel of the Kings Regiment complete with his mess bill in the pocket which he returned because he was known to treat the IRA sympathetically. We may ask what else would he want a British Colonel's uniform for, except deception?

We must also take into account the several reports, including that of the only British survivor - Cadet Forde - that the IRA wore British uniforms complete with British steel helmets. I doubt all the IRA were so equipped but for added deception they would not need to be; a few men in army overcoats with rifles and steel helmets would create the necessary effect, particularly if, as reported, the Auxiliaries knew the army was operating in the area at the time. There would be no problem in obtaining any number of army greatcoats, because thousands of demobilised solders in Britain and Ireland were given the option of keeping their coats or handing them in at a railway station where they would be paid £3 for them.

There is another reason why Barry was chosen to stand in the road and flag down the patrol. A man has to be used to wearing a uniform to look right in it and this can often be seen from the extras in the background of many war movies. If you look closely you can see by the fit of the uniforms and nature of their movements they are not soldiers but actors dressed up. That Barry had been in

British uniform for five years meant he could look relaxed in it, when any other IRA man in a British officer's uniform would just not look right and this would be apparent to the crew.

With the disguise of the uniform and natural military bearing Barry might well have had a few steel helmeted men in the background giving the impression he was commander of a friendly unit. Having stopped the vehicle he could have instructed the commander D I Craik to get his men off the wagon to join him for any one of a dozen reasons. Once they were out of sight of the second vehicle they could have been ordered at gunpoint to drop their weapons and surrender. They would almost certainly have done so because the shock of what they thought were British soldiers under a British officer suddenly turning weapons on them would completely disorientate them.

The IRA probably expected the crew of the second vehicle to close up on the first when they could have been similarly deceived but they did not allow for the auxiliaries' professionalism. Instead of just driving up to the first vehicle or wandering down the road like a rabble they took the precaution of forming up and advancing in fighting order.

"We threw a grenade which landed in the driver's seat and killed him outright."

This is possible even though it is very difficult to throw anything into the cab of a moving vehicle, particularly in the dusk. To be fair there is a sport in rural Ireland where they throw a ball the size of the grenade along the road and bet on the outcome, so anyone who was good at this could theoretically throw a grenade into a cab.

However this can be discounted because grenades are extremely dangerous and quite impartial as to the identity or cause of both thrower and victims. They pose a serious risk to anyone in a 25 yard radius and for this reason they are only used when the thrower is behind some kind of cover. They are normally only thrown into enclosed places such as bunkers, trenches or the rooms of houses, in fact anywhere the blast is confined.

If a grenade had landed in the cab it would still pose a considerable risk to anyone nearby, including Barry who claims he was standing by the road as the lorry drew up. Had it bounced off the lorry and into the road Barry would have been at least injured or even killed. If it had landed in the cab, an explosion in such a confined space would be more than likely to rip the driver and commander to pieces. Not blow them away, just tear them to shreds, making it difficult to remove the remains without a shovel. A body could fall or be blown out of the driver's seat into a messy heap on the road - but no bodies were found in the cab or on the road near either vehicle and the body of the patrol commander who would have sat next to him was found several yards away on the track by Barry's "Command post".

Even if a grenade was thrown into the cab as it slowed down, the vehicle would have continued forward for at least a short distance and gone out of control as the driver was killed. But it was halted on the correct side of the road by a junction and the explosion would have instantly alerted the second vehicle a few hundred yards behind.

Given the impartial nature of hand grenades it would be interesting to speculate whether their own grenade caused at least one of the IRA casualties - just a thought.

The only logical explanation of this phase is to consider Barry's statement that he flagged the first lorry down at the place where it and the bodies of the eight or nine men - who we can assume were its crew - were found.

We have said that they were tricked into stopping and the grenade story is improbable. What is not apparent on the plan, but is very clear on the ground, is that these eight or nine bodies were in a depression behind a rocky hillock about four to five metres high. Even allowing for the tree planting which has taken place since 1920 it is obvious they were screened on three sides, four if you count their own tender and they could not have been seen from the second vehicle.

It is possible that Barry alone flagged the vehicle down and when the commander dismounted to talk to him held a pistol to his head and invited him and his men to surrender, but the greater deception with uniformed men in the background is more likely. What was going on would not be obvious to the second vehicle even if they were in sight because it was late afternoon in November and going dark.

But crucially, consider the one thing that proves Barry a liar. The one thing that no in-depth interview with veterans, no general's memoir, no detailed research, no records official or unofficial, no cover story considers, no historian thought of and no book, written dissertation or printed word can ever convey. What is this single piece of evidence that destroys his credibility?

NOISE!

We are so used to "noise pollution" today that we cannot understand how quiet the countryside was then and in the more remote areas is still. A city dweller who settled in East Anglia was in his garden and sensed something unusual. After a few minutes it dawned on him what it was - the silence compared to London.

Had "battle commenced" the noise would have been heard up to a mile away and the crew of the second tender would know instantly what had happened. Any gunfire, let alone the noise of an exploding grenade, would have alerted them at once! So there was no grenade and no battle. But what then?

Well, this is where we see just how professional the Auxiliaries were, but it did not save them.

Remember in this situation vehicles stay in contact, but as far apart as possible and if the first vehicle is seen to stop the last thing the rest of the party or convoy will do is drive up to it to see why.

Hence the position of the second vehicle 250-300 meters back. Having stopped well back, the commander would then go forward or send a party forward to discover what was happening and why the first tender had stopped. Remember also it was late afternoon in November and going dark. Had there been any gunfire, let alone the noise of an exploding grenade, the commander would instantly have had the crew take up fire positions around the vehicle and assessed the situation before trying to counter attack or even approach the first vehicle. He would then have immediately occupied the rocky hillock on the north-eastern (left) side of the road with up to half his force to cover the first vehicle and the approaches to it before sending anyone forward.

This is absolutely standard procedure and, as we know, if this had happened they would have stumbled into the IRA positions on the hillock and the shooting would have started then. That they did not do so tells us there had been no shooting and they did not appreciate they were already inside the ambush area.

As we have said, eight bodies, Webster, Baylby, Crake, Cleave, Graham, Bradshaw, Poole and Wainwright were found in a group where they would have been out of sight from the second lorry. So we can assume they were the crew of the first vehicle.

Close by were those of three more men, Cadets Hugo, Lucas and Hooper-Jones and it is reasonable to assume that these were from the second vehicle and had moved forward to investigate the reason for the stop.

We can again take it for granted that there was no firing up to this point or they would not have moved down to the first vehicle let alone got so close.

We are now into phase two and from here we are into the area of conjecture as to the detail of when the shooting was started and by whom.

It is improbable that the eight men from the first vehicle started it, as they were certainly prisoners at the time. The bodies of four of what can only have been some of the crew of the second vehicle were about 100 metres back up the road from where the main group of eight bodies (prisoners) were found.

Again it is highly significant that three bodies, those of Ford, Pallister and Taylor were in line abreast, an equal distance apart because that is the correct tactical formation for infantry advancing when an enemy may be encountered. The standard procedure is to advance in a straight line keeping as much distance as possible between each man to make the most difficult target. Nearby, but on the opposite side of the road, was the body of Pearson, who might have either been the fourth man in the line or could have been a little way behind it. I would guess it most likely that he was on the end of the advancing line and was shot while trying to get back to his vehicle when Ford, Pallister, Taylor were killed.

That Ford, Pallister and Taylor's bodies were in a line tells us they were cut down in the first burst of firing and literally dropped on the spot where they stood. Otherwise they would have gone to cover or run forward to attack as the situation demanded. They fell before they could do either.

There are several scenarios as to how the shooting started.

For example one could say the three men who reached the first vehicle shouted a warning to the rest of the party following. This is unlikely given the position of the four bodies 100 metres back up the road, particularly those of Ford, Pallister, and Taylor. If one looks at the plan one can see that Taylor was about to climb the hillock occupied by some of the ambush party when he was shot dead and to have got so close before he was killed is not unusual in a well-concealed ambush, particularly in poor light.

There could have been no firing until this point or the second group of Auxiliaries would never have got so close. I would guess, and it is no more than that, three men Hugo, Lucas and Hooper-Jones reached the first vehicle with the rest of the crew following in support at least 100 metres behind. At this point the IRA opened fire when this support group of four men, including the line with Ford, Pallister, Taylor were about to overrun one of their ambush positions.

It is anyone's guess what happened in the second phase but it would have taken less than a minute.

Again, the three men (Ford, Pallister and Taylor) were cut down immediately and allowing for those IRA guarding the prisoners, the remaining five were being fired on by up to 20 rifles at point blank range, in some cases from as little as 25 metres. In bad light even an amateur can hardly miss at that range. The three men nearest the first vehicle could have arrived there simultaneously with the outbreak of firing and died quickly at the hands of the IRA nearby.

Returning to the use of the hand grenade. Looking at the position of the second vehicle it would seem possible it was thrown into its cab at this time. Assuming the driver stayed at the wheel with his engine running and probably in gear, which again is normal in this situation, the arrival of a grenade in his cab would have meant he would leave it at some speed. Grenades are fused to go off between four and ten seconds after the pin is pulled and this is a long time for a quick-witted man, let alone veterans like the Auxiliaries to get clear. In the movies, of course, the driver would have picked it up and thrown it out or thrown it back but in real life anyone who has fumbled around the floor of a car looking for something knows he would be better using the few seconds available to jump out - which is probably why this vehicle was found run off the road and with an empty cab. This is what one would have expected to have happened to the first lorry had Barry been telling the truth.

It would also be reasonable to assume the two bodies of the men nearest the second vehicle - Barnes and Jones - had been left to guard it when the rest moved down the road. When the shooting started and a grenade landed in the cab the only thing they could do was run to join the main group 150 meters down the road in the semi-darkness. The plan shows they did not get far.

It is at this point that Barry took the three casualties for which he blames himself - attributing them to his honourable and chivalrous nature, which was betrayed by the mean and treacherous British. He may very well have been responsible for his own casualties but it could be asked if the British actually killed all of them.

Among the many "Irish" jokes circulating in England a few years ago was a cartoon of an Irish firing squad with the victim in the centre of a circle with the firing squad around him pointing inwards. This is in fact a simplified plan of Berry's ambush, a brilliant ambush if we are to believe Dr Bowyer-Bell. Any corporal in a modern army would be reduced to private at once for such unbelievable stupidity because the men on either side of the road were in each other's line of fire. Even in daylight the risk of hitting their own men in the confusion was high, let alone in the dusk when the ambush occurred. In fact, this layout does make sense if one feeds in other fragments of information that allow you to discern a darker purpose.

My first thought was that because Ireland's Legendary Guerrilla Leader's military experience was gained in the Royal Field Artillery he did not have the necessary experience to mount an ambush. In the British Army the infantry call the Royal Artillery "The five mile snipers" because that is about as close as they get to front line combat. Barry would not know the capability of infantry weapons, otherwise the men would never have been set out on either side of the road where they were in each other's field of fire. Why did he make such a basic mistake? Originally I thought inexperience and his service in the British Army, because at that time regular armies had not studied ambushes. They were not part of the business of European war that thought only in terms of manoeuvre against similar armies with regiments of infantry, artillery and cavalry.

Ambushes were for "colonial" warfare with "natives" attacking columns typically on the North West frontiers of India where the British Army got most of its combat experience before the First World War. In that environment the way he set his ambush would make sense. Tribesmen several hundred feet up an Afghan mountainside, firing down onto a road on the valley bottom were not going to shoot their compatriots on the opposite hill. There were a lot of Indian Army units in Mesopotamia with Barry and he would undoubtedly have met men who had served on the frontier and heard their experiences of Afghans firing down from the hills and thought: "That's how it's done"!

But adding in a little more obscure, but critical, detail I realised this apparently poor - even suicidal - disposition was ideal for another even darker purpose. The layout of the IRA men at Kilmichael broke every rule in the book for a conventional ambush because they should have been concentrated in groups that allowed the maximum fire on the Auxiliaries while they were still in their vehicles. Not only were the men too spread out, 36 men was too small a force to take on 18 veteran Auxiliaries.

A week previously at Rineen in County Clare 50 IRA men had been concentrated under the command of an ex-Irish Guardsman to wipe out a six strong RIC patrol that was also making a routine journey. On this occasion the IRA used explosive bullets and not only finished off the wounded at the site but took the trouble to track a wounded constable into the countryside and kill him too. So from this one incident I had to conclude that the IRA knew how to carry out an ambush properly It is worth mentioning that at Rineen, with the exception of one Black and Tan, all the RIC were Irishmen with between one and eight years' service in the force There has never been any suggestion that they were killed to save the local people from a reign of terror or that they were killed as a reprisal for firing on the IRA after a false surrender. They were still massacred and their wounded murdered - just a thought.

Rineen tells us that the IRA had learned to do things properly, by targeting a routine journey and taking the time to prepare and select the ambush site, but most importantly taking sufficient men to ensure the patrol could be overwhelmed without difficulty.

Then I asked myself why the haste to attack what had become a very routine patrol? There was no need to ambush them with men who had only a week's training because they knew the route had become routine. They could have waited another two or three weeks, or even another month. Or they could have called in more experienced men and, more importantly, more men. Therefore, I deduced that time was imperative and being an Irishman and understanding the national taste for symbolic revenge coupled with the manner of the Auxiliaries' deaths, I looked for a reason.

When examining any incident one must ask *why* something happened and my initial conclusions were based on two assumptions. The first was that the near 100% casualty rate was unusual and had to be a result of deliberate action to finish off the wounded. I subsequently found out that in guerrilla warfare it is often the practice to massacre the enemy in an ambush and this occurs from time to time in conventional warfare.

So finding massacres were more common than I believed, I then came to the conclusion that Barry killed the prisoners in revenge for his own casualties. This too is common, as men seldom show mercy to the killers of their friends and comrades and this is the reason Barry gave. He was provoked by the treacherous behavior of the Auxiliaries in shooting down his men as they went to accept their surrender.

However, having studied a plan of the ambush and the position of the bodies I could see that this was absolute nonsense.

The story about the grenade being thrown at the start did not make sense and the second lorry did not just "happen along", they were travelling together. Barry and his men lacked the experience, training and communications to move up to it as a "command group". By his own admission, while he gave different reasons at different times, only half of his men took part in the fighting anyway. It was in the course of my research that I stumbled across something else which looked more like the real reason he shot and hacked his prisoners to death in cold blood - for that is what was done.

The Sunday morning a week before Kilmichael, the IRA, under the direction of Michael Collins, killed 12 British Army officers in their homes or hotel rooms around Dublin in a co-ordinated mass assassination. The event is well known and well documented and like Kilmicheal it is always mentioned, but it has never occurred to anyone that the two incidents might be linked. The officers were described as spies and torturers who planned to assassinate the entire leadership of Sinn Fein and destroy the independence movement. Michael Collins in a "brilliant counterstroke" destroyed them in a single blow and he in his own words "put out the eyes of the British in Ireland".

As usual this is utter nonsense, but explaining why is not the subject of this chapter. The Republican writer and playwright Ulick O'Connor tells the story of their deaths as follows:

"By about 9:30am the killing everywhere was over as yet the military were not aware of what had happened. At about 9.20 General Crozier was passing 22 Upper Mount Street with a group of Auxiliaries when they heard shooting. It was probably the execution of a spy named McMahon who had been warned more than once by Collins not to come back to Ireland. General Crozier jumped out and ran towards the house. Two auxiliaries who went to the back were shot by Tom Keogh who burst out through the cordon as they came towards him."

Details in Britain's Public Record Office that were in a closed file until 1970, tell a different story. The notes begin by saying that unconfirmed reports were coming in of officers being shot all over the city. A later note states that they seem to be mostly intelligence and legal officers. Then another note records that two of the new Auxiliary police are missing and during the course of the day increasingly anxious notes record that they had still not been found. Finally, with some shock, it is recorded that their bodies have been found in a back garden and what obviously happened is that they had set off in pursuit of the killers of one of the officers and overtaken the IRA pickets. Finding themselves outnumbered they surrendered and then they were disarmed, put against the nearest wall and shot. It concludes by saying that these are the first of the "New Police" to be killed and the manner of their deaths has made a very deep impression on the whole force.

Actually the report in the Public Record Office was written on the day and as often happens with initial reports, it is wrong. A later investigation found that the two men were making their way back to barracks for help when they were stopped and questioned by the IRA, then taken into the back garden put against a wall and shot through the head. As they would have been able to identify their captors this can be passed us off as military necessity and a quite acceptable action when done by freedom fighters. However, in war it is always considered a crime and inevitably provokes reprisals from the victims' comrades.

One can assume that these were the two auxiliaries *"who went to the back were shot by Tom Keogh who burst out through the cordon as they came towards him"* described in O'Connor's book. After all no one could expect Tom Keogh to say *"We took their weapons questioned them and shot them through the head to prevent them identifying us"*. In Western societies such action is just not acceptable, so he was required to give and in this case create, an "acceptable" explanation for the deaths. In time he may even have come to believe it himself as people often do in these cases.

Everyone is of course aware of two other deaths that occurred on the same day when two IRA men held prisoner in the guardroom of Dublin Castle were killed by their Black and Tan guards, probably with bayonets. The room in which they were killed was subsequently dedicated to their memory as a museum cum shrine. The time at which these men were killed is unknown but it is reasonable to conclude that they were killed by the guard in response to the execution/murders of their friends when they heard their bodies had been found. At least one Irish writer quietly acknowledged this when he stated the two IRA men were killed in revenge, but with typical economy of truth he did not specify who or what they were killed in revenge for - leaving open the implication that they were in response to the massacre of the officers This is certainly not the case, because as far as the Black & Tans were concerned the regular army officers killed by the IRA on that day were of no concern to them because they were not "their" comrades.

The Dublin Castle killings were passed off by saying the two men had attempted to escape. This is a political explanation which most Irish writers treat with understandable contempt, but just why the guard would kill them needs further explanation. To scream "that's not fair!" may be the view of most people but it is not enough.

In the Second World War it is estimated that a prisoner's chances of survival in the hands of front line troops be they British, American or German were no better than 50/50. When soldiers carry out an attack that leaves their closest friends dead and dying they are not inclined to give the killers directions to the nearest Prisoner of War camp. One officer related how in Italy one unit bayoneted surrendering Germans with the *traditional* response "too late chum". Quite simply if you made a serious attempt to kill an attacking soldier and failed he would certainly kill you. To put it in modem terms: "No chance, you tried hard to kill me, now it's my turn."

It does not excuse the Castle killings/murders but for the first time the IRA were not dealing with the civilian policemen of the RIC or teenage soldiers who had never seen action. Now they were faced with veterans of Flanders trenches who did not take things such as the killing (murder?) of comrades lightly. To quote Coppard again, "Whatever they (the Germans) did to us, it was meet and proper we did it back to them" and for the first time the IRA were faced (repaid?) with what Professor Beckett called the hard currency of terror.

Consider again the action of the men of the Manchester Regiment on the first day of the Somme in 1916. Having suffered over 400 casualties in the few hundred yards advance across no man's land they set about killing every German they could find regardless of whether they wanted to surrender or were even armed. One man who had retained some humanity was appalled when the first German he saw staggered out of a dugout shocked, half dressed and terrified offering him his gold watch in return for his life. When a comrade came up he asked why he had not bayoneted the man he said, "Look at him!" and was told he was getting soft. He told the German to "bugger off", in this case meaning, get out of here, but the German did not get far before he was shot by someone else.

Knowing Collins' nature it is logical that he instructed immediate and characteristically ruthless retaliatory action for the Castle killings. I think that is the truth of Kilmichael; it was a deliberate act of policy to show the new police - The Black and Tans - that anything you can do I can do worse.

As such it was mistaken because the men he was dealing with were a type he had never met before. Collins might fool the leadership of Sinn Fein, lead the British intelligencia a merry dance and have the International press eating out of his hand, but the "Tans" were among the hardest and toughest men in Europe at the time and well able to show him what ruthlessness meant.

This led me to look again at the disposition of the men at Kilmichael because a new detail had come to light. All the propaganda about young men with only one weeks training was untrue because some were quite experienced and described by Hart as "hard men". Consequently if they were looking to carry out a conventional ambush to inflict heavy casualties they knew how to set one up. Ambushes do not start by flagging down the leading vehicle and then opening fire, they start by bringing the leading vehicle to a halt and then opening fire with every possible weapon before the crews can react.

The normal IRA method of stopping a vehicle was to dig a trench across the road and at Kilmichael they had plenty of time to do this. That they did not do so suggests they did not wish to alert the crew because a trench across the road would have brought the vehicle to an immediate halt. Even if there been no firing, the crew would instantly expect trouble and would rapidly disembark and disperse in the surrounding area until they were sure there was no danger.

It was with some shock that it dawned on me what the reason was for the uniform and deception!

THEY WANTED THEM ALIVE!

They needed their victims alive so they could be butchered as an example to their comrades if they did anything similar to the Dublin Castle killings again! In this context one can look again at the layout of the IRA and realise it was not as amateurish as I first believed. They were not setting up the normal ambush where they could butcher and bolt.

IT WAS NOT AN AMBUSH, IT WAS A CORDON!

The intention was to prevent anyone from escaping because they wanted to take as many as possible alive. They also it knew it was inevitable that a few would not be caught in the main trap and took the necessary precautions to prevent their escape.

- That was why they used men with only a week's training - time was important.
- That was why they had so few men - it was all they could muster by the Sunday deadline.
- That was why no trench was dug that would have alerted the crews.

- That was why deception was used against such a large group - their requirement was for prisoners who could be killed as an example.

There can be no other rational explanation why the experienced "hard men" would have allowed such a disposition of the force. As for Barry, for all his talk on this occasion he was not in command - he was just the front man, the dupe who did not know what was planned and was not responsible for the disposition of the force.

There is an oral tradition in Cork which holds that because of his background as the son of a long-serving policeman and a former regular soldier, Barry was not actually in command at Kilmichael. It is said that another senior IRA man present was specifically there to keep an eye on him and he was effectively still on probation.

If we accept that the IRA hard men had been instructed to massacre the Auxiliaries as an act of revenge, the fact that he was put in this position shows a very sophisticated understanding of human nature. When the French were fighting the Algerians in the 1950s some of the most effective and ruthless troops they had were former guerrillas who had been "turned". The French achieved this by implicating the guerrilla in an atrocity against his former comrades as soon as possible after he had changed sides. Then they could be sure there was no going back and he was on their side for the duration.

There is no suggestion that Barry was a double agent, nor has there ever been, but he went on to be a quite ruthless killer after the IRA used him as front man at Kilmichael. According to Abbot, some months later he and others were preparing an ambush in Bandon when he encountered a group of RIC coming from the cinema. When the IRA fired on them one of the constables sought shelter in a house but Barry followed him in and killed him.

That Michael Collins would order such a massacre is completely in character. Like most Irishmen Collins was very keen on both anniversaries and revenge. When an RIC District Inspector whom he believed had killed a Sinn Fein leader in County Cork was transferred to Northern Ireland, he took the trouble to trace him and send two selected assassins to kill him. That the subsequent murderous revenge of the Unionists was visited on the local Catholics was not something that would trouble him greatly. He had been brought up from childhood to think killing was the only thing in politics that counted and Robert Kee noted that he wrote of his frustration with members of Sinn Fein in Dublin who were moving towards compromise and negotiation.

It can be argued that there is nothing in writing to prove these propositions but then there never is because no competent politician ever commits anything contentious to writing.

There is not a shred of evidence that Collins ordered the murder of Field Marshal Wilson in London in 1922 but this has long been accepted as a fact. The nearest thing to confirmation was given by one of his closest associates in *Curious Journey*. Just after Wilson was killed he quietly asked him if it was an "official killing" as distinct from the many "unofficial killings" by enthusiastic patriots over the past two years and Collins just nodded.

It is a measure of how little he had learned about politics, let alone the business of government, that he thought he could send his men to murder the Commander in Chief of the British Army and expect them to get away with it. In his crude and murderous logic he undoubtedly thought that as he had got away with murdering army officers in Dublin by the dozen, civil servants, the chairman of a national rail company and hundreds of police and soldiers then nobody would worry too much about a Field Marshal.

Of course he could not be more wrong. Police and soldiers are ten a penny, murdered civil servants and leaders of society are a grave political embarrassment, but no government can excuse the murder of the Commander in Chief of their army. That is just too big for any government - even the pragmatic and cynical British Government - to let pass.

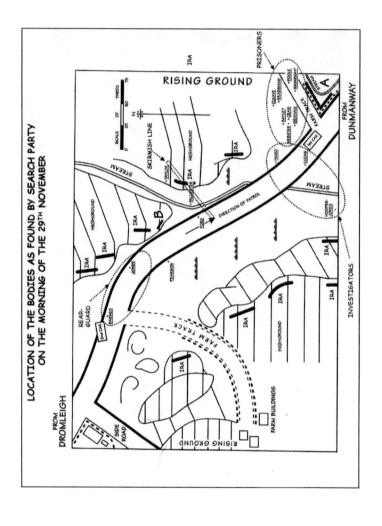

LOCATION OF THE BODIES AS FOUND BY SEARCH PARTY ON THE MORNING OF THE 29TH NOVEMBER

CHAPTER 13

CASUALTY INJURIES

There have been vast social changes since the early part of the 20th century and prime among them has been a complete change in the style of press reporting. From the first newspapers until the 1930s newspapers printed the most gruesome and lurid details of accidents. For example, from an English local paper of 1903: "We are sad to report the child's brains were dashed out on the road by the cart's wheels to the great distress of the driver." The same applied to the reporting of assaults and murders, so it is no surprise that a press report gave the details of injuries suffered by the cadets at Kilmicheal that would never be printed today.

Taking into account the position in which the bodies were found, the location of the IRA, the most likely sequence of events and the physical effects of the various weapons, we have four sources of information to collate and analyse. The first thing to do is to look at the casualties in four separate groups as follows:

1. THE SKIRMISH LINE

The first group I have described as the skirmish line was advancing in open order towards the first tender and almost certainly the first to be shot. These were Cadets

Pallister, Taylor and Forde whose wounds were listed as follows.

William Pallister (25) Capt. West Yorks. - wound over heart caused by expanding bullet; fracture of skull inflicted by heavy instrument after death.

Frank Taylor (21) Lt. RAF - lacerated wounds in chest and shoulders; fracture of bones to face, inflicted by heavy instrument.

Forde - wounded in head and survived.

The initial wounds Pallister and Taylor suffered are consistent with being shot by rifles at close range and severely wounded, after which their skulls where smashed in, probably with rifle butts. This is an effective, if messy and laborious, way of finishing someone off. There is no mention of bullet wounds to Taylor's body, but if his chest was later cut about with bayonets or most probably hacked at with axes, any sign of these would have been obliterated. That his face was smashed in suggests he was lying on his back at the time.

Ironically, Forde probably owes his survival to the fact that, among other injuries, he suffered a bad head wound and they did not think it necessary to finish him off. Irish accounts sometimes reported that he was brain damaged and spent the rest of his life in a wheelchair. This is at best only half true because he gave an account of the ambush to the press. It is said that about 40 years later he responded to statements that he had been killed at Kilmicheal by writing to inform people that he had not and was still very much alive.

As his survival was widely reported at the time and a photograph of him sitting up in bed with a bandaged head was printed in The Freeman's Journal on 17 January 1921 Barry's claim that Forde never recovered consciousness is just one of his many outrageous lies. It is certain that the entire membership of the IRA also knew of Forde's survival but we may assume they would not mention it because it would draw attention to someone who knew what actually happened.

2. THE INVESTIGATORS

We should next look at the three men from the second tender who went to investigate the reason for the halt and who were killed as they reached the first vehicle. These were Cadets Hugo, Lucas and Hooper-Jones and their wounds are given as:

Fredrick Hugo (40) Maj. MC & Ment'n RE Ind. Army - compound fracture of skull, compound fracture of thigh bone.

Earnest William Lucas (31) 2/Lt. Royal Sussex - gunshot wound in head, several other wounds in head neck and body.

Stanley Hooper-Jones (27) Lt. Northumberland Fus. - wounds in back.

Hugo's body was found by the side of the road about 25 yards behind the first tender and, as with Cadet Taylor who was part of the skirmish line, there is no mention of any wound inflicted by a firearm. We can only speculate why this is, but a compound fracture of the thigh is when the shattered bones come though the flesh. The thigh is the longest and strongest bone in the body and if it was shattered, say by a heavy calibre pistol bullet, as he fell the resulting tearing of the flesh as the bone came through would again remove all evidence of the bullet. A shotgun blast at close range would have a similar effect. In either case he probably died very quickly from loss of blood. However the body might still show signs of life, so they probably cracked his skull open for good measure.

Lucas' injuries are interesting because he had a "gunshot wound to the head" and this is where changes in terminology are important. Today a gunshot wound means any wound inflicted with any type of firearm, from a pistol to a machine gun, but at that time shotguns were called "guns" because they were/are quite distinct from rifles. So if, as seems likely, Lucas was hit in the head by a shotgun it would have been at very close range, as his body was found three to four yards from the back of the first vehicle. Again, the circumstances under which he was killed can only be a matter of speculation, but for him to be hit in the head by a shotgun the firer must have been very near to him.

One IRA account has Hooper-Jones dying in a suicide charge against their positions 50 plus metres south west of the road. Utter nonsense.

He survived the first burst of fire, including the deaths of Hugo and Lucas. By that time there would have been heavy firing as the skirmish line was brought down and close range fire was opened on the second vehicle. He was doing the only sensible thing by trying to escape the killing ground into what he thought was open country when he was hit several times in the back by the IRA near the "command post". If the IRA in the position he was moving towards when he died had fired on him they might have hit their own men opposite. Perhaps they did - in these situations, who knows?

3. THE CREW OF THE SECOND TENDER

The third group to consider are the remaining crew of the second tender, Cadets Barnes, Jones, Pearson and Guthrie. The bodies of the first three were found either on or close to the road where the memorial now stands. The fourth, Cadet Guthrie, is generally accepted to have been the driver who initially escaped the ambush only to surrender to two IRA men on his way back to Macroom. He was shot and buried in the bog the following day. Most Irish accounts agree that this happened, but one actually claimed he was a coward who abandoned his comrades, so his killing was no more than natural justice. The exception is of course Barry, who in one of his many accounts has Guthrie crawling away wounded before dying and sinking into a bog hole.

William Barnes (26) Lt. DFC - gaping wounds in back, four other bullet wounds, gunshot (shotgun?) wound over heart inflicted after death.

Albert Geo. James Jones (33) 2/Lt. Shropshire's - bullet wound in back, six other bullet wounds. (The calibre of the bullets and location of the wounds is not stated.)

Horace Pearson (21) Lt. Yorkshire Regt. - wounds in head, lacerated wound in top of arm.

All three men suffered bullet wounds consistent with being caught in the open in front of the main ambush position. Barnes was probably ordered to stay back as bodyguard for the driver, while Jones and Pearson could have been on the right hand end of the skirmish line and, being furthest away, survived the burst of fire that brought down Cadets Pallister, Taylor and Forde. They could also have been going forward to help Pallister, Taylor and Forde when they were brought down - who can say now?

Either way, two of them had wounds in their backs that suggest they were trying to escape the killing ground. Barnes was hit at least four times in the back and then finished off with a shotgun, while Jones' total of seven bullet wounds seems to have made further attention unnecessary. Pearson had several head wounds but as sometimes happens, a man can survive these for several hours, so it is possible they started to use bayonets on him and someone said not to bother as he was finished anyway.

In almost all his accounts, Barry told how he was narrowly missed by a pistol shot from an Auxiliary who was immediately run through with a bayonet that severed an artery, giving out a spurt of blood that caught the IRA man in the mouth. There are a number of scenarios whereby this could have taken place. The most logical would be the failure of the IRA to fully disarm all the prisoners from the first tender in the natural confusion of the initial capture. When they realised they were going to be killed, one man who still had his revolver, decided to go down fighting. Another possibility is that the same man who still had his revolver decided to use it when the investigating party of three men from the second tender were shot on reaching the first.

However, I think the most likely possibility is that the IRA went to finish off the wounded from the skirmish line when one of them drew his revolver and fired it. This was either to defend a comrade who was being killed or more likely a last desperate attempt to save himself from the same fate. My guess would be that this is what happened to Cadet Pearson who was found alone by the side of the road with a lacerated wound to the top of his arm. That would be consistent with being bayoneted when his arm was outstretched holding a revolver and a wound there would be likely to sever an artery.

4. THE PRISONERS

Cecil James Bayley (22) Lt. RAF - large bullet wounds behind ear and in chest.

Leonard D Bradshaw (22) Lt. RFA - perforated wounds over liver. Gunshots fired at close range.

Francis William Crake (27) Lt. Hants - gunshot wounds in head.

James C Gleave (21) Lt. RAF - gunshot wound over heart; chest wound from expanding bullet, inflicted at close range.

Philip Noel Graham (31) Capt. RN Fus. - explosive wounds through neck.

Arthur F Poole (21) Lt. RAF - bullet wounds in chest and shoulders; fracture bones of face, inflicted by heavy instrument.

Christopher Wainwright. (36) Capt. R Dublin Fus & RIR - wounds in chest and other wounds.

Benjamin Webster (30) Lt. Black Watch - wounds on shoulder and fractured shoulder bones.

Note the references to "guns". As explained in the weapons section, there are several advantages to using shotguns in this situation. At close range they not only produce a devastating wound, the pellets are unlikely to go right through the victim and hit other people. Also shotguns are still classed as an "agricultural tool" and common in the countryside, so from a logistics point of view the cartridges would be easier for the IRA to obtain than rifle ammunition.

Do we really need to examine these men's injuries in detail? Their bodies were found grouped in a small area by Barry's "command post", an area enclosed by rising ground, a rocky hillock, a wall and their own lorry. They were the crew of the first vehicle who had little option but to surrender, and almost every one was found shot through the head or body with shotguns at close range.

There is a Latin legal term - Res ipsa loquitur - *"The thing speaks for itself."*

Let it, and let us have no more nonsense about who said what to whom or wrote what in 1921 or 1928 or 1949 or 1972 or any other year.

Reasons why in descending order of importance.

Is there any other evidence to add to a collection of technical information, conjecture and an old plan giving the location of the cadets' bodies? Yes, I believe there are other strands of information, details which are nothing in themselves but which added together lead a thoughtful person towards the conclusion that there is "something nasty in the woodshed". Consider:

1. It takes time to die. If there had been a prolonged gun battle at least half the police would have survived, even if they had all been wounded. Unless you know how to do it properly, killing someone quickly is difficult. People think you can shoot, bludgeon or stab a person to death instantly, but inflicting a fatal wound can take several attempts but most of all, even with the most appalling wounds, dying takes time. That is unless you have practical experience that soldiers acquire, not only from killing, but from seeing comrades die of all manner of injuries. They can tell as well as any doctor from the location and severity of a wound whether if is fatal or not.

2. The location of the bodies as set down and the plan is clear evidence in itself. Half the bodies were found close together by the first tender. They were in an area that was not only out of sight of the remainder of the patrol, but out of sight of most of the IRA. It is inconceivable that they could be in this location and be engaged in any kind of open battle with firearms.

3. Most of the bodies in the hollow by the "command post" had been killed by bullets or shotgun blasts fired at close range into the head and chest - in the case of Dl Crake a bullet behind the ear.

4. In the initial treaty negotiations, the British Government wanted the men who carried out the attack at Kilmichael excluded from the general amnesty. I do not think for one minute they thought they would be, but they knew very well that Black & Tans had carried out a few unofficial killings and in a sense they were getting their atrocity in first. In

simple terms they were pre-empting any Sinn Fein demands for prosecution of the Black & Tans by saying if you make a fuss about - for example - the killings of McKee and Clancey in Dublin Castle we will make a fuss about Kilmichael.

5. What is interesting about the drawing of the ambush is that it did not go into the official archieve where it would have been hidden away and perhaps even destroyed. Almost unbelievably, it was kept in the personal papers of a senior civil servant, Francis Hemmings. In due course these were passed to his College at Oxford University. Anyone who knows the British system of administration knows this would be quite easy for him to do, particularly as it was not an official document or part of an inquiry. The reason? Even by the quite brutal standards of "The War of Independence" Kilmichael stands out as an act of unparalleled and cold-blooded savagery. It was politically impossible for him to tell what actually happened in his lifetime, but in that quiet English way he thought the truth should be known. He knew that some day someone would look at the drawing, understand its significance and finally accord a degree of justice to the victims. It should be made clear that Hemmings was not just appalled by Kilmicheal. It is to be expected he would express his horror and disgust at what was being done by the IRA - but his notes also record efforts to apprehend members of the security forces for what he uncompromisingly calls criminal acts. However, he is most appalled by the fate of the ordinary and quite helpless Irishmen who were being murdered for the most tenuous association with the

government. On one Election Day the IRA, whom he describes as Sinn Fein, killed eight civilians, including five ex-servicemen, in his words "to demonstrate its power". But I am sure he was mistaken and proper research would show they were all spies, torturers, traitors and of course the ex-servicemen were simply traitors.

6. One of the most telling fragments of information is the handwritten note on the typed list of Hemmings' papers by the English librarian in 1968. Against item 8, Plan of Ambush at Kilmicheal 1920, is written, "This item is not to be shown to members of the public." This is the only item thus noted and strongly suggests the librarian at that time understood the significance of the plan. Fortunately, by the time I asked to see it in 1992 the reason for his notation had been forgotten, but I could see clearly why it was being suppressed in 1968.

7. The memorial erected on the ambush site in 1966 was paid for by Cork County Council and dedicated by the parish priest. This begs the question, "Why was a monument on the site of such famous victory ignored by national politicians and churchmen?" No Prime Minister, no bishop - let alone an Archbishop – visited the memorial, just county councillors and the parish priest. Given that Irish politicians share the national fixation with memorials, dedications and opening ceremonies, this is particularly significant. There were still a lot of leading IRA veterans in senior government positions in 1966, including the Prime Minister and President and one would normally expect them to be present on the site of such a famous victory. Unless of course they knew the truth and

thought it wise to stay away. Indeed, it seems that until questions began to be asked by Dr Hart in 1998 about what really happened the commemoration was a local event that anyone in national politics carefully ignored. Now of course senators and TDs (MPs) are rushing to defend the glorious memory of Ireland's legendry guerrilla leader and his greatest exploit. They might pause for a moment to ask why their fathers and grandfathers stayed away.

8. According to Mr DeValera, the IRA was the National Defence Force and therefore the army of the Irish Government. So why has the Irish Army, which claims to be the successor to the IRA, never been represented at the site of its greatest victory? Why has the Irish Army - who according to the official Irish version of history carried out the attack - never been present at a commemoration? When they put up a near identical monument in 1966 to Barry's other victory a few miles away at Crossbarry, where by good luck he escaped from a military cordon, the Irish Army Reserve provided a guard of honour. But so far as we can ascertain, neither regular nor reserve army units have ever been represented at Kilmichael. When I enquired of the Irish Department of Defence in the 1990s if they provided a guard at the annual commemoration of Kilmichael their reply was, "The regular forces were not represented". Ambiguous. I had enquired if the Irish Army attended without any qualification. To reply "The regular forces were not represented" might have three interpretations, i. The Regular Army does not, but I don't know about the reserve and it would be too much trouble to find out. ii. The

Regular Army does not, the reserve forces do, but we don't want too many people to know, iii. The Regular Army does not, but I want to imply that the reserve forces do, because I know what your looking for and there is no way I am going to say any more. This all suggests the Irish army knows that one day the truth about Kilmichael will come out and they did not want to be too closely associated with it.

9. Barry was never accepted into one of the political or government jobs reserved for top IRA members after De Valera came to power in the 1930s. He remained a national figure but he never made any great play in Irish politics for the rest of his life. It could be fairly said that this was because he was an extreme republican who took the losing side in the civil war. However, this overlooks the fact that the equally murderous Dan Breen, having skipped to the United States for a few years until things cooled down, returned to Ireland in the late 20s to become a senator and later a TD - comfortable positions he held for the rest of his life. Barry remained an official of the Cork Harbour Board, a position he used from time to time to smuggle in weapons for the IRA and perhaps organise the murder of a British soldier transiting the docks to the British Naval base located in Cork harbour until 1938. One can perhaps trace a strand of bitterness in Barry's writing that he never enjoyed a political sinecure like Breen and others, particularly as Breen was, if anything, an even more brutal and opportunistic killer of police and servicemen. Perhaps too many people in power knew that the truth about Kilmichael might come out one day and

they too did not want to be too closely associated with the man who did it?

10. About the only commendable thing in the whole affair is the fact that Barry, or one of the other leaders, ordered the young IRA men to carry out drill to recover their supposedly shaken morale. What shook their morale was the sight and sound of men being shot, battered, stabbed and hacked slowly to death and they were so appalled at the sight that they were moved to protest.

11. I was discussing this book with a friend of 40 years and while he's not from County Cork he was countryman and I said I was writing about the Black & Tans in County Cork. He leaned across the dinner table quietly, touched my hand and said, "They butchered the Black & Tans in County Cork". I was naturally surprised and asked, "Have you ever heard of Kilmichael?" He said, "No, but they slaughtered the Black & Tans like animals in County Cork". Folk memory is seldom correct on fine detail but there are many instances in history when it is the only source and proves remarkably accurate.

CHAPTER 14

THE REASON WHY

The problem is that, in common with most incidents at that time, Kilmichael is looked at in isolation. But these events do not just spring out of the ground.

Yes, there were incidents when patriots got carried away such as the occasion an ardent young man saw a house across the road being quietly searched by the army. This was too much, so got a pistol and blew off most of the skull of the policeman who was sitting on the front wall and passing the time of day while he oversaw the search.

That is an isolated incident, but many incidents linked. I have told how the local Sinn Fein/IRA had killed two policemen in Balbriggan before the police came back in the form of the Black & Tans and killed two of their people.

When examining any incident one must ask why it happened and my initial conclusions about Kilmicheal were based on two assumptions. The first was that the near 100% casualty rate was unusual and had to be a result of deliberate action to finish off the wounded. I subsequently found that in guerrilla warfare it is not unusual to massacre the enemy in an ambush.

This occasionally occurs in conventional warfare as Major, later Brigadier, Pendergast of the Indian Army related in his memoirs. He learned his soldiering in a hardest school on earth - the mountains of the North West Frontier - and for this reason was attached to the British Army during the short campaign in Norway in 1940. There he set an ambush for a German cyclist column of about 100 men and so completely surprised them that they were shot down before they had a chance to stop, let alone unsling their weapons. Nevertheless, he ordered his men to keep firing and make sure they were dead. One could say this was a result of his experience on the NW frontier, where a prisoner could count himself lucky if the tribesmen killed him with knives shortly after capture.

Another allied veteran took part in the ambush of a German patrol by partisans in Italy in 1944 that ended with the shooting of the sole survivor who had escaped and buried himself under manure in a farmyard.

Finding massacres are not that unusual. I then concluded that the Auxiliaries were killed in revenge. This too is not unusual, as men seldom show mercy to the killers of their friends and comrades. This is the reason Barry gave, but with the specific justification that it was the treacherous behavior of the Auxiliaries shooting his men as they went forward to accept their surrender. However, having studied a plan of the ambush and the disposition of the bodies anyone can this was absolute nonsense. The story about the grenade did not make sense and the second lorry did not just "happen along", they were travelling together. Barry and his men lacked the experience, training and communications to move up to it as a "command group" and by his own admission only half of them were fighting anyway.

It was in the course of my research that I stumbled across something else which looked more like the real reason he killed his prisoners so brutally in cold blood - for that is what he did.

So what was that real reason?

As mentioned earlier on a Sunday morning, a week before Kilmichael, the IRA, under the direction of Michael Collins, killed 12 British Army officers in their homes or hotel rooms around Dublin in a co-ordinated mass assassination. The event is well known and well documented. They were described as spies and torturers who planned to assassinate the entire leadership of Sinn Fein and destroy the independence movement. Michael Collins, in a "brilliant counterstroke", destroyed them in a single blow and he, in his own words, "Put out the eyes of the British in Ireland". This is of course utter nonsense as was explained in the last chapter.

Most English commentators seem to be unaware that the government had opened up communications with Sinn Fein and Arthur Griffiths late in 1920. This was through an intermediary in October 1920, a full month before Kilmichael. It is understandable that Irish commentators, who had been programmed by their education system to see the British Government as inept and duplicitous, would ignore it. Nevertheless, Robert Kee is one of the few people to tell how a businessman and friend of Griffiths named Moylett, while on one of his private journeys to London, approached Lloyd George's Civil Service Secretary. He subsequently met the minister heading cabinet committee on Ireland and was able to report back to Griffiths that:

"Lloyd-George might be prepared to meet three or four men nominated by the Dail in a conference at which the republic and the union would be "left outside the door" like coats to be assumed again by the two parties if necessary when they left. As this implied partial recognition of the Dail, Griffiths was much moved Collins was notified of the tentative moves and approved. Though an event was to occur which suggests that he did not attach great importance to them. Moylett returned to discuss the possible calling of a truce between the two armed sides"

But according to O'Connor, in October 1920 Collins had detected a plot to assassinate Griffith - by whom we are not told. As the finger is not pointed at the government we must assume it is the patriots and liberals' all-time favourites, those undefined "rogue officers". Precisely what the assassination of Griffith would achieve is never explained, nor is how they could expect to get away with it. Nor is it considered what the British press, let alone the international press, would have made of such a murder. To say all hell would have broken loose is one of the great understatements of all time and I would go so far as to say it would be another event that would have brought down the government. The revenge killing of two low level Sinn Feiners by Black & Tans in Balbriggan on 20th September 1920 caused uproar in London and across the world and a visit from an independent American Commission of Inquiry. Consider the fallout from the assassination of a prominent man like Griffith, let alone members of the Dail cabinet. Of course if anyone dared to ask these questions, they can be answered by simply reminding everyone that the British Government is invariably inept and therefore capable of anything.

This begs the question why Collins did it. O'Connor tells us that his original list of spies contained 32 names. This was passed to Cathal Burga as Minister of Defence and nominally Collins' boss. Burga, as political head of the IRA, is said to have deleted 20 names, as there was insufficient evidence against them. Given Burgas' record as a man committed to violence, I think this is unlikely, but he may well have pointed out that it would be just as effective and a lot easier to kill 12 than to kill 32. Could it not also be that 12 is a nice round number? Accepting O'Connor's research is accurate it is interesting to point out that:

1. If almost two thirds of Collins' list was wrong he was nothing like as good at counter intelligence as everyone believes.
2. If he was right and all 32 were spies, most of the British intelligence network survived thanks to an interfering politician.

In one of the finest examples of political propaganda in the 20th century, Sinn Fein labelled - or as we now say packaged - the men who were eventually killed as the "Cairo gang".

They were supposedly recruited following successful, and by implication, dirty work against Egyptian nationalists in Cairo and brought to Ireland to deal with the IRA. But, of course, however good they were in Cairo, thanks to Michael Collins, the IRA were too clever for them. To be fair, more serious historians ignore the label but to the press and ordinary people it provides a hook on which to hang politically useful assumptions. In "Cairo" we are presented with men from the mysterious East and "gang" implies a criminal group out of control. O'Connor tells us that General Richard Mulcahy, chief-of-staff of the IRA at the time, assured him they were, "A murder organisation, their murderous intent was directed against effective members of the government as well as against GHQ and the staff at the Dublin Brigade."

Well he would wouldn't he?

This is why we were told that their massacre "Put out the eyes of the British in Ireland" but very few appear to have been in Ireland for any time so they could not have known too much.

It is true that barring the army veterinary officer included by some stroke of genius, most were intelligence and legal specialists but by no means irreplaceable in an army which had thousands of similar men left over from the war. Collins is frequently quoted as saying that the IRA could never match the government in firepower and resources and the value in killing police and soldiers was in the newspaper headlines it created. No one would disagree with this, so why should the elimination of a dozen men, however skilled, be such a fatal blow? Has it ever occurred to anyone to ask whether these men were replaced? Why is it assumed they were not? They had to be replaced by other more careful men and almost certainly were.

Another detail that is judiciously ignored is the fact that at least one, but probably several, of the men killed that day were legal officers. As part of its attempt to reassert some control, the government was introducing military tribunals in certain areas to overcome the total non-function of the civil courts as a result of IRA intimidation. That these men in particular were killed also suggests that they were included to make up the nice round number of 12, regardless of any involvement in intelligence.

This truth is that Collins had already infiltrated the Dublin Metropolitan Police political G division and killed or wounded all those detectives who would not come over to him. It would be a poor government that did not appreciate that even if those who had not been shot could be trusted, their morale would be so shaken as to render them ineffective. It was therefore necessary to replace them with "clean skins" and it was these replacements that Collins decided to destroy.

It was not only army intelligence and detectives of G Division who were targeted. Few appreciate that Collins' campaign to destroy the government's information sources was as perceptive as it was ruthless and went right to the bottom of the chain. Like all detectives, the men of G Division would have their contacts who could be called informers if one wanted to justify killing them - people they could chat to over a friendly (sic) pint and would tell them anything that was going on in the area.

O'Conner relates how Collins dealt with them:

"One day Joe Dolan and another squad man were sent up from Abbey Street in a taxi to get a porter of the Wicklow Hotel who, it had been discovered, had

betrayed a number of people to the British. Though the Wicklow was only five minutes' walk away they hired a taxi. When they reach the hotel they asked the porter to take their bags. Once he was burdened they shot him."

I have already explained how everyone doing a job develops a range of quite unique skills from their day-to-day experience. In the case of hotel and boarding house staff these include the ability to instinctively spot any irregularity in a guest. They may not know what it is, but they can tell when a guest is not the person they say they are and this would be the first alert for any detective. A non-political example of this skill is the keepers of English seaside boarding houses who could tell the difference between married and unmarried couples when people cared about these things. One was having a holiday while the other was having a weekend of passion. It did not matter that they might wear wedding rings; they could still spot an illicit relationship. Signs like one not knowing if the other took sugar in their tea or how much sugar they took in their tea was a simple and obvious giveaway.

Killing this unfortunate man whose name was probably given to him by Broy or Nelligan was Collins' way of serving notice on the hotel staff of Dublin to stop talking to the police. It is very doubtful if he would have known anything about the IRA and he probably cared less. It was also a very well planned killing because the distance between Abbey Street and the Wicklow Hotel was irrelevant. They needed to arrive by taxi so they could ask the porter to take their cases and ensure he was burdened to make killing him easier. I would go so far as to say that killing and frightening these people was far more important than the murder of any number of British officers. Unlike the officers, they could not be replaced and, being the very foundation of any intelligence network, their skills were priceless.

It would be an interesting footnote to know why out of all the possible police contacts in Dublin hotels he was selected for death. Perhaps he was well known as a friend of the police among his colleagues so his killing would serve as a particularly good example. Who can tell? He might have been a single man with no family and selected by Collins' informants Nelligan or Broy on humanitarian grounds - although Collins' men in G Division were not usually that sensitive.

On one notorious occasion they arranged the murder of one of their colleagues who had come up to Dublin to identify the body of an IRA leader Sean Treacy, who had been shot the previous day. This was Sergeant Roach who was stationed in Tipperary where Tracy came from and like all RIC officers he knew who the IRA men in his area were. He was also to help identify the body of a man who had accidentally blown himself making a bomb and was thought to be one of the top IRA gunmen, Dan Breen. Sergeant Roach was a man with 45 years' service and there are several accounts of how Nelligan assisted in his murder.

O'Connor's account shows Nelligan to be particularly cold-blooded and does not actually name him, but tells us that the IRA men detailed to kill him: *"...saw Collins' spy with Sergeant Roach chatting away. As they walked along the street the detective held his finger over Roach to identify him. Daly fired. The detective calmly turned back and went to the castle to report he and his companion had been attacked by gunmen and that Roach was dead".*

However this is quite different from the account Nelligan himself gives to the DTA in Curious Journey. There he calls Sergeant Roach "Comerford" at the request of the sergeant's daughter: "The Sergeant had already identified the body of a man thought to be Dan Breen who had accidentally killed himself experimenting with explosives. As Nelligan tells it Roach said "That's not Dan Breen I know Dan Breen's ugly old mug anywhere".

Nelligan agrees - "Dan wasn't a very beautiful looking character" - which any photograph of him will confirm. He continues: *"As bad luck would have it I had a meeting with Liam Tobin that night in one of his joints and I was indiscreet enough to mention these two RIC men and my appointment with them the following day. So didn't four men of the squad show up the next day to say they had orders from Mick Collins to mow down the Sergeant? I nearly died, I said for Christ's sake what's he done? 'I don't know what he's done' said one of them, 'But I've orders to shoot him and that's what I'm going to do'."*

His account of the killing is:
"I begged them not to do it and I could already see, Comerford and Fitzmaurice coming along the quays and the next thing of course there was a murderous flare-up

and the poor Sergeant crumpled up and fell down dead in the bloody road. It was the most terrible episode of my life."

He concludes: *"I never found out what poor Comerford (Roach) had done to deserve his fate but it was the one day I regretted the role I was playing. There were too many killed. I often wonder if the whole bloody thing was worth it at all. That's God's truth and I often ask God to forgive me for having anything to do with it."*

I would guess the truth of what happened lies somewhere between these two accounts as there can be no doubt that Nelligan told the IRA of the meeting and identified his colleagues to the IRA on the day. As to his claim that he didn't know why Roach was killed - that is selective amnesia, as he has already told us they were brought up to Dublin to identify members of the Tipperary IRA who were active in the city. As a detective he would know this was a perfectly good reason for having them killed. It often happens that it is only later in life that men develop conscience about these things, which accounts for his attempt to distance himself from responsibility in "Curious Journey".

Collins' infiltration of G division is presented as a mark of his genius, but it does not occur to anyone that there might be more to it than that. If the government was looking to pull out and, contrary to popular mythology in any reasonable assessment it was, an obvious indication of its intention would be their soft peddling on Sinn Fein and the IRA. The detectives of G division would be the first to know this and the more astute ones would make provision not only for their survival but also for their futures. This was certainly the case with Edward Broy and David Nelligan.

Broy, reborn as Commandant Eamon Broy, was to set up and lead the Free State's own political police in the 1930s. He so dominated political policing in the Free State that the IRA referred to his department as the "Broy Harriers". David Nelligan took the Free State side in 1922 and was a ruthless operator against the IRA in Kerry during the civil war. As noted in later life he doubted the wisdom of the whole campaign and regretted his part in it but I would say that in both their cases patriotism and pragmatism went hand in hand.

It is also true that at the time the government was gearing up for a fight, but this was political to show they meant business. Flexing their military muscle for the first time in years, while at the same time suggesting Sinn Fein might like to talk, is a normal political manoeuvre. Unfortunately, this preamble to talks triggered in Collins the idea that he should also demonstrate his strength in the only way he knew. He did not have the time, organisation or resources that he had six months later when he could kill up to the stroke of midnight as the truce came into effect. In October/November 1920 he had to act with what he had. Throwing everything into a "spectacular" in Dublin was the best he could manage. That his action cut whatever political ground there was from under Lloyd George's feet may or may not have occurred to him.

In any organisation every member first and foremost has their own agenda and as a guide to Collins' character and his possible agenda, consider the reasons he might have:

1. He was aware of peace moves and wanted to demonstrate his strength.
2. He may have thought that the destruction of the existing political structure was insufficiently advanced for Sinn Fein to take over a wish to polarise opinion still further.
3. If you wanted to wreck what he considered premature peace moves a co-ordinated massacre would be the best way to do it. The officers were just a group at the time and place for which he could produce a politically acceptable cover story.
4. His innate restlessness and duplicity. He did after all have the Commander-in- Chief of the British Army murdered in 1922. This was two weeks <u>after</u> signing the treaty – a detail most Irish commentators carefully fail to mention.
5. He had no time for politics, as soon as the treaty was signed he sent his most effective guerrilla leaders into Ulster to continue and expand the campaign there.
6. Reducing activity into the run-up to peace talks is not desirable if you're running what is essentially a campaign of political violence. Then you must show you are strong up to the last minute. If that means killing to within seconds of the ceasefire that is what you do.
7. Collins' charm and intelligence are such that few people appreciate what a truly unpleasant and dangerous man he was. I am not qualified to classify someone as a psychopath, but I have been told that charm and intelligence are two of the indicators. I can

say that I have been fortunate to meet only two or three truly evil men in my life and all were exceptionally intelligent and regarded the rest of humanity with contempt.

Despite all the evidence that high intelligence is no proof of humanity, people insist on believing it is. The best example would be the SS officers running concentration camps who were invariably intelligent and often cultured men but neither of these positive traits in any way inhibited them in carrying out their daily work.

Nevertheless, people still insist on believing that an intelligent man like Collins must inevitably be a good man acting out of necessity. It is a mark of his ability to deceive otherwise intelligent people that to this day he is the subject of favourable comments from the British intelligentsia. He is invariably portrayed as a great man, a visionary tragically lost to Ireland when she needed him. I would say that for his part he probably regarded them as the fools they were and delighted in using them. He was, after all, raised from childhood to hate Britain and specifically England and the DTA tells us how as his father was dying he told his son "Ireland may not be free in my time but perhaps it will be in yours". As his file in the Public Record Office noted he was from "A very disloyal family'.

His record of duplicity is shown by the circumstances in which he left his London office. It started early in 1916 when he told his approving colleagues that he was going to enlist in the army and took the month's pay they gave him in appreciation. In truth he had been active in the extreme Irish Republican Brotherhood all the time he was in London and was leaving because resident in mainland Britain as a single man he would have been liable for conscription from 2nd March 1916. It finished with his ordering the murder of Sir Henry Wilson in London six years later.

It is therefore entirely possible that O'Connor is right that as he was briefing his squad for the Bloody Sunday massacre he emphasised they were not to open fire before 9 o'clock. This is actually commonsense, as a simultaneous attack would have the element of total surprise. A series of attacks even over as little as half an hour would allow some victims to escape and inevitably bring the police and army onto the streets and endanger his men. It is not the instruction that gives a key to his character but the way he said it: *"This is to be done exactly at 9 o'clock neither before or after those hoors (whores) (the British) have got to learn that Irishmen can turn up on time."* Note that hoors in Ireland is an expression of extreme abuse and to call someone of either sex a "hoor" is not only an extremely violent insult but an expression of loathing and contempt. This gives an in insight into his mind because for all his charm at that moment the mask slipped and he expressed the deep and ingrained hatred inculcated by his family from birth.

He fooled Englishmen then and continues to fool them to this day. In London, to negotiate the treaty he was the darling of the intelligentsia and fashionable artists, reportedly sleeping with a few of their wives. His problem was that fooling the intelligentsia and the international press was, and is, a lot easier than fooling the government.

CHAPTER 15

BURNING OF CORK

It is interesting at this point to look at another major incident at that time which is usually linked to Kilmicheal - the burning of Cork city. While James Boyer Bell's account is as lurid as the rest of his writing on the "glorious fight for freedom" it is nonetheless the fairly standard account given by historians and includes the main points.

"There was an ambush on December 11th in which one auxiliary was killed. That night the auxiliaries took their revenge. Running through the streets of Cork they literally burned the city down. Vast areas were gutted as firemen, their hoses cut by the auxiliaries, stood idly by. The damage was estimated at £3 million. In the House of Commons when first questioned, Sir Harmer Greenwood, chief architect of the hardline, at first denied that British troops and police had been involved," insisting that the citizens of Cork had burned down their own city. Even the British public fed on a steady diet of Irish gunmen and murder gangs would not swallow that.

Let us consider the main points in turn.

1. The auxiliaries "running through the streets of Cork". This is a fairly standard description but some writers add

that they were "looting, burning and drinking" for good measure. The interesting thing is that a police report on the fire in the British Public Records Office which has been open for more than 30 years makes the following comment,

This (incendiarism or arson) could not be the work of a large body which would have come to the attention of the police."

So much for *"Hundreds auxiliaries pouring into the town, looting burning and drinking".*

2. *"Vast areas were gutted."*

Not a single historian seems to have taken the trouble to look at the map of the burned area. While it does contain most of the commercial and business centre of Cork, it could hardly be called a 'vast area' and according to the official report, a total of 28 businesses were destroyed.

Not all histories mention the burning of the Carnegie Library and those that do seem to suggest it is another example of "Tan barbarism" to burn down a library. Again, if anyone took the trouble to look at the map they would see that the Carnegie Library, like Cork City Hall which was also burned, is on the other side of the River Lea from the rest of the burning, so it had to be specifically burned down.

City Hall was the home of Sinn Fein/IRA at the time, so one can see why it might be burned, but why would the Tans burn down the Carnegie Library? Why should they single out this one large building donated by a Scotsman who made his fortune in America and distributed his wealth in philanthropic bequests throughout the British

Empire and the United States? To burn down the library at that location one would have to have a reason and what reason apart from the general wickedness and barbarism would the Tans have to burn down a charity library? None - unless they thought it was a Sinn Fein building because of its proximity to the Town Hall.

Of course, it is quite impossible that the IRA - champions of freedom, progress and enlightenment - would burn down the library. Or is it? This is where snippets of information, insignificant in themselves, might provide an answer. During the 1916 rising in Dublin, citizens who performed heroic acts in support of the British troops and generally aided government, received rewards from a charitable foundation. The charitable foundation was the Carnegie Fund for Heroes. Given the famously long Irish memories and the regrettable national taste for revenge it is quite possible the IRA would have burned down a library provided by a foundation that rewarded their enemies. Of course there is no evidence of this but it is worth considering.

3. *"The firemen, their hoses cut by the auxiliaries, stood idly by."*

Again this is a pretty standard account, but if one looks at the files which, again, have been open for over 30 years in the Public Record Office, one will see that "Captain Hutson of the fire brigade reported that a fire hose was cut". NOT fire **hoses** but "a" fire hose - just one - was cut. It might also be of interest to point out that Captain Hutson did not say by whom it was cut - it might have been the Black and Tans, but that is an assumption. It could just have well been civilian looters or the IRA.

4. *"The damage was estimated at £3 million."*

This figure is quoted in just about every history, but it seems that nobody has ever bothered to analyse it. Referring again to the file that has been open for 30 years in the British Public Record Office, one will see that the 28 businesses which were burned down included grocery shops as well as offices. If you divide 28 into £3 million you get an average valuation of £120,000 for each business, which is a lot of money for a grocery shop in Cork in 1920. For £120,000 in 1920 you could build two decent size town halls and £3 million would build one and a half battleships. I doubt 28 shops and two public buildings in Cork were worth more than a battleship.

Historians again overlook the fact that the government was paying compensation for all damage and there was no incentive for individuals to underestimate the cost.

The burning of Cork was much more extensive than most arson at the time but otherwise is not exceptional if one takes the trouble to read the police reports of this period. Time and again much of the damage being attributed to the IRA or "the Tans" is in the opinion of the authorities an attempt by individuals to profit from compensation. Typical minor cases include a farm manager who reported a hayrick burned by the IRA but in the opinion of the police he had sold it for his own profit. Even government employees were burning things when they thought it would be to their advantage. One postmaster reported his handcart burned by the IRA but the police thought he had probably burned it himself because he wanted it replaced with a motor car.

And finally from Bowyer-Bell.

5. *"In the House of Commons when first questioned, Sir Hamer Greenwood chief architect of the hardline, at first denied that British troops and police had been involved insisting that the citizens of Cork had burned down their own city."*

It is doubtful that the citizens of Cork would actually burn down their own city, but they would certainly take advantage of the opportunity to loot once the fires had started. This was the immediate public response to the 1916 Rising in Dublin. On a personal level, my father told me how my uncle, always the family scallywag, would go looting in Dublin whenever possible. I particularly remember him telling about the chocolates from an exclusive confectionery shop that stood on the comer of Grafton Street until the 1960s. We often passed this as children and I lost count of the times he told me of "the lovely chocolates, the beautiful chocolates" my uncle had looted from there. He was 14 at the time and had never tasted anything like them before or since.

Damage and theft is invariably blamed on the undisciplined Black & Tans, although from police records one can see that the ordinary people of Ireland had no hesitation in taking advantage of The Troubles for personal profit. Some victims of looting had a positive interest in blaming the police and the army, as in the case of Mr O'Connor, described in the records as a "red hot Sinn Feiner". When his shop in Castleisland, Co. Kerry, was burned out and looted in December 1920 - supposedly after the attempted murder of a police constable ten days before - he claimed £1,000 for malicious damage. To quote the report, *"Most of the property was looted by "criminal classes" but he blames the police and will not identify the recovered property."*

However, while that might be true, it is also probable that if he admitted it was the work of looters, it would have been recorded as a normal criminal offence and the government would not compensate him. If as is possible in Co. Kerry in 1920 he had no insurance on a political and business level it was in his interest to lie and blame the police.

It might be interesting to return briefly to the claim of £3 million for the supposed damage done in the burning of Cork centre. I have not been able to research the value of real estate in Cork at that time but if a burned out and looted shop in a town in Kerry could be rebuilt for a £1,000, then let us say that twice that would be sufficient for a shop in Cork. One could also say that as a "red-hot Sinn Feiner" and a businessman, Mr O'Connor would not have been scrupulous in his estimates of the damage to his shop. So, if 28 shops and businesses were destroyed in Cork, simple arithmetic would put the total value of the damage to them at £56,000. Just a thought.

One might ask why the file on the burning of Cork is still closed until 2020? Surely it must contain some terrible evidence of misconduct by government servants? Robert Kee cites this as prima facie evidence of the security forces' guilt, to which I would say not necessarily. Contrary to popular opinion, at the time, Britain was not desperately trying to hold on to a recalcitrant colony to preserve the integrity of the Empire. Anyone who takes the trouble to analyse their actions and records, rather than their words written and spoken, can see that they simply wanted to get out. In those circumstances they adopted a policy that could at best be called conciliatory and at worst be called appeasement. Traditionally, the British Government does as little as possible when it is faced with a really unpleasant problem. Not only that, if possible it will do nothing at all and hope things work themselves out. As a leading English historian wrote, *"There is nothing the British political system finds so thoroughly disagreeable as a decision"*.

The truth is they had stood back from Irish affairs as much as possible to give Sinn Fein its head. The problem was that while Sinn Fein might have the British press eating out their hand, it still had no experienced political organisation. Nor was it prepared to negotiate with the government on any handover of power.

The founder and leader of Sinn Fern was Arthur Griffiths, a humane and civilised man but in political terms a complete crackpot. His policy was based on a personal interpretation of events in the Austro-Hungarian Empire in 1848.

He thought Hungary had obtained a considerable degree of independence from the Austrian Empire by setting up a parallel administration to the Imperial Government. This had been recognised by the Hungarian people and the Imperial Government's institutions had simply been ignored - boycotted in fact - and this alone had compelled the Austrians to accept the de facto existence of a separate Hungarian administration. Again this is utter nonsense, but the point is that Sinn Fein could not govern the country, nor would it talk to the government about running the country.

At the same time the IRA was doing its utmost to prevent the government running the country and as a consequence there was a near complete breakdown of law and order. The fact is government only seriously commenced fighting the IRA a year after the "war of Independence" started. Until then they had gone out of their way to give Sinn Fein as much political leeway as possible. This included withdrawing the police and not intervening in the arbitration courts Sinn Fein had set up to displace the Crown Courts.

The still closed report on the burning of Cork was prepared by an army officer. However while 1960s liberals might sneer that "military intelligence is a contradiction in terms" that is a measure of their stupidity and ignorance. The military intelligence officer has to be the most objective and honest reporter of events if he is to do his job properly and avoid a major disaster for his army and his country.

Nothing must be left unsaid or played down. The truth must be presented as clearly as possible without any reservations. With this in mind suppose the report on the burning of Cork read as follows:

"This event is the culmination of 12 months in which the government has done absolutely nothing to counter the growing tide of lawlessness throughout the country. Individuals who are well known to the authorities have killed police and soldiers and even when the electoral system has been blatantly corrupted no action was being taken. Therefore, it is perfectly natural that the citizens of Cork or any town have concluded they may do whatever they wish and there will be no intervention by

the police or the authorities. The burning was probably started by a few soldiers but continued by the criminal elements and Sinn Fein/IRA and is therefore the inevitable result of government policy of minimum reaction prior to our planned exit."

In conclusion, the consensus is that the fires were started by some of the military but where and how is the crucial question. As in Balbriggan, a fire started as a specific unofficial reprisal spread, and as I believe happened with the mill at Balbriggan the IRA may have taken immediate reprisals against "enemy" property. Anyone looking at the records can see that the definition of "enemy property" like that of "spies and traitors" was pretty wide.

As the fires took hold the citizens of Cork took advantage of the situation to do a bit of looting – just as Dubliners did in 1916.

CHAPTER 16

THE BATTLE OF CROSSBARRY

It is surprising when you begin to research something what you can turn up. My initial interest in Ireland's legendary guerrilla leader's other great victory at Crossbarry was triggered by the newspaper report that the memorials at Crossbarry and Kilmichael were dedicated at the same time in the 1960s.

What attracted my interest was that the Irish army was represented at Crossbarry but <u>not</u> at Kilmichael. Having already deduced the truth about Kilmichael I thought this was extremely interesting and it did not make me "smell a rat", so much as confirm the existence of one.

It suggested that the Irish Army and government at least knew what had happened there and were discreetly ignoring that particular event. This is where cultural differences come in, because while the unveiling and dedication of plaques and memorials in England is a very local matter and usually passes without notice, in Ireland it is quite different and politicians queue up to take part. To this day a small project that in England would be completed with the builder simply handing over the keys, in Ireland would probably have an opening ceremony involving a cabinet minister or a least the local MP. Consequently, when I noticed the memorial to a famous victory like Kilmichael was only dedicated by the parish priest it was particularly significant.

So far as I was concerned that was all that was worth knowing about Crossbarry because I accepted the accounts in all the histories I read as fact and did not think there would be any details that would alter the story. The examples I would quote are from:

Robert Kee's *Ourselves alone*

Barry inflicted a severe reverse on the two battalions sent against him

Ulric O'Conners *A Terrible Beauty*

At Crossbarry on March 19th, 1921 - a determined effort was made by Crown forces to eliminate Barry's Flying Column. Over 1,000 Troops drawn from the 1st Essex, 2nd Hampshires and 1st Manchester's and 120 auxiliaries from the Macroom Castle began a massive sweeping operation - their aim was to destroy the column completely. Barry, as a result of the sweeping operation, found himself under attack from three directions at once. Instead of retreating he decided to take on the enemy full face though he was outnumbered 10 to 1. At Crossbarry on the old main road to Cork city he ambushed three detachments of soldiers and police. Twenty-nine British were killed and 47 were wounded, while the IRA lost only three.

Throughout the engagement a piper walked up and down playing Irish War tunes to encourage the men of the column.

Kenneth Griffiths' *Curious Journey*

In March Tom Barry engineered another remarkable victory at Crossbarry, some 12 miles south of Cork city and a massive encircling operation involving over 1,000 troops and 120 Auxiliaries was mounted to finish off once and for all his troublesome column which at that time was operating at the fully extended strength of 104 men with only 40 rounds of ammunition each. With troops closing in from all directions Barry took the calculated risk of a stand-up fight and deployed his men into strategic ambush positions at Crossbarry. From the morning of the 19th March, with a bagpiper blaring out marching tunes from the opening shots, they met successive British attacks and drove them off, leaving the road strewn with corpses and the surrounding countryside crossed by straggling lines of retreating troops. At the end of the fight there were 39 British soldiers dead and 47 wounded, as against three IRA men dead and just a couple of wounded.

The British receive even more casualties in a lurid account on the internet which sings the praises of the piper whose heroic presence was worth a regiment. For good measure it declares that the victory of little over 100 IRA men facing 1,000 British troops as happened at Crossbarry showed that the IRA could never be defeated. This victory was instrumental in forcing the British Government to sue for peace six months later. Even by Irish standards this assertion is jaw dropping, breathtaking, hair-raising nonsense and that's within the limits of acceptable language as there are less acceptable terms one could use. But even allowing for lurid language, it did not occur to me to question the basic facts that government forces suffered a serious reverse when caught off balance by a much smaller force - until I read Brian Abbot's account of an incident at

Lissagroom in County Cork on 19th March 1921, when a police constable was killed and another wounded.

This account was as follows:

On St Patrick's Day - 104 men led by Tom Barry had been in an ambush location between Kinsale and Bandon, at Shipool, to ambush a military patrol that travelled along the main road.

Shortly after leaving on this patrol the military became aware of the ambush and returned to Kinsale and the plan was formed to attempt an encirclement of the IRA. On realising that the military had returned, and fearing that an attempt would be made to capture the column, Barry moved his forces to Crossbarry. Here he prepared an ambush on the encircling military and police patrols and mined the roadway with two devices and had the column split into seven sections. Six were used as an attacking force with the remaining section in the rear of the main force to protect it.

On the 19th March, 1921 military and police were moving towards this IRA column from three directions. As they went, the security forces searched the houses and other buildings they came across, dividing the forces between foot and mobile units.

At Barry Murphy, a few miles from the column, soldiers searching a house found Charlie Hurley, Cork No. 3 Brigade Commander. He tried to fight his way out of the house he had been staying in but he was killed. As the military closed in on the IRA unit, they left some vehicles with their drivers and moved forward. The IRA unit fought its way out of the encircling police and military forces and as they were leaving the area they came upon the vehicles and their drivers. Six soldiers and one RIC constable were killed before the main party of the military could come to their aid. This was the largest action during the period with the largest flying column the IRA had at that time being involved. An IRA man Peter Monahan, a deserter from the Cameron Highlanders, was killed whilst others were wounded.

It was obvious to me that his account of Lissagroom and the accounts of the Battle of Crossbarry were describing the same incident. As there was no reference to the shooting of police or drivers in any historian's account, Irish or otherwise, I wondered if these fitted into the often quoted casualty list of 39 British and security forces killed. Nothing more than curiosity caused me to ask whether these seven were in addition to the casualty list of 39 killed or were they included in it?

At Kilmichael I thought Barry was entirely responsible and was lying to cover up a very nasty deed but I stress that took all the accepted accounts of Crossbarry at their face value.

Seeing that the main regiments involved were the Essex, the Hampshire and Manchester, the obvious first point of inquiry was the Essex Regiment Museum at Colchester. I outlined the basic details of Crossbarry and the date in an email with a request to advise me of the regiment's casualties. I promptly received an email in return stating that "the Fenians have got carried away again" and a list of their four casualties killed at Crossbarry on 19th March.

A further soldier was listed as dying of wounds a couple of days later and being the pedantic sort I enquired if these were received at Crossbarry and a second email confirmed this. So the total Essex Regiment casualties at Crossbarry were five. There might only have been four killed had not the IRA stopped to smash a wounded sergeant's head in with rifle butts. All the IRA accounts say they were short of ammunition and beating a wounded man's head in with a rifle butt saves at least one round. As a matter of interest, to do this properly they would have had to remove his steel helmet first, so time cannot have been a serious factor. I expect he was a well-known rapist and/or torturer.

At this point I still fully accepted the accounts I had read and, using basic arithmetic, I thought seven police and army drivers, five casualties from the Essex - total 12 - subtract 12 from a total of 29 or 39 and this means that Hampshire must have had 17 or 27 killed.

Consequently I emailed the Museum of the Hampshire Regiment and received a reply to the effect that they had lost so many men in March 1920 and a few more in May. I thought my enquiry might been misunderstood so I telephoned the curator and the conversation went something like this:

Me - *I emailed you recently about your losses at Crossbarry, Cork in 1921. Can you give me your actual casualties there please?*

Curator - *Well didn't you get my e-mail?*

Me - *Yes thank you very much, but it never mentioned Crossbarry. Could you tell me what your casualties were then?*

Curator - *But those **are** the total casualties we received in the period you inquired about. You have to understand that in that sort of thing there's a lot of patrolling and nothing very much happens. The main losses were when the regimental band was blown up, that's quite a well-known incident.*

Me - *Thanks.*

End of conversation.

Reaction? I was absolutely speechless with amazement and tried to take it in.

Looking at the plan of the "battle" published on the internet it occurred to me that it also told a story - particularly when linked to Brian Abbot's account, the casualties incurred by the different regiments and the note on Barry's file in the Public Records Office at Kew. This simply mentioned that Barry was believed to have been in charge of the column that was dispersed by the police and army at Crossbarry. Not defeated, not engaged and not trapped, just *dispersed,* chased away.

One of the boring details about Crossbarry is that in their haste to get there the 120 police who should have closed the cordon round the IRA went to ROSSCARBARY - although some say it was Kilbarry - instead of Crossbarry. Either way, it is accepted they went to the wrong place.

Far from being a magnificent victory with far-reaching political implications, Barry escaped due to a simple communications breakdown on the part of the security forces. Not surprising, when one considers the size and urgency of the operation at a time when dispatch riders were the main means of military communication. Radio was in its infancy, while telephone and telegraph lines were inadequate and insecure.

The police and army could not assemble 1,000 men quickly and, realising what was going on, Barry took the perfectly correct decision to escape as quickly as possible. One of his groups probably caught and ambushed the unfortunate men of the Essex Regiment and he then made off to the south with his main body. In doing so, quite by chance he ran into the transport column whose drivers are reported to have been sitting having a quiet smoke. This is confirmed by the fact that of three bravery awards the army gave that day only one went to an infantryman. The other two went to sergeants in the RASC (the Royal Army Service Corps).

In both cases they had rescued wounded and Acting Sergeant Mepham's citation read:

Seeing the officer in charge of the convoy and several others lying wounded in exposed positions, he made his way back to the lorries and drove off one in which he took all the wounded to a place of safety.

Having shot up the lorry drivers and assuming the main force was behind them he then retreated north and had the good luck to find the open-side of the cordon and escape.

I think he was speaking about Crossbarry when Barry declared the British Army casualties were so heavy that they were concealed, so as not to further undermine the morale of an already badly demoralised force.

If this were true it would undoubtedly be Barry's most outstanding military achievement, because the British Army was the only army to go through the First World War without a major mutiny. These men had in 1916 seen 60,000 of their comrades killed and wounded in a morning on the Somme, in 1917 lost a quarter of a million dead in the unspeakable mud and horror of the third battle of Ypres and had gone on in 1918 to defeat the Germans at Amiens in the first modern combined arms battle. So, this army was said to be completely defeated and demoralised by Tom Barry and a few hundred men in West Cork.

With this claim in mind anyone looking at his record must conclude that his statements and writings should all begin "once upon a time", but because contrary to all reason, historians, writers and journalists insist on believing his version of the middle, the ending cannot be "and they lived happily ever after".

They might however consider the cryptic note about Barry in his file at Kew Public Record Office: *Suffers from "swollen head"*.

CHAPTER 17

AMBUSH AT FERMOY

Lest one should think that Kilmichael and Crossbarry are the only occasions where the truth was utterly distorted, one should look again at the almost equally notorious Fermoy ambush on 8th November 1920. This also merits a mention in most histories and was the first attack on the army since the 1916 rising.

O'Connor's typically lurid account of the incident is as follows:

Many statements have been made by ministers and generals in various countries on the necessity for long periods of training before even an infantry soldier is ready for action. This is utter nonsense when applied to volunteers for guerrilla warfare. After only one week of collective training, this flying column of intelligent and courageous fighters was fit to meet an equal number of soldiers from any regular army in the world, and hold its own in battle, if not barrack yard ceremonial.

The first Column attack in the South was by Court No. 2 Brigade led by Commandant Liam Lynch who was later to command a first Southern Division. He and his group ambushed a detachment of the Kings Shropshire Light Infantry on the way to Church Service. As the soldiers marched in fours down the road,

Lynch blew a blast on his whistle and called on them to surrender.

When they refused, the volunteers opened fire and killed one soldier and wounded four. All Lynch's men made their escape, after relieving the ambushed soldiers of their arms and ammunition. Next day the Shropshires went berserk and looted and burned the town of Fermoy, causing damage to the extent of over £3,000. This engagement took place in September 1919 and set the pattern for other IRA attacks. Soon the ambush of troops and police became commonplace in the countryside.

Again, the account from Kenneth Griffiths' the DTA's *Curious Journey*:

The Cork No. 2 Brigade under Liam Lynch ambushed a party of the King's Shropshire Light Infantry who were on the way to church in Fermoy, disarmed them and escaped with 13 rifles, leaving behind a dead British soldier the operation showed all the panache and resourcefulness that would characterise the IRA's new campaign under such men as Tom Barry, Ernie O'Malley and Sean McEoin, and the British humiliated and bewildered, by an enemy which was in all ways indistinguishable from the native populace away simply seemed to vanish into the countryside, struck back by sacking the town in a fit of impotent rage. The war became one between increasingly undisciplined British troops and the increasingly resistant people of Ireland.

From Robert Kee's *The Green Flag - Vol 3 - Ourselves Alone*

One of the other casualties had been a soldier killed in Fermoy, County Cork, in a daring assault on a party of troops marching to church on Sunday 7 September. This raid had been formally authorised by Collins and the Volunteer GHQ in Dublin, although on condition there should be no casualties. It was brilliantly executed by Liam Lynch, revealing guerrilla professionalism of which he was one of the earliest volunteer exponents. Eighteen men at the King's Shropshire Light Infantry in the Church party were swiftly overpowered and 13 rifles loaded into waiting motorcars which were immediately driven off. Military vehicles which took off in pursuit found the roads blocked by fallen trees which would have been sawn through during the night and held back by ropes until the escaping raiders were safety past. Only one detail of the operation had gone awry, for in the scuffle one of the soldiers was shot dead and three others seriously wounded.

The jury at the subsequent inquest unanimously expressed horror and condemnation for this appalling outrage "in the midst of a peaceful and civil community between whom the most friendly feelings have always existed", but they did not find a verdict of murder because the raid's intention had clearly been to get the rifles and the killing had been unpremeditated.

For this oversight, in spite of their additional expression of sympathy with the dead man's relatives, they were made to pay a heavy price. That night undisciplined troops broke out of barracks and did considerable damage to the town, smashing shop windows, particularly attacking the house of the foreman of the jury.

Nobody has ever bothered to look at "the British version", written by someone who was actually in Fermoy when the attack took place and was directly involved in the aftermath. This less heroic account is included in the memoirs of Lt Col Hughes-Hallett who was a Lieutenant with the KSLI in Fermoy:

WITH 2/KSLI IN IRELAND 1919-22

I joined 2/Bn at Fermoy, Co. Cork, in August 1919, from half-pay, and served with them in various stations until early 1922. Fermoy had been a pre-war station for the Regiment and a number of Regimental wives came from there. It had, I gather, always been a happy station. One of my uncles had commanded his Regiment there and my sisters had much enjoyed visiting their aunt and family there. When I first arrived, all seemed to be at peace - tennis parties and so forth in the surrounding countryside. Then - one Sunday - while the main body of the Battalion was falling-in in front of the church, after church parade, a hatless soldier rushed up, calling out that he had a message for the CO. After being jumped on by the RSM, he was fortunately seen by the CO, who called him up. His story was that he was one of the Wesleyan Party, going to their chapel in Patrick Street, some "baker's dozen" strong. As they filed into the chapel doorway (he was last man in the file and a cross-country runner) a gang of locals, sitting lounging around - in ambush - on various walls, suddenly produced revolvers and 'loaded' staves from their sleeves, and opened up on the backs of the troops at point-blank range. The troops were carrying their rifles (for safety, just as was the custom in India) but no ammunition. One soldier (Re Lloyd) was killed on the spot and the rest knocked down. Their assailants seized their rifles (13,1 think) and drove off towards Cork (where they had come from). Trees, which had been sawn thro', were pulled down to block the road from pursuit. All the houses round at once barricaded themselves in, and - except for the Wesleyan Minister and his wife - who did everything they could to help - not one soul was prepared to assist the injured men, even with a glass of water, although many of them must have known what was 'in the air'. The last soldier in the queue, who saw what was about to happen, knocked down several men and leapt the wall across the road, into the cattle market and ran to where he knew the Battalion would be parading. As he ran through the built-up area he threw his rifle to an old woman ordering her to hide it. Hatless, he raced towards the CO. Lieutenant Norton was ordered to rush his platoon down into the town and round to the scene of the outrage; but it was too late. The murdering thugs had bolted. A coroner's Inquest was ordered, and, owing to the machinations of a priest, it brought in a verdict of "Accidental death, unpremeditated".

That was too much for the troops, many of whom were 'war' soldiers awaiting demobilisation. That evening we were at dinner coatless, when the Mess Sergeant rushed in to say that the troops were in the town. The sound of breaking glass was heard, from the town, a few hundred yards away across the river (there was only one bridge giving access). Everybody hurried to exchange mess-jacket for tweed coat and cap and hastened into the town. The Sergeant's Mess had been equally surprised and knew nothing of what was to occur. The troops had worked out a plan. First they sent a screen ahead of the main body to clear the streets -

ordering everybody, who was on foot, into their houses and to stay there.

Then the demolition party proceeded to every shop, place of business of the coroner and the members of the jury, who had brought in their infamous verdict.. I can't recall all the details, but the Jeweler (Barker?), the Boot Shop (Tyler), the Wine Shop and particularly the Foreman of the Jury, etc., were all faithfully dealt with. Trays of rings and watches were soon being flung into the river. A chain of men supervised by a Captain, (?) who was to become later Chief Constable of Devon, smashed bottles on the pavement, and drink flowed in a stream down the gutter. The Boot Shop produced one incident that could only be Irish. An old woman - looter - like jackals they had soon got wind of matters - had filled a sack with boots and shoes, but when she had reached the exit-door she realised she had no laces. She hurried back to collect some, only for another looter to make-off with the sack. There she stood shouting for the police, as somebody was "after stealing her boots".

The Fall-in was sounded at 10 pm. Not a man was absent, and, so far as was ever known, not a penny-worth of loot had been brought into Barracks and nobody was drunk. Next morning the Divisional Commander (Strickland) from Cork addressed the Battalion. He said we had had a damned dirty trick played on us and had had an adequate revenge. But enough was enough. It was his job to see discipline observed and there would be no more. In the meanwhile the Battalion would be confined to Barracks. That was observed by all in the Regiment. However, that evening a large party of Gunners, who had not been privy to the first revenge, had spent the day making petrol torches etc., as they intended to burn down the church of the offending priest. They assembled outside our Barracks, while our men just sat on the wall. The Gunners kept calling out 'What's the matter with the Shropshires? Aren't you coming with us?' But our people said 'No - they had done their bit'. Meanwhile I and Lieutenant Norton were sent to double down to the town (leaving Barracks by a side exit, so the assembled Gunner lot would not see us go). Norton had to man the bridge over the river with fixed bayonets. I had to go into the town and clear St Patrick Street from end to end and keep it clear with my platoon in an open-order of 4'8 (fixed bayonets) covering the road from pavement to pavement, and slowly sweep it clear, and keep it so. How long this lasted I can't recall, but at one time a senior RIC Police Officer said to me that he hoped the troops wouldn't get across the bridge as at least 500 armed men had moved into the town during the day and were in every house round us and round the threatened church.

I'm glad to say they did not get across the bridge. The next move was that the Battalion, with Band and Colours, made a demonstration march thro' the town, it having been made very clear to the authorities that they had never yet apologised for their outrage and had not expressed one word of sorrow for the death of the soldier being killed in his chapel door-way, etc. The march was carried out and they grovelled. But Ho, how stupid can authorities be? After a few days when we were top dogs again, they suddenly moved us to - of all places - Cork, from where our assailants had come. We moved into Victoria Barracks (since burnt down) alongside the Ox & Bucks. We had a double-company detachment about six miles out at Ballincolig. I was with that lot - about *half a dozen Subalterns under a Major, who was resigning and emigrating. Except for me, all the Subalterns were ex Cavalry war-time promoted 'rankers' (a splendid tough lot). We had to take turns to dine in Mess at En HQ on 'Guest Nights'. I well remember my turn as I had to cycle in Mess kit. As I cycled back in the dark, I rounded a comer between high hedges slap into a Parade of "Sinn Feiners" drilling. They were as much surprised as I was, and they all turned outwards and hung their heads so that I should not see their faces.*

Don't doubt my hair stood up a bit as I rode silently through. Our Fermoy incident was, I believe, the first incident of bloodshed after the quelling of the "1916 Easter rising" (looked on by us as a stab-in-the back, but differently by them!) Cork was not a happy station.......

In the aftermath, questions were asked in Parliament and the answer given by Winston Churchill Is as follows:

HANSARD 1803-2005 -* 1920s   1920-> November 1920 -> 8 November 1920 -»Written Answers (Commons) -»IRELAND.

REPRISALS (POLICE AND MILITARY)

HC Deb 08 November 1920 vol 134 ccaSf~JW851W S Mr. DEVLIN

asked the Chief Secretary for Ireland whether on the night of 8th September, 1919, some hundreds of soldiers left the barracks at Fermoy and proceeded to wreck the town, under the leadership of some of their officers in mufti, by way of reprisal for the shooting of a soldier in an attack on a military party some days before; whether over 50 shops were wrecked and looted and a great deal of the property thrown into the river; whether no attempt was made by those in authority to stop them, though several of their officers resided in the Royal Hotel near where the wrecking occurred; whether the men who attacked and shot the soldier did not come from Fermoy, but were all from outside districts 20 or 30 miles away, as they have all been arrested or are certainly known to the authorities; whether the shops wrecked belonged principally to people who belonged to no political party—for example, the local branch of the Munster and Leinster Bank and Messrs. Tyler's boot shop, Messrs. Tyler 852W being an English firm, suffered damage sworn to over £1,000; whether the persons injured claimed compensation, and decrees running into thousands of pounds were ordered to be paid by the ratepayers, including persons whose property was destroyed; whether these decrees were made by the Recorder of Cork, and several of them were on appeal confirmed by a High Court Judge sitting as Judge of Assize; whether the Government were represented on the hearing of all these cases by a legal representative; whether, in view of the fact that absolutely innocent persons were injured and absolutely innocent persons have to pay for the damage, the Government have done anything, or intend to do anything, to compensate these people; whether they have not been paid the amount of compensation granted by the Recorder; and why was no punishment meted out to the troops for this outrage, although many were ready to come forward and identify the officers and men who were implicated?

Mr. CHURCHILL.

My Right Hon. Friend has asked me to take this question, and I will answer the points seriatim. On 8th September, 1919, a party of the King's Shropshire Light Infantry, after hearing the verdict given by a Coroner's jury, broke shop windows and did considerable damage to the property of the members of the jury. The verdict given at the coroner's inquest was to the effect that Private Jones died from a gunshot wound when attacked by a party of civilians, who wished to obtain rifles, but did not intend to do any harm. Private Jones was murdered on the way to church in Fermoy on Sunday, 7th September, 1919. The soldiers were not led by officers in mufti. Some officers in mufti who eventually arrived prevented further damage, and got the soldiers back to barracks with the assistance of a picquet. Approximately 39 shops were damaged. There is no evidence to show that property was thrown into the river. Some of the men arrested in connection with the murder came from the neighbourhood of Fermoy. I am informed that claims for compensation were made by a number of persons, including those named by the hon. Member.

Messrs. Tyters' claim was for £1,120, and they were awarded £158, but the claim is the subject of an appeal now pending. I have no knowledge of the politics of the em- 853W ployes of the two claimants mentioned. The total compensation awarded amounted to about £3,000, including costs. The decrees were made as stated, and some were confirmed at Assizes. The Government has no locus standi at the hearing of such cases. The responsibility for payment of the sums awarded rests with the local authority, and I understand that they have

*not made any payment up to the present. No civilian
witnesses would give evidence, although invited and
encouraged to do so. As there was no evidence against
any individual, no disciplinary action was taken.*

One has to say that Churchill was deploying his
considerable political skill in giving this answer but it
contains several interesting pieces of information. It is
worth pointing out that the MP who raised the question,
Mr Devlin, was the Unionist representative for Belfast
Falls and later from 1929-34 sat at Westminster for
Fermanagh and Tyrone. As Sinn Fein refused to take
their seats, one has the interesting paradox of an
Ulsterman and a Unionist taking up the cause of the
people in County Cork whose own MPs had denied
them a voice.

Mr Devlin (an Ulster Unionist!) also states the Sinn Fein
allegations almost word for word:

1. Hundreds of soldiers left the barracks at Fermoy and
    proceeded to wreck the town, under the leadership of
    some of their officers in mufti.
2. Fifty shops were wrecked and looted and a great deal
    of the property thrown into the river.
3. No attempt was made by those in authority to stop
    them.
4. The men who attacked and shot the soldier did not
    come from Fermoy, but were all from outside districts
    20 or 30 miles away.
5. But most incredible of all to anyone such as the DTA
    who speaks of the IRA as "an enemy which was in all
    ways indistinguishable from the native populace

away simply seemed to vanish into the countryside", the attackers "have all been arrested or are certainly known to the authorities".

Within days, those suspected were arrested! Of course this is now the standard damage limitation exercise when a government is faced with a public demand to take action. Round up some suspects in the immediate aftermath to show you are doing something and are in control of the situation. Then in a week or so when the hullabaloo has died down and people have forgotten, release them for "lack of firm evidence" or "pending further enquiries". These arrests are <u>never</u> mentioned in Irish accounts, which implies several things,

1. They picked up most of the guilty men otherwise they would scream that they were "innocent men arrested by bungling British!"
2. They were quietly released unharmed and without charge otherwise they would scream "innocent men mistreated and tortured!"

Finally, of course we have an Ulster Unionist demanding compensation for the townspeople and punishment for the perpetrators who could be identified. It is worth mentioning that the people of Fermoy were prepared to identify the soldiers involved in the reprisal but not the IRA involved in the attack. Nor is mention made of the fact that local people would have been fully aware of what was going to happen as things like that cannot be kept secret but, like any people in these situations, all they could be expected to do was keep their heads down.

However Churchill's reply does fall back on the good old "no evidence" ploy when he said: *"There is no evidence to show that property was thrown into the river"* because Colonel Hughes-Hallett clearly states that the soldiers did so. This was to make clear they were not using the murder of their comrade as an excuse to loot but taking measured revenge against specific individuals. As the Colonel says there was looting by the townspeople, but then there always is in these cases.

Also he told the house that, *"no civilian witnesses would give evidence, although invited and encouraged to do so. As there was no evidence against any individual, no disciplinary action was taken"*.

The truth is that to punish the men for such a controlled act in the aftermath of murder would have meant examining the whole affair in court. This would bring the details of the vicious business to the unwelcome attention of the British public whose sympathies would not only be with the soldiers but demand government action which must make the bad situation vis-a-vis Sinn Fein politically worse.

MY ANALYSIS

Perhaps the most important thing that all these writers have paid little attention to - and the Irish writers and Griffiths understandably so - was that before the attack Fermoy was a happy and peaceful town. Not only that, there had been no attack on the military anywhere in Ireland for over four years; the regiments stationed there and the local population got on well with each other. Colonel Hughes-Hallett's account, which has been missed by all historians, is the only a first-hand British account to come down to us and he confirms that Fermoy had always been a "happy station".

Perhaps that was why it was singled out and there was certainly some thoughtful planning. Until the 1950s church parades were compulsory in the British Army, but men were allowed to attend their own denomination. The parade for most of the Shropshires would be held in the barracks or on the barracks square by the battalions' own Church of England chaplain. The Methodists were allowed to make their own way to the local Methodist chapel under an NCO or senior soldier. Officers were seldom Methodists as Methodism in England was essentially a working class movement. If a small military detail was to march in fours there would normally be a minimum of 16 men - 13 men would most probably march in single file. They were not marching in the road as "heroic" Irish accounts claim, but appear to have been quietly entering the chapel when the attack started. Lynch targeted a group of men who could be surprised and overpowered when they were isolated and most vulnerable. They were more vulnerable because relations between the army and the town had always been good and it seems when the KSLI had been stationed there before the war several of the men had married local girls.

There are many things that British historians are unaware of and Irish historians and writers, if they are aware of them, choose to ignore. The most important thing that was overlooked here, and what I had always suspected when I read about it, was that the ambushed soldiers at Fermoy had rifles but no ammunition.

As Lieutenant-Colonel Hughes-Hallett said, it was normal practice for men to keep their own weapons with them, but no ammunition. During the war soldiers often took them home on leave as, apart from security, each man's rifle was in everything but the legal sense "his". Its sights adjusted to his eyes, its unique balance and "feel" understood by him alone. Keeping it with him as much as possible maintained his "relationship" with it and ensured it remained with the man to whom it had been "fitted". This practice also simplified security and continued into the 1960s when one of the last men to do British National Service told me that while in training his rifle was kept padlocked in his bedside locker with his personal property.

As to Liam Lynch obeying Volunteer GHQ's instructions to avoid casualties, we must ask how much this was political window-dressing for the consumption of the British press. It does not seem to have occurred to anybody that the men of the Cork IRA who were quite prepared to kill two policemen at Solebeghed in January 1919 just to stir things up were quite capable of killing a few soldiers in October for the same purpose. Politics being the dirty business it is, they targeted a peaceful town where relations between the military and citizens were good.

Innocent men who are set upon by people they have considered friendly and to whom they have done no harm are most likely to produce the violent reaction the patriot requires. In view of the universal shock and condemnation of the Solebeghed killings - ambush is too grand a word for that murderous incident - it made political sense to have a cover story ready whether they intended to kill someone or not. I believe they intended to kill someone, as it is difficult to shoot four unarmed men by accident.

Collins' instructions about not causing casualties were pre-emptive propaganda, given the inevitable negative public response to shooting men who were in, or going into, church.

The story that it was "an accident", later mutated to "they refused to surrender", has served very well to deflect opinion away from what was in truth premeditated and cold-blooded murder.

None of the Shropshires could have done more than club the IRA with their rifles even if they had them in their hands at the time. By contrast, the IRA were all armed with pistols or "loaded staves" i.e. weighted clubs. Again, one could ask why it was necessary to shoot more than one soldier but they managed to shoot four and all the wounds inflicted were described as serious. The rifles were as much an excuse as anything. Nor was it was it important how many men the IRA killed as long as they killed or wounded some to get the ball rolling. The soldier who died was by all accounts the last man in the file entering the church and it would be logical for the IRA to wait until the men had broken rank to go into church before they acted.

The key would of course be to know where the men were shot. It is reported that the man who died was shot in the back as he was entering the chapel. In those circumstances it seems possible that bullet that killed him passed through him into the man or men in front. The IRA, having shot him, could then burst into the chapel blazing away at men already there and were able to make their getaway while everyone was in shock.

Unfortunately, at the time in Ireland there were people who might not think it particularly wrong to shoot someone in a Protestant Church. In Sean O'Casey's play *The Plough and the Stars* set in the 1916 Rising some of the main characters are told they are to be taken to a church to be questioned and propose to take a pack of cards with them to pass the time. There follows an exchange in which they ask if it is a Protestant or Catholic church as there is "probably nothing derogatory in playing cards in a Protestant church". One has to be fair and say in this respect the IRA was not sectarian. They not only shot English Methodists, they later shot RIC men coming from mass and an RIC Sergeant in the doorway of a church as he was going to Evening Mass.

In one respect I would agree that O'Connor's account is right about the level of military training required by volunteers in guerrilla warfare as he observes:

This flying column of intelligent and courageous fighters was fit to meet an equal number of soldiers from any regular army in the world, and all its own in battle, if not barrackyard ceremonial.

Whatever is required to shoot unarmed men in the back as they go into church, it does not feature widely in military training manuals. It is seldom mentioned, but Lynch himself was the only IRA casualty when he was accidentally shot by one of his own "intelligent and courageous fighters", at which point he might have regretted not spending a little more time on training. Indeed this alone might have saved the lives of more soldiers as the shock of shooting their own commander would certainly have diverted their attention from their purpose. It would certainly have diverted Liam Lynch from his murderous task and one can assume the shock distracted him from the main purpose. It would be interesting to know what he said to the "Intelligent and courageous fighter" who shot him.

Finally, considering again the credibility of the supposed "no killing" instruction from Collins, one should be aware that Liam Lynch was a particularly ruthless, and indeed murderous, individual. Along with Cathal Brugha, he proposed the bombing and machine-gunning of civilian crowds in theatres and cinemas as a way to assisting the polarisation of opinion. The Dail Cabinet is said to have rejected this as "impractical". Note, this is the same Cathal Brugha who O'Connor tells us refused to sanction the killing of 20 out of 32 British officers in Dublin two months after Fermoy on the grounds of insufficient evidence. It would require a degree of stupidity denied to the writer to believe that a man prepared to murder civilians in theatres and cinemas would miss the opportunity to kill "armed" soldiers going into church.

It is worth pointing out again that despite repeated tales of the whole town being sacked by berserk soldiers allegedly the worse for drink, it was a targeted and well thought out response. By the colonel's account, the men waited until all the officers and sergeants were at their evening meal before going into town and specifically attacking the shops of the jurymen who refused to return a verdict of murder. According to him, they did not loot the shops, although the shops were severely looted by the townspeople making the most of the opportunity.

Everyone who knows anything about civil unrest would know that the public is quick to take advantage of the chance to loot - particularly if they are poor. However, this is probably another British lie as everyone in Ireland knows all the looting at that time was done by berserk soldiers and Black & Tans.

As to the officers in mufti or civilian clothes directing the assault, he agrees they were there but they were trying to restrain the men. In this situation that is about as much as officers and sergeants can do.

When men consider themselves rightly angry they can only be persuaded to restrain themselves. When the officers got word days later that artillerymen were proposing to burn down the church of the priest who "leaned on" the jury, they were able to put an armed picket in place to stop them before they got going. However, he does say that at the height of the wrecking the men were directed by a captain who later became Chief Constable of Devon. Whether he is speaking of a captain as in the case of say, the captain of a rugby team or an officer with the rank of captain is not clear, but research into the background of later Chief Constables of Devon would clear this up.

All in all, the British authorities' response was about as much as could be expected. In these situations it is questionable whether any political authority could have responded with court martials and jail sentences. Had they done so, not only would they have risked a mutiny, as the details came out public opinion in Britain would almost certainly have supported the troops. This would raise public anger in Britain and lead to demands for vigorous action against the IRA and make the political situation even more difficult.

As it was, the General in command accepted that they had had a dirty trick played on them, but told them frankly that one act of revenge was enough. They were allowed to march through the town behind the band with fixed bayonets and colours flying and then they were quietly withdrawn to Cork to make absolutely sure there would be no further trouble.

I should also say that I have a great deal of sympathy for the Fermoy jurymen, who were in a simply awful position. The government at that time was trying to maintain the normal administration of justice and therefore had to hold an inquest. Even without the alleged involvement of the parish priest, had they returned a verdict of murder that would have sanctioned the government's right to try and in due course hang the IRA. That would be inviting their own summary execution by the IRA as traitors to the Republic. Whilst they were not enough to quell the anger of the troops their statements of regret can be taken as genuine and were probably as far as they dared go in the circumstances.

Of course, Irish writers do not think it necessary to record that appropriate claims for compensation were made in the civil courts. One must assume these were paid as had they not been it would have been emphasised in their accounts.

Let us again look at and dissect the accounts of Griffiths and Kee.

First from Kenneth Griffiths' *The DTA's Curious Journey*.

The Cork No. 2 Brigade under Liam Lynch ambushed a party of the King's Shropshire Light Infantry who were on the way to church in Fermoy, disarmed them and escaped with 13 rifles.

Poetically speaking it was an ambush, but in plain language they were set on by men with clubs and pistols when they had not the slightest reason to expect it

"leaving behind a dead British soldier"

One unarmed man shot dead and three seriously wounded?

the operation showed all the panache and resourcefulness that would characterise the IRA's raw campaign under such men as Tom Barry, Ernie O'Malley and Sean McEoin...

Panache and resourcefulness? Shooting unarmed soldiers going into church and running away?

British humiliated and bewildered...

Humiliated and bewildered? Hardly surprising; who would not be in the circumstances?

An enemy which was in all ways indistinguishable from the native populace away simply seemed to vanish into the countryside...

Indistinguishable? Churchill stated in the House of Commons that several men were arrested in connection with the incident. What happened to them is not reported but I would suspect they were quietly released for "lack of evidence" when the fuss had died down.

Struck back by sacking the town in a fit of impotent rage...

No, the men were careful to direct their rage not by sacking the town, but by wrecking the property of specific individuals. They may have been wrong but they were not inclined, and indeed could not be expected, to make allowances for the position the jurymen were in. They destroyed property but it seems the actual looting was done by the townspeople of Fermoy.

The war became one between increasingly undisciplined British troops and the increasingly resistant people of Ireland...

Increasingly resistant people of Ireland? On the contrary, on occasions when these incidents occurred the army was surprised by the increase in information they got from local people. This is normal in any guerilla situation, as a British Field Marshal writing in the 1980s said effectively: "The people support the side they fear the most".

And when the civil law remains largely intact to restrain the security forces this is invariably the freedom fighters they fear.

Looking again at Robert Kee's account, one sees the problems a writer who is being as fair as possible has. Writing a complete history of the period, historians cannot be expected to examine every incident in detail, so poetic licence invariably creeps in:

One of the other casualties had been a soldier killed in Fermoy County Cork in a daring assault on a party of troops marching to church on Sunday 7 September.

No need to say again that clubbing and shooting an unsuspecting and isolated group of unarmed men going to church cannot be called daring.

This raid had been formally authorised by Collins and the Volunteer GHQ in Dublin although on condition there should be no casualties...

Political manoeuvre - you do not shoot four men out of 13, or even 18, by accident when you know they are unarmed - or if you do it is as a result of nerves and/or indiscipline.

It was brilliantly executed by Liam Lynch, revealing guerrilla professionalism of which he was one of the earliest volunteer exponents. Eighteeen men at the King's Shropshire Light Infantry in the Church party were swiftly overpowered and 13 rifles loaded into a waiting motorcars which were immediately driven off. Military vehicles which took off in pursuit found the roads blocked by fallen trees which would have been sawn through during the night and held back by ropes until the escaping raiders were safely past.Only one detail of the operation had gone awry, for in the scuffle one of the soldiers have been shot dead and three others seriously wounded...

As I have said several times already - you do not shoot four unarmed men out of 13, or even 18, by accident, or if you do, it is as a result of nerves and/or indiscipline. It is also interesting that he describes it as a "scuffle" which suggests he knew the soldiers had no ammunition for their rifles. Also, he makes no mention of "marching in the road", "whistles" and "calls to surrender" which suggests his research has discovered what actually happened.

The jury at the subsequent inquest unanimously expressed horror and condemnation for this appalling outrage. In the midst of a peaceful and civil community between whom the most friendly feelings have always existed" but they did not find a verdict of murder because of raids intention had clearly been to get the rifles and the killing had been unpremeditated.

If the IRA did not encourage them to this verdict it is certain the local priest did.

"For this oversight, in spite of their additional expression of sympathy with the dead man's relatives, they were made to pay a heavy price. That night undisciplined troops broke out of barracks and did considerable damage to the town smashing shop windows at particularly attacking the house of the foreman of the jury."

What else could be expected of jurymen or troops in the circumstances? The jurymen dared not return a murder verdict and unfortunately there is a limit to what "discipline" can achieve if soldiers are to have any worthwhile spirit left in them. According to Lt Col Hughes-Hallett's account, many of the men were war veterans awaiting discharge and therefore accustomed to dealing out measured revenge for what they considered acts of malice outside normal behavior. By all accounts damage was limited, compensation was paid and no small amount of the looting was done by the townspeople themselves.

So let us conclude with the details:

1. The people of Fermoy knew what was afoot, but to be fair, could and dared not, do anything.

2. A group of 13 unarmed soldiers were set upon by IRA armed with pistols and clubs.

3. The IRA did NOT blow a whistle or ask them to surrender.

4. The soldiers had no ammunition for their rifles and the IRA would know this.

5. There had been no attacks on the army for four years.

6. Fermoy was a happy station and relations between the men and the townspeople were acknowledged to be good.

7. The soldiers did not wreck the whole town, but attacked only the shops and homes of the jurymen.

8. They were not drunk but stone cold sober and well organised.

9. One officer may have accompanied them. This is not necessarily a bad thing as he could direct and limit their anger.

10. The commanding General told them they had been victims of a dirty trick but told them there should be no more trouble.

11. Setting aside details of nationality and the glorious fight for freedom, the reader is invited to speculate on what his or her response would be if a friend were shot down in a similar manner, allowing for the fact that the justification for their murder is that the government was oppressing the people with whom they had been living in perfect harmony for some time.

In the final analysis men can only be expected to take so much without lashing out. A similar and indeed more cruel murder occurred in Cyprus in the late 1950s with the probable intention of provoking the same response.

During a campaign which O'Connor is quite proud to claim was inspired by the IRA of the 1920s the EOKA freedom fighters shot two soldiers' wives shopping in a supermarket, killing one. On hearing this the British soldiers went into town and proceeded to beat up every Greek they could find until the officers and NCOs got into the town and persuaded them to calm down and return to camp.

The niceties of law and legal retribution administered by men who have very little contact with the brutal realities of "freedom fighting" are not well suited to these incidents.

We must of course quote the account of this incident given by Bowyer-Bull:

"Slyly, without formal recognition, the British chose to permit unofficial countered terror. In September; a column of Cork No 2 under Liam Lynch ambushed a detachment of the King's Shropshire Light Infantry near the Wesleyan Church at Fermoy. An infantryman was killed, but the coroner's jury refused to return a verdict of murder, finding only that death had resulted from a bullet wound. Two hundred British soldiers rushed into Fermoy and wrecked the houses of several jurymen, doing £3,000 worth of damage. No effort was made by the RIC or the Shropshire officers to stop the unofficial raid. It was the first indication of a pattern that was to develop over the next two years - assassination, indignation, retaliation."

The reader is invited to compare this with the matter-of-fact account by Colonel Hughes Hallett in his memoirs.

But let us analyse the account of this "wise and wary professional historian" in detail:

Slyly, without formal recognition, the British chose to permit unofficial counter terror...

The attack and response was wholly unexpected and I repeat, the General commanding the area called a special parade and told them he understood their feelings. It was a dirty trick, but there were to be no more attacks on the town. Just in case, the regiment was withdrawn as soon as possible afterwards to prevent any reoccurrence. To anyone other than a "patriot" or a "wise unwary American historian" that does not sound like "sly approval" of counter terror.

In September; a column of Cork No 2 under Liam Lynch ambushed a detachment of the King's Shropshire Light Infantry near the Wesleyan Church at Fermoy. An infantryman was killed...

About a dozen unarmed men quietly making their way into the Wesleyan church were set upon with clubs and revolvers.

The coroner's jury refused to return a verdict of murder finding only that death had resulted from a bullet wound...

No! The jury returned a verdict of manslaughter, accidental killing, and again while I have sympathy with them for the pressure they were under it was no accident. You do not shoot three unarmed men, killing one, by accident.

Two hundred British soldiers rushed into Fermoy and wrecked the houses of several juryman, doing £3,000 worth of damage...

Two hundred is a nice round figure, but certainly a lot of soldiers went into town on a well-planned raid to take it out on those who refused to call the murderers of their comrade, murderers.

No effort was made by the RIC or the Shropshire officers to stop the unofficial raid...

There is very little the RIC could do in the face of a hundred or more angry soldiers, but the officers for the most part did their best to stop the damage and make sure that nothing like it happened again.

It was the first indication of a pattern that was to develop over the next two years - assassination, indignation, retaliation...

Well, it had to be the first because it was the first attack and the pattern was just what the murderous Lynch and his comrades intended to initiate. Intellectuals and "wise and wary historians" can never understand the refusal of men, be they police or soldiers, to allow patriots and revolutionaries to kill them and walk away.

This is pretty much the standard way Bowyer-Bull presents his information - leaving out any detail that might embarrass the IRA.

One can well understand why he is so beloved by Republicans, but how anyone else could consider him a "professional historian", let alone "wise and wary" is beyond comprehension.

CHAPTER 18

THE BRITISH CAMPAIGN IN IRELAND, 1920-21

This is the title of a book published by the Oxford University Press and it is now very difficult to obtain. I tried to buy a copy on the internet for over a year without success but it contains a great deal of data, which challenges the normal perception of the military action of the period.

It has been described by one Irish historian as a "revisionist" account, which in this case is a compliment.

This is probably because it debunks many of their long-held assertions that have been accepted as facts - in particular the claim that resignations from the RIC in this period were a serious problem and the lack of new recruits led to the formation of the Black & Tans. In his book "The British Campaign in Ireland" Dr Townsend claimed that his research established that while resignations were at a higher level than normal, the government had no problem recruiting replacements. Even in 1920 when the situation was at its most serious they were still able to recruit Irishmen - although many were ex-soldiers recruited from the Irish community in Britain.

Actually, the origins of the assertions that resignations from the RIG were widespread are quite fascinating;

an excellent example of Michael Collins' ingenious manipulation of liberal opinion and what we now call the media.

Rather like the Borgias in medieval Italy, he understood that things are better done by a third party and you do not administer a deadly poison to people you want to kill. You administer a poison that creates what appears to be a medical condition for which their doctor will prescribe a medicine. You know this will react with the poison, and that is what will kill them.

Consequently, most historians cite a letter printed in an Irish newspaper, which was read out by an English Member of Parliament in the House of Commons. He informed parliament of the concern of Irish people about the high level of resignations in the RIC which were not being matched by recruitment. The underlying suggestion is that even the police had lost confidence in the government and were either afraid of, or even sympathetic, to the IRA.

However. there is a copy of a letter written by Collins in the Public Records Office at Kew - again in a file that has been open for more than 30 years. The letter passes on some information to Sinn Fein's English director of propaganda, Erskine Childers, hoping it will be put to good use. He adds that he has an arrangement with correspondents in London who can be relied upon to publish any figures he gives them "pretty much to our advantage". Freethinking liberal correspondents were ever thus.

So it would appear that the origin of the "mass resignations from the RIC" story was a letter written on Collins' instructions to a Dublin newspaper.

Its publication by the editor is not so much an indication of public opinion and even less the paper's concern to inform the community. The editor would be well aware that - in the manner of Vito Corleone - printing a letter at Collins' request was a request he could not refuse (at least one Dublin newspaper editor had received a warning visit from "the squad" about his unsympathetic attitude to the IRA) .

Consequently, the RIC resignations story went into the House of Commons records and then into every history book as an unquestioned fact.

Any readers who are not prepared to believe this may look in Kenneth Griffith's hymn of praise to the IRA, *Curious Journey*, in which one IRA veteran tells how he and others called on this unsympathetic newspaper editor. The veteran tells with satisfaction how the editor considerably changed his attitude to the IRA afterwards. The editor was lucky he was in Dublin.

When the Cork IRA were concerned about the Cork Examiner's continued opposition to violence and its advocacy of peace they decided to take action first by trying to wreck its presses and burn its building down. That failed, so in the small hours of the morning they waylaid four of its printers - ambushed is too grand a word - and threw a bomb that blew the legs off one unfortunate 22-year-old and seriously wounded another man. While the innocent and helpless men were lying in agony in the road they opened fire on them just to make sure.

As I recall, two of them were killed, including the double amputee who died in hospital the following day. I do not think the Republican propaganda bureau put out a communiqué about this but had they done so it would probably have ended with their usual phrase "there were no IRA casualties". Freedom fighting, don't you love it?

Dr Townshend is also revisionist in that he declares the IRA had in fact won the guerrilla war and, naturally enough, even the most extreme Irish historians do not challenge this piece of revisionism. This is contrary to the general opinion of historians who have declared the war to be a draw, citing Collins' own statement that the IRA was "on its back" at the time.

The research Professor Townsend uses to support his claim is quite the most fascinating reversal of an argument I have ever heard outside Ireland (where argument reversal is a national talent). It is simply this. On the basis of casualty figures the majority of government or Crown casualties were suffered in the six months before the ceasefire, therefore the IRA, in inflicting these casualties in the last period could not have been losing.

Casting one's net far and wide and linking up data, consider the opinion of respected historians regarding British casualties in the Second World War.

There is a general perception in Britain that the army's casualties in the Second World War were much lighter than in the first. In fact, the casualty rates were just as heavy and the lower total figure is accounted for by the fact that the allies only engaged the main German army in France for 10 months between June 1944 and April 1945. In the First World War they were committed against the main German army for four years and when you compare the casualties in the relative periods they were just as bad in the Second World War as the First.

If that were not enough, most people believe the worst casualties the British Army suffered in the First World War were in 1916 and 1917, the years of the Somme and Passchendaele. In fact the army's worst year was 1918 when it was engaged in the most successful campaign in its history, the 100 days that ended the war.

It is strange that Dr Townshend actually missed a document in one of his quoted sources that categorically declares the government had no wish to fight a guerrilla war and only did so as a last resort in the six months leading up to the ceasefire.

The briefing paper for the Cabinet prepared early in 1921 states clearly "casualties have been heavy but this is a measure of the intensity of the fighting not the course", or in plain English, "We are winning".

Any military historian would tell him that the casualties received, while tragic for the individual, are not as important as the objective for which they were incurred. The test of success is not the number of men lost, but whether the objective has been achieved and if it was worth the relative expenditure in lives. A military historian also knows that the most successful and effective units suffer the heaviest casualties. The normal cinematic portrayal of the disheveled and perhaps slightly wounded victors standing above a pile of enemy corpses is utter nonsense.

The majority of government or Crown casualties were suffered in the last six months because as in the last 10 months of the war in Europe 22 years later that was when the government realised it had to do some serious fighting. For over a year it had been just too busy in the wider world and, in any case, had no wish to fight anyone or do anything except proceed with the political programme agreed in 1914.

A more accurate measure of the effect of the Government's campaign would not be the additional number of servicemen and police killed. It would be interesting if there was a reduction in the number of ex-servicemen murdered simply for being ex-servicemen and any reduction in the number of wretched civilians shot as "spies and traitors". Or those killed because they witnessed some IRA action and "might" give evidence. One would hope that the patriots' need to look to their own security might have reduced their capacity to kill what most would regard as innocent people.

Dr Townsend also drew attention to the boycott by Irish railway workers on the movement of military stores and troops. This had the support of the trade unions and he suggests their action is yet another example of the grass roots support for Sinn Fein. As a result of this the workers were penalised by the authorities with loss of pay etc. etc. and this great contribution to the national cause had never been recognised in Ireland. When I first read this I accepted it but did not think the government action was unreasonable; after all many of the railways in Ireland were subsidised. Why should the government continue to pay for something which was not being done?

That was until I chanced on a report in the Irish Times from July 1920. This was headline news and reported that three young men entered the offices of the Dublin and South-Eastern Railway. They demanded to see the chairman of the company, a gentleman in his sixties, a leading member of Dublin Society and a Privy Counselor. Naturally they were refused and then asked where he was. On being told he was in his office they pushed passed the staff declaring *"we'll deal with him in there then"*. They clearly knew the layout of the building and made their way to his office, drew their revolvers and proceeded to blow most of the top of his head off when he was either sitting at his desk or trying to escape. I think this had a rather greater influence in Irish rail workers' attitudes to the IRA than simple patriotism. Disagreeable as it may seem, this probably made it unnecessary for Collins to have railway workers killed and may therefore have saved a few lives. One cannot say that Collins was not responsible because while there were many unofficial killings around the country, in Dublin it was a different matter, as his control of the patriots' murderous enthusiasm was much closer. As Flash Gordon's adversary the Emperor Ming the Merciless declared, "Nobody dies in my palace without my orders", we can say with certainty that few men died in Dublin without Collins ordering it.

If one casts the net ever wider, Dr Townshend's book is full of fascinating details for anyone who cares to analyse it. Interestingly, he confirms that the army was not really involved until a comparatively late stage and, as his book is unobtainable, I have to rely on memory. He notes that there were no training courses on guerrilla warfare for regiments serving in Ireland until late in 1920. Even then they seldom lasted more than three days and were voluntary and were simply available for any regiment that wanted to send their men on them. The fact that regiments were not sending regular cadres and carrying out intensive training indicates that fighting the IRA was not considered a priority. The reason is obvious, about everyone from the colonel down do the ordinary private knew that they would be leaving Ireland and the IRA shortly so why bother?

There are quite different confirmations of this. The first is from Professor Townshend's book in which he records that Field Marshal Sir Henry Wilson was annoyed to find that his instructions to armour vehicles against pistol and rifle bullets had not been carried out. We first have to say that Field Marshal Wilson, a committed Unionist and sometime supporter of the UVF, was one of the few top members of the government who did not understand what was going on. Had there been any serious need for these vehicles to be armoured, the soldiers, never mind the regiments, would have done it themselves. Soldiers are always careful of their own lives and quite reasonably pay no attention to orders and costs when these are at risk.

There are many examples, but to cite one from Vietnam, the US Army found that the suspensions and engines of armoured infantry carriers had a very short operational life. When this was investigated it was found that the soldiers were covering the floors with layers of sandbags as extra protection against mines and this additional weight was what seriously overloaded the drive systems.

It is interesting to cross-reference Townsend's comment about his research with the note by the historian

Pakenham in his book *The Year of Liberty* about the Irish rebellion of 1798. Pakenham stated that his work was bound to be unbalanced because while there are thousands of government documents about the 1798 rebellion there were very few rebel documents. Townshend quotes the exact opposite, noting that while there were thousands of books, writings and interviews by and with people on the Republican side to research the British side he had trawled through mountains of regimental histories for the sake of a few paragraphs here and there.

This is hardly surprising because in 1919-1922 the British army had major wars in Russia, Iraq and Afghanistan and the really serious threat of a renewed war against Turkey. It is also forgotten that there was a considerable degree of unrest in mainland Britain. It was so serious that when a policeman was shot and seriously wounded in a failed IRA raid on an army reserve Drill Hall in Scotland the group initially thought to be responsible were "Bolsheviks" and not the IRA.

As to whether the period called by the Irish people "The Troubles" - but since recycled into the "War of Independence" or "The Anglo-Irish War" - was actually a war depends on your point of view. What is a war is actually relative to what you experience.

Sixty years ago, leading English historians wrote that however much it might be denied, the "Irish War of Independence" was a "war" because not only that the IRA were fighting a great army, but an army which had just returned from a victorious war. Much as I am influenced by the Irish maxim that one should never speak ill of the dead I must do so here and as this historian has undoubtedly passed away and as I cannot be sued, I am obliged to state that he is/was a complete idiot.

The British Army, in common with the rest of British and European society, was trying to make sense of what they had just gone through and the people were trying to come to terms with the appalling casualties. There was by all accounts a quiet pride in what they had been told was a great achievement but there was also terrible pain caused by the losses they had suffered. In these circumstances arrogance in victory and contempt for opponents is not possible. Consequently, while the renewed war with Turkey I mentioned was thought to be politically and strategically desirable in the long term, at the time it was *politically* impossible - the people of Britain and the Empire would just not allow it.

I would say that yes, the politicians and patriots of Ireland have a great interest in calling it a war and a War of Independence if you like. The academics of England might like to call it a war, but what of the soldiers who were there?

To again cite the Manchester Regiment's experience, does anyone honestly think the men thought it was a war compared to its 500 dead out of a 1,000 strong battalion on the first day of the Somme in 1916? Their 1st Battalion was in Cork at the same time that the 2nd Battalion was out in Iraq where it suffered 500 casualties in 18 months - just under 200 of them dead, including a posthumous VC. Does anyone honestly think these men operating in the area with the highest level of IRA activity, a province that boasts it killed more policemen and soldiers than any other part of Ireland, could consider the two men killed from a random shooting and an officer abducted and murdered - assassinated if you like - as a war? Does anyone honestly think the drafts sent from Cork to reinforce the battalion in Iraq breathed a sigh of relief because they were no longer going to have to face Ireland's legendary guerilla leader?

They were not alone. The Hampshire Regiment operating alongside them who were supposed to have suffered such heavy casualties at Crossbarry, lost just eight men in a whole period. Half their casualties occurred when the IRA electrically exploded a shell under the regimental band when they were marching to the rifle range on routine training. Yes, the politicians, historians and academics might insist this was a war, but as a curator of that Hampshire Regiment Museum said when I was so surprised at their small losses. "You've got to understand that in these affairs there is lots and lots of patrolling and not very much happens."

It is worth repeating the IRA propaganda bureaus report of the mining of their Regimental Band:

May 31 was a red-letter day for the IRA when another blow was struck for the freedom of Ireland by her gallant sons against the unbearable tyranny of England. Six of the 2nd Battalion Hampshire Regiment were killed and 20 wounded in a decisive action which took place about two miles from Yougal, Cork in which the IRA suffered no casualties.

Several of the dead were 16-year-old band boys and the only sight of the IRA were the two men who exploded the mine running away. Quite sensibly, as it happens.

294

People have pointed out that the British Army's casualties in the entire "War of Independence" were less than a month's normal wastage on the Western Front. I would say some battalions serving in Ireland probably lost as many men in accidents as to IRA action. No, the British Army who in the previous eight years had seen thousand strong battalions disappear without trace, quite literally blasted off the face of the earth by artillery, didn't consider Ireland in 1920-22 to be a war worth talking about.

It is interesting that he also makes two observations which suggest a lack of psychological and military understanding. He reports that the IRA suffered heavy casualties in one clash when for some "inexplicable reason" one of their men opened fire too soon. But of course there is nothing inexplicable about this.

It takes a great deal of training and very strong nerves for anyone to hold their fire as an enemy comes within the 50 yards and less required for a successful ambush. All that happened on this occasion was the build-up of nerves was intolerable and the only way one IRA man could reduce the tension was to open fire, with disastrous results for him and his comrades.

He also states that "Irishmen proved to be natural adepts in fire and movement". This is the tactic whereby up to half the unit's strength stays in firing positions to cover the movement of the remainder. This is challenged in a report on an ambush that took place on 16th June 1921 almost at the end of the "war". An army officer concluded that the mines and tactics used in this ambush were good but the IRA was "not at all formidable in fire and movement".

CHAPTER 19

IT'S THE WAY WE TELL THEM

George Bernard Shaw was a Fabian socialist and like all intellectuals of the 1930s an outright supporter of Stalinist Russia.

With other Establishment figures he went there to investigate reports of a famine caused by the Communist collective farming program and to paraphrase his conclusions, he told the world on film "there was no famine, it was all a Capitalist lie". It was not. Millions died and he had been fooled.

But on Ireland, its history and leadership he was much more accurate, describing the Irish maxim, "England's difficulty, Ireland's opportunity", as the old spiteful excuse for stabbing England in the back when she was occupied somewhere else.

This sharp judgment was confirmed by his assessment of Michael Collins who was an admirer of Shaw and met him in London during the treaty negotiations in 1922. After they had dined together Shaw told his friends, "They should not worry about the prisons filling up under any government run by Michael because under Michael the burden would fall on the cemeteries".

Anyone who cares to study Collins' career must conclude that he was unquestionably one of the most evil and dangerous men Ireland has ever produced. A man of considerable charm and intelligence, he understood absolutely what he was doing but had no long term vision, very little appreciation of the wider effects of his actions and no moral scruples whatever. The remarkable thing is that he is very much regarded as a hero and not only to many people in Ireland but the absolute darling of the British intelligentsia. When a British company made a "blockbuster" film called simply Michael Collins in the 1990s I chanced to see a documentary made by Irish television. I was quite surprised. Whereas the British film portrayed him as the great hero and lost leader betrayed by lesser men, the Irish television view was much more circumspect. I now believe being closer to the facts and living with the results of his handiwork they had reason to be less enthusiastic.

The very narrow understanding of history and life given to Collins by his family corrupted his considerable talents. His file at the Public Record Office notes that he came from "a very disloyal family" and while many might sneer at this observation it is valid because it tells us he was programmed from childhood to take a particular attitude.

He is the perfect example of the Jesuit maxim "give me a child until he is seven and I will give you the man". Education and experience made no impact on his understanding. He worked in the City of London for several years and integrated perfectly with his English colleagues who had no reason to suspect he would have killed any of them if he thought it would further "The Cause".

He returned to Ireland early in 1916 because as a resident of mainland Britain he would have been liable to conscription on 2nd March that year. When his employers asked why he was leaving he had no scruples about telling them it was to enlist in the army. It is a measure of how little they knew of his character or political attitude that he was given a month's pay in recognition of his patriotism. In fact, he actually went back to Dublin to take an active part in the Easter Rising.

People in Ireland often talk about "the English mind" and this is valid when it recognises that the average English perception of affairs is quite different to that of the Irish. However, too many people in Ireland use the expression to suggest that the English mind is somehow perverse; most just like to see the English as stupid. In whatever context the expression is used there can be no doubt that Collins understood the English mind perfectly and his time in London was invaluable and allowed him to master the English way of thinking.

One cannot be unfair and say that he used his talent for misleading, deception and outright lying on the English alone. He had no scruples whatever about lying for his own purposes, regardless of whether he was dealing with the Irish or English - but his exceptional understanding of educated English thought allowed him to manipulate it at will. Despite evidence of his murderous duplicity, one only has to hear modern British film producers and writers eulogise about him to understand the extent of his skill.

Shaw was not the only contemporary Irish writer to understand the negative side of the Irish character. Samuel Beckett, winner of the Nobel Prize for literature, described his countrymen as "a vicious bunch".

Irishmen are naturally proud of Becket, but this quote is seldom remembered and while I do not particularly agree with it, I can understand what he meant.

People do not understand that for all the similarities there are fundamental differences in character between the English and the Irish, even though we speak the same language. English is a language the Irish have mastered and in fact understand far better than the English. The Irish are absolute masters of language and know that words do not always mean the same thing and often present poetic licence as factual truth.

When they wish to make a point, Irishmen are like competent lawyers and seldom lie. But they do leave out troublesome details and provide just the right amount of truth to allow you to reach the conclusion they require on your own. This natural talent can be very useful. l was occasionally asked to draft "difficult" letters for my English colleagues who were perfectly intelligent and literate men. I would occasionally draft their CVs for them because they told me I could make a boring mundane job sound important. Looking at my draft of one tricky letter one of my staff said admiringly in his Lancashire dialect - "Eeee tha's called him a bloody fool and a liar as plain as day! An tha' has'na put fool nor liar anywhere in it!" This is what we now call spin and is the basis of much "history" - not only in Ireland.

There are other differences and it was the Jewish writer Gerald Kresh who, with the clear perception one would perhaps expect of a Jew, wrote - "When Irish eyes are smiling, the wise man will run for his life or grab the nearest bottle by the neck". Those who consider this to be racially offensive should be advised that when my father read it out from the Manchester Evening News 50 years ago he dropped the paper and laughed so loudly I can hear him laughing to this day.

Ireland is transfixed by its own heroic perception of itself and can never accept anything else. Napoleon's dictum that "History is a collection of lies upon which everyone is agreed" or Henry Ford's misquoted observation that, "History is bunk" are incomprehensible to Irishmen. What Ford actually said was "The teaching of history is bunk", a quite different thing and anyone who has studied history in detail knows he was right. It has been said that the human mind can only manage a limited amount of truth before it loses direction and must resist or more usually ignore information that contradicts its basic beliefs. Irish history, more than any other, is the core programme of Irish culture.

The great European statesman Tallyrand, when asked if Napoleon's judicial murder of a young nobleman was a crime, responded, "It was worse than a crime, it was a mistake".

Most writers dismiss this as an example of his cynicism, but it is nothing of the kind, it is the expression of a fundamental political truth. Crime is an essential part of political life and therefore crime is excusable - mistakes are not. When one looks at the IRA campaign of 1919-1922, it completely wrecked a political solution acceptable to the majority of the Irish people North and South. Yes, I know the Republicans say the people were fooled by their politicians of the Irish Parliamentary

Party who were not "true patriots" - but whether you believe the murder, lies and general mayhem of the campaign were criminal or not is irrelevant, because as a political policy it was worse than any crime - it was a mistake.

In discussing the nationalism of any country the stupidity and ignorance of television executives, writers and producers never ceases to surprise me. There was once a short television documentary in which an earnest Englishmen held forth about the greatness of the Welsh. I do not particularly dispute the greatness of the Welsh but in the course of the programme he had a particularly ill-informed Welshman declare, "I do not wish to be British! What is that? I am a Welshmen I want to be Welsh!" I was sufficiently annoyed to write and point out to him that the word "Welsh" is derived from the Anglo-Saxon word "Welash" meaning foreigner and Wales is not Wales in Welsh but Cymru. He was in fact demanding to be described not by a Welsh word but by the Anglo-Saxon word for foreigner.

Britain, of course, like all countries, possesses a tiny minority of the idiots, bigots, ignorant people and sundry self-righteous fools immune to facts and reason. Collectively they are known as the intelligentsia.

The Irish capacity for misleading about history by omitting detail is so general it could be classified as lying. If you go to Dublin in the middle of O'Connell Street there is a statue to one William Smith O'Brien who was responsible for a minor fracas, which resulted in the deaths of two people in 1848. There have been bigger and nastier incidents in England before and afterwards but this is counted as one of the great occasions when the Irish "struck a blow for freedom" - even though at the time it was referred to as "The Battle of Widow McCormack's Cabbage Patch".

Smith-O'Brien was educated at Harrow and Cambridge, had been a Conservative MP and until very recently his statue bore the following inscription:

William Smith O'Brien sentenced to death for high treason, 1848.

Perfectly true, but it would be more truthful if they added that the British Government had no intention of hanging anyone, particularly an upper-class man over such a minor incident. If nothing else it would have been unparalleled political stupidity, so parliament rushed through a bill abolishing the automatic death penalty for high treason and the sentence was rapidly commuted to transportation to Australia. While in Australia he did not work as a convict but lived in reasonable comfort in a cottage which is still preserved and like some of his fellow rebels was only required to remain within a 20 mile radius of his "prison". He was granted an unsolicited pardon after four years on condition he did not return to Ireland, but after a further four years he received a full pardon and returned to Ireland eventually dying of natural causes in North Wales eight years later.

But that is not what you would think when you saw his statue. One Irish writer declares that he died "broken in health" which suggests to the reader that his time as a "convict" caused his early death, but he was 58 and at the time that was considered a reasonable age. This was not the impression given by the inscription on his statue in the centre of Dublin before the date of his actual death was added in the 1990's.

Few Irish writers or historians bother to mention the later career of a fellow rebel, Charles Gavin Duffy, who was transported to Tasmania with him. It is just too embarrassing for them to record that he settled there, entered politics, went on to become Prime Minister of Tasmania and was knighted for his services by Queen Victoria.

Anyone who reads history must conclude that the moral politician is about as much use to society as a chaste whore. That is not to say they must be completely promiscuous but like a high class whore they must ply their trade with moderation and discretion for the sake of their own health and the client's good.

Very few people know enough about anything to analyse information and form their own conclusions. Our minds are full of pigeonholes in which we place information and it is natural to try to make new information fit into these. We seldom or never think of opening a new file or cross-referencing files. In modern jargon very few try to think outside the envelope.

An apolitical example of this would be the writer Charlotte Bronte's father, the Reverend Patrick Bronte, who was an Irishman. Charlotte told her friends that when she was a child her father used to fire a pistol out of his bedroom window every morning and thought it was terribly amusing. Her friends simply considered it eccentric, but 20th century academics considered it to be clear evidence that her father was slightly insane and this to some degree explained the literary genius of his daughter.

In fact he was anything but mad. A modern writer who understood the wider picture pointed out that when she was a child England was not the peaceful happy place people believe it to be and anyone with any sort of property kept a loaded firearm by the bed at night in case of burglars.

The only way to unload a pistol then was to fire it, so what the supposedly insane clergyman was doing was making sure there was never a loaded pistol in his home during the day that might endanger his children. For this and several other reasons it was a very intelligent thing to do but through ignorance of the social situation and the firearms of the time people concluded the exact opposite. Far from being insane, or even eccentric, his action was not just that of a rational man but of an exceptionally careful, well-informed and intelligent man.

The point is by failing to look at and take into account technical and social information we reach entirely the wrong conclusions.

Sinn Fein was founded by Arthur Griffith a journalist and intellectual. A decent man who hated violence and whose political ideas were based purely on what he thought had happened in the Austrian Empire in the mid

19th century. He declared that the Hungarians had not rebelled against Austrian rule but had set up a parallel administration to carry out the functions of the Vienna government which the Hungarians had then simply ignored. This was done peacefully and the Austrians had been left with the option of launching an aggressive war on a popular movement or recognising the de facto Hungarian administration. Whether this is what actually happened is open to question, but the account is very popular with Hungarians - to the extent that when an English historian asked a Hungarian colleague "What really happened in 1848?" he was advised to "read Griffith".

Leaving aside the detail that there had been a vast increase in the duties and scope of government in the 70 years since the supposed events in Hungary it has escaped most writers' attention that the bedrock of his policy was no negotiation whatever with the government. The British Government was simply expected to walk away from Ireland in embarrassment regardless of its strategic importance to what was still a world power. It is therefore incredible that Irish writers and so-called historians have been allowed to blame the bloody events of the "War of Independence" on the arrogant British for refusing to negotiate with Griffith and the other elected representatives of the Irish people.

Griffiths' incompetence in the day-to-day realities of politics was compounded by the fact that he was surrounded by poets and psychopaths who likewise knew nothing about government but believed everything could be solved if you shot enough of the right people.

(And did not worry too much if you shot a fair number of the wrong ones). Griffiths may not have understood day-to-day politics but he did have a grasp of strategic and military reality and it was never his wish to "Drive the British Army out of Ireland". Almost the first words he said to the Prime Minister and the British delegation when he arrived in Downing Street to negotiate a treaty in 1922 were, "We don't want total separation, we have to rely on you for defense".

Could anyone tell me what sense it makes to attack and drive out the army and navy that your political leader considers essential for your defence?

It is extremely difficult to talk to anyone in Ireland in a rational manner about Anglo-Irish history. If you put an Irish atrocity to them they seldom argue, but immediately ignore what they have just been told with an instant "that doesn't matter!".

If they do agree what you have said is true they immediately counter with "Yes! But what about…?", citing what they consider to be an English atrocity so it is rather like a game of political poker - I'll see you and I'll raise you.

You can rarely pin them down on any point and even an ingenious political operator like Lloyd George remarked that negotiating with De Valera was like "trying to pick up quicksilver (mercury) with a fork". Fifteen years later the writer of the brilliant satirical book on English history "1066 And All That" made the same observation, saying that Gladstone had "spent his life trying to guess the answer to the Irish question. But just as he was getting warm - the Irish changed the question".

Only the other side's atrocities are of any use in politics and this is not only true in Ireland. Take the example of Cawnpore Well in India. In the 1850s, during what the British have always called the Indian Mutiny but which the Indians now refer to as the First Great Rebellion and are currently re-packaging as the "First War of Independence", a local ruler had over 100 British women and children killed. They were hacked to death by a market butcher and their bodies thrown down a well. The British response when they recaptured the town was to hang a similar number of Indians from a large tree beside the well and erect a monument on the site by a leading Victorian sculptor. On attaining independence in 1948 the first thing the Indians did was demolish the monument, concrete over the well and as the tree was still there, fix an inscription in the form of a lament by the tree speaking as an Indian of the saddest day in its long life. Mourning for "her children" who had been hanged on her branches. Naturally this lament did not make any mention of the British women and small children buried beside it whose remains the Indian Government had quietly concreted over.

An interesting example of the Irish way of dealing with unpalatable truths is the case of Sir Roger Casement, an Irishman and a career diplomat who was knighted for his work in publicising Belgian colonial atrocities in the Congo. At the start of the First World War, while still drawing his diplomatic service pension, he travelled to Germany to arrange a shipment of arms for the 1916 rebellion.

The shipment did not get through and he was arrested after landing on an Irish beach from a German submarine, tried at the Old Bailey and subsequently hanged. However he was very well placed in social and literary circles and considerable pressure was put on the government to secure him a reprieve on the basis that he was simply a decent patriot. This pressure more or less collapsed when the government produced some of his diaries detailing a lifetime of rather sordid homosexual encounters.

Every true Irishman knew at once that the diaries were complete forgeries put together by the filthy British intelligence services to discredit an Irish patriot. For over 80 years Irish writers and politicians raged about the Casement diaries and held them up as an example to the world how rotten and devious the British were. None of them bothered to take into account completely independent evidence from German sources.

The German security services naturally took a close interest in a British diplomat arriving in Germany on a neutral ship in the company of a rather rough Norwegian sailor. Their file included details of the exploits of Casement's Norwegian companion in the homosexual bars and clubs of Berlin and most people would consider this reasonable evidence of a homosexual relationship. However, this was nothing to Irish politicians and writers who kept insisting the diaries were forgeries until 2004 when Tony Blair directed they be subjected to forensic tests, which proved them genuine. This has not produced the slightest embarrassment in Ireland and the Irish side has never considered it necessary to apologise for calling the British Government forgers despite 80 years of vitriol.

The extent to which Englishmen have been taken in by the conventional "800 years of oppression" line was brought home to me when I remarked to one that for all practical purposes the 1916 rebellion was unnecessary. An acceptable deal had been passed into law in 1914 and was only suspended for the duration of the war. "But," said the Englishman instantaneously; "the government doesn't keep its agreements with the Irish!"

It did not matter that the Government of Ireland Act had passed into law and, of course, I would not expect him to know that the work of organising a separate Irish administration went on throughout the war. His instant response was that "the Government had no intention of keeping its agreement".

Even more incredible was a local Liberal politician who said quite forcefully that he considered the IRA campaign of 1969 onwards to be entirely justified when one considered what Ireland had suffered at the hands of the British. I was so surprised that I asked him did he know who Patrick Pierce was? What did he know about the 1916 rebellion? Had he heard of The Troubles in the 1920s? The answer to all these questions was "no" but his ancestors had been driven off their land in Ireland by the English and that was as much as he needed to know. He was the director of one of the largest specialist companies in the region and enjoyed all the trappings of success, a large house, a top-of-the-range Mercedes and a flat in the centre of Madrid, so his Spanish wife could keep in touch with her family. When one considers all this, one would have thought a rational man would want to bless the wicked landlord that drove his family out of Ireland.

Of course, this shocking ignorance of Irish history and Irish attitudes is not confined to successful businessmen and local politicians. Alan Clarke was a leading minister in the Thatcher government and one of the most intelligent and articulate members of the Conservative Party. He was also a thoroughly unpleasant, selfish and arrogant man, but that is beside the point. Some time in the 1990s he publicly declared that the way to solve the Ulster problem was simply to shoot 500-600 of the IRA. As an Irishman I was shocked that any politician in Britain could openly say this, as it was tantamount to sentencing himself to death.

He did not understand that that alone promoted him from the status of "legitimate target" to "prime target" for the IRA. It came as no surprise to me that a week or two later he made an equally outspoken statement declaring that elected members of Sinn Fein should be allowed to take their places in the House of Commons without swearing allegiance to the crown. It was obvious to anyone who knows the Irish mind that the second statement had cancelled out the first and he would therefore be demoted back to ordinary legitimate target status. That he should have effectively retracted his "shoot 500-600" comment suggests that the security services and perhaps his fellow politicians had a quiet word with him about the workings of the "Irish mind".

Despite all the ranting of the wickedness and duplicity of the English I have always found them to be an exceptionally honest and open people. Yes, I have met one or two unpleasant and treacherous ones but they're very much the exception. If you look them in the eye and speak sincerely they usually believe you and Irish Republicans have never hesitated to exploit this rather naive aspect of their character.

They regard most Englishmen in the manner a deaf and dumb boy was treated when I was at Technical College. He was attached to the group around the class comedian and when I said to this individual that it must have been hard work communicating with someone whose conversation was restricted to grunts his response was, "No - you can have some good fun with him, you look him in the face and say you're a right thick bastard you aren't you? And as long as you smile when you say it he thinks you're being nice". Likewise, you can lie through your teeth to most Englishmen and provided you smile and sound sincere they think you are decent and being honest.

Many years ago I briefly looked at a hagiography on the life of De Valera in which the author informed the reader "the growing military success of the IRA in 1920 meant that the British authorities in Dublin Castle could no longer refer to him as the illegitimate half breed Spaniard". I cannot imagine British civil servants who were educated in the classics at the great universities referring to anyone in such a coarse manner. So it was very interesting to read De Valera's file in the Public Record Office that has been open since 1972. Having outlined the fact that he was born in New York and was the son of Kate Coll of Buree Co. Limerick etc it included the following notes:

Mr De Valera is a very earnest man - a dreamer or who sways a crowd - convinced of the justice of Sinn Fein but

*will not come down to practical politics. No orator as
Mr Gladstone was a great public speaker - his fervor and
sincerity carry a crowd by their conviction.*

No mention of the circumstances of his birth or the
slightest reference to him being "an illegitimate half-
breed Spaniard" and why should there be? What
possible relevance were these things to the political
situation at the time? There was absolutely no possibility
that a government headed by the sex-mad Lloyd-George,
reputed to have several illegitimate children himself,
would take the morally upright view Gladstone had
taken of Parnell's affair 30 years earlier.

Regarding the British Army, one should remember that
in Britain the army is usually regarded with contempt.
The officers are all stupid and the men are only to be
pitied as having intelligence only slightly above that of
the Neanderthals.

Thirty years ago I was present at a lecture on Northern
Ireland by a leading television producer who informed
the meeting "that the army was recruited in the poorer
areas of cities like Manchester and Birmingham and not
much could be expected of such people".

This attitude is typical of the intelligencia but it is
not the opinion of many distinguished soldiers over
countless wars who understand that the soldier is
nobody's fool and cannot be a fool because fools can cost
him his life. Those writers who have served in the army
know the truth and Robert Graves wrote that it was
amazing how quickly the men could take the measure of
a new officer or NCO. Within 24 hours they knew

exactly what they could get away with because above all they were and are "street wise".

The fact is that for most of the "War of Independence" the British Army was just not fighting and the burden fell on the armed police. The number of soldiers killed in the period amounted to less than 200 - many when they were unarmed and in the streets, in public houses and going about their normal business.

When an army lorry was moving along the road, patriots did not actually "ambush" it in the sense of mounting an organised attack to destroy it, but took pot shots at it in the course of its journey.

The 1st Manchester Regiment was sent to Ireland specifically to fight the IRA in Munster which was the area of the most intense IRA activity. In the course of six months it lost two men to random sniping from hillsides while they were driving about the country and their intelligence officer was murdered. He left the barracks (alone) to go to his quarters by motorcycle and was found a day and a half later blindfolded in a field and shot seven times through their head and body. Again this is nothing compared to the 2nd Battalions 167 killed in Iraq at the same time. Which campaign do you think figured largest in the consciousness of the Manchester soldiers?

Barry's capacity for a fantastic invention bears no limits. I seem to remember in one account of his exploits - naturally published by a British company - he told how at one stage his men had to avoid an artillery barrage laid down to cover the advance of British infantry. Artillery barrage in Ireland in 1922! When the government was even more than usually terrified of inflicting civilian casualties? Pull the other one Tom - I've never heard of it anywhere else. I believe it was in the same book that he told how when he attacked one convoy the soldiers did not fight but simply ran away across the fields to escape - one trusts taking their weapons with them. The author of this book recorded that Barry expressed his utter contempt at the behavior of these British soldiers in terms so strong they did not think it possible to print them.

I'm sure that every true patriot will agree with Barry, as did that author, and this may well be the origin of Barry's contention that thanks to his heroic efforts the British Army was a demoralised force.

I would however invite you to consider another possibility. The possibility that if some army officers in Cork were asking Barry for safe conduct when they wanted to go fishing, the vibes as we say nowadays would certainly reach the men.

The British intelligentsia might regard the soldiers as Neanderthals but in common with their officers and the civil service they could see what was going on.

Field Marshal Rommel observed that "the ordinary soldier has an extraordinary nose for what was true and what was not" and the British soldiers' noses told them that the battle was not lost - but not really being fought. Consequently, they had no intention of losing their lives in a battle they knew had no purpose as the end had been decided months if not years earlier. I do not know if the soldiers shouted anything as they ran away but had they done so it would probably have been on the lines of, "Sod off you daft bastards we're not playing!"

On the subject of soldiers' intelligence at the time, it is worth quoting the comment which found its way into the Public Records Office, presumably from a censored letter. The author is not named but he wrote,

As long as the Irish Republic confines itself to murder, robbery and arson it is taken seriously, but as soon as it begins to meddle in statecraft one sees the empty pretence of the whole business.

It is a measure of the commonsense of the supposedly ill-educated British people that 90 years ago they had an understanding of the political realities that the 'intelligentsia' have yet to attain.

One can see why the intelligentsia regard the British people with such contempt. They are just too rational.

CHAPTER 20

LAST WORD

At the beginning of this book I described the different
attitudes of English and Irish people to history, citing in
particular how my schoolmates poured out of the
cinema on the dot of 4 o'clock regardless of the
requirements of patriotism.

Also, there was the Irishman who lived in England most
of his life with an English partner who became enraged
when the patriotic version of the Kilmichael ambush was
challenged. There was a sequel to both incidents.

In the case of *The Dam Busters,* when I related the
cinema incident to an Irish history graduate she did not
pay too much attention to the point I was trying to make
but asked me if knew that over 1,000 Russian slave
workers had drowned in a camp below one of the dams.
As it happened I did, it was one of the points Britain's
Guardian newspaper had made a particular play of
when reporting the 50th anniversary in 1993.

I am sad to say that the Russian prisoners were also
irrelevant because if the strategic return on any military
operation is worth it, logic decrees that you carry it out
regardless. Had there been an orphanage under the dam
they would have gone ahead anyway. She was certainly
unaware that the Russians regarded any of their men

who allowed themselves to be taken prisoner to be deserters and traitors. Marshall Zukov actually wanted Moscow to execute the families of men who allowed themselves to be taken prisoner, but that was too much even for Stalin. Had the Russians themselves had the capacity to carry out the raid they would have done so and not turned a hair about their slave workers. I also pointed out that my brother had attended the same secondary school just three years later. When the raid came up in modem history they were told that regardless of the ingenuity and courage involved the raid had not achieved its objectives. It was therefore almost a total failure. Not only was the casualty rate among the aircrew exceptionally heavy, the aircrew lost were the most experienced aircrew in Bomber Command and it could ill afford to lose them.

Sad to say, none of this registered and all I was asked over and over again was what about the Russian slave workers? It was only in 2006 that I came across a satisfactory answer that reflects considerable credit on the British people when they knew nothing about Russian slave workers. Throughout the war the Mass Observation organisation left diaries with a range of ordinary British people so they could record their reactions to the war and its progress. Regarding the Dam Busters raid, the correspondents noted that while they took pride in the skill of the operation and admired the airmen who took part, they were very concerned about the fate of the German civilians who were drowned as a result.

But I'm afraid an Irish historian did not want to listen to any of this but instead fastened on to what they considered the most discreditable aspect for Britain and refused to budge until they had an answer. The simple and truthful answer was that in the grand scale of things, a 1,000 or so drowned Russians were neither here nor there. But this would only have served to confirm their prejudices about the British.

All this confirms my point that the British have a far more commonsense attitude to patriotism, which we could well learn from. Three years after the cinema turned an unsuccessful bombing raid into a glorious victory, history teachers were cutting it down to size with cold facts. There were no great academic arguments, no fury and vitriolic letters from patriots, no acres of writing refuting or discounting facts and no abuse or threats. Ordinary history teachers in suburban secondary schools were telling the simple truth. An acknowledgement that regardless of the effort and losses of those involved the whole business was at best a partial success. Added to that is the people of the time were genuinely troubled by the deaths of German civilians and we have an example of truth and humanity which far too many Irishmen need to learn.

There was also a sequel to the incident of the Irishman who became incoherent with rage when I outlined details of Kilmichael to him.

For over a year afterwards he refused to meet us, even though my wife had been a close friend of his partner for 45 years. However, he eventually relented and invited us over when they moved to a new and larger house. We had no sooner stepped into the living room than I noticed a large photograph of Michael Collins on the sideboard, the popular half profile photograph of his head that is seen in many books.

It was difficult to miss because it was probably the largest size in the largest frame that could be conveniently placed on a suburban sideboard. Of course, I understood what he was doing but I could never understand how a large photograph constituted response to a historic proposition.

Consequently I ignored it, which was the only polite thing to do. But when talking later, my wife pointed to it and to my fury at the time asked her friend, "Who is that, your granddad? She giggled with slight embarrassment when her friend who clearly knew what was going on and was embarrassed herself, replied, "No it's Michael Collins".

I should say that my wife was a woman of exceptional intelligence and education, very good at mathematics, literature and a talented artist, but with no interest whatever in history. Sometime afterwards I reflected that her honest, innocent, question was quite amusing and a far better response than my quiet resentment.

CHAPTER 21

WHY TELL THIS NOW?

Everyone commits atrocities. And as human savagery goes Kilmichael is small beer and the men who committed it are all as dead as their victims. So why raise the matter now?

In political terms it makes perfect sense that during the lifetime of both the perpetrators and the victims' relatives that the truth should be suppressed. What makes it so appalling is that it is still commemorated as a noble feat of arms - although not only the Irish and British governments have known the truth from the beginning, but many people in Ireland know as well.

It has been said that the victor writes the history. This is only true in that the victor writes the history he wishes the world to know . . . but usually this account is challenged, if not by the loser then by historians.

One of the most remarkable things about the British is the manner in which only the misdeeds of their own people are worth picking over. They constantly pick over the wickedness of their Colonial past and elevate the most primitive peoples to the status of liberals, socialists, but most of all victims. An English historian will bewail the murder of the Spanish/Italian soldiers by Englishmen at Kinsale in 1598 but consider improper to record that in the 1950s Egyptian guerrillas/freedom fighters buried British soldiers up to their necks in the sand with their genitals sewn in their mouths.

Concealing the truth about Kilmichael only serves the murderous mythology that has plagued Ireland for centuries. Myth is an essential component of nationalism and as a half understood fable it does no harm creating a vague common feeling in the state or community. Then the standard half-truth that passes as history is useful but when it is the basis of a political programme or guide for national policy it is a blueprint for disaster.

All states are prone to believe their own mythology, not least Britain, where one leading historian noted, the worst military blunders can be attributed to the fact that politicians often believe one British soldier is worth two of any other country.

It seems little original research or thoughtful analysis goes into many "history" books. Most seem to read what has been written by other historians and the same selection of letters and memoirs before recycling it all as a factual account or a "new assessment". The most vociferous survivor, or the victor, tells the story in the manner required to justify his actions and is believed - nobody questions this or looks any further.

An example of this would be a book published in Britain in 2001 *The Military Heritage of Britain & Ireland*. This lists battle sites in Britain and Ireland with a summary of the action and devotes two-thirds of a page to Kilmichael and this is substantially a statement of Barry's account. It is as follows:

In the autumn of 1920 the activities of the RIC Auxiliaries against the civilian population made it imperative for the IRA to take action. Commandant General Tom Barry recounts that he was aware that his enemy made regular use of the road south from Kilmichael and that in addition the road kinked East for 150 yards

I will spare the reader main detail but it concludes:

Cold, wet and with little to eat or drink, they waited. It was not until 4.05pm that the sentries gave warning of the Auxiliaries' approach from the north. Coming towards the concealed command post the driver was puzzled by the appearance of a man in an IRA tunic. As he slowed down a Mills bomb was thrown, a whistle blew and riflemen opened fire. A savage fight left 11 Auxiliaries dead. The second lorry did turn the corner before halting and the men in it managed to take cover and return fire as Barry and his companions moved to take them in the rear they heard shouts of a surrender, only to see the IRA men shot at again as they rose to take their prisoners. In the ensuing battle no prisoners were taken, the Auxiliaries were wiped out. Three of Barry's men lost their lives.

It is virtually word for word Barry's story.

Quite simply, an Englishman has taken Barry's account at face value and, to add insult to the matter, Richard Holmes who was Britain's leading television military historian and a former Brigadier in the British Army, supplies a preface endorsing his work.

Their entry for Barry's other exploit at Crossbarry is little better and also worth quoting:

The British forces were operating in units of some 300 men early in 1921 and Tom Barry's Brigade Flying Column decided consequently to consolidate all available men and weapons in a single group. On 19th March it became apparent that the British were mobilising at least four units to surround and destroy Barry's force. The operation was not however closely co-ordinated and Barry was able to set up an ambush at Crossbarry to deal with the first thrust which he knew was coming from the West.

The old road from Bandon to Cork passes through the little town and two roads from north to south across it some 30 yards apart. Barry placed his men to the west of these crossroads deployed to defend all sectors except the East, which was lightly guarded. Instructions were given that all sections should hold a position unless expressly ordered otherwise, to guard against attack by other columns. The plan worked perfectly. One by one the British units came in, first from the West and, each after a convenient interval, from the other points of the compass. Each was repelled with serious casualties, until the attacks ceased, Barry was able to withdraw to the West in good order, only three of his men having been killed. The impact on the civilian population is not recorded.

Such bland acceptance of the received account by British writers is standard. I accept that the book is a guide, with only a couple of paragraphs on every battle in Britain for over a 1,000 years and for that reason one could not expect it to be extensively researched.

But one would have hoped that at some time or other someone would have made a simple phone call to the Museum of the Essex Regiment who were the most heavily involved. That was all that was needed for the average sort of person to start asking serious questions.

Imaginative fiction is much more interesting and exciting than simple truth and politically much less useful.

Much of what passes for Irish history is about as close to reality as the Western, where an entire idea of a period of American history is the result of bad journalism and the vivid imaginations of writers who never left the East coast.

As I have said, anyone trying to dispute the millions of words written about Kilmichael is faced with the same task that the sorcerer's apprentice had when he tried to stop the broom carrying in water. When he chopped it in two he was faced with two brooms and when he chopped those in pieces he was faced with a dozen brooms each carrying water and making the problem worse. What was needed was the return of the sorcerer who knew the spell to stop every broom.

Looking at the clear evidence of cold-blooded murder and quite possibly premeditated political murder against the so-called accounts and analysis by writers and historians - not to say hysterical shrieks of patriots backed up by implicit threats of violence - we definitely need a very powerful spell to rid us of the madness.

That spell can only be learned by yet again taking a cold hard look at:

1. The moral, social and religious need of those who had done it to deny or justify their action if they were to retain their status as civilized Christians. This is not unusual in western society where people have to convince themselves that their enemies are evil men and by killing them they are actually doing good. The difference in Ireland at that time is most of them would really believe they would spend eternity in hell unless the men they killed were evil.

2. Technical matters such as the effect of the time and season on visibility.

3. The skill needed to load and fire a Lee Enfield rifle.

4. Where those rifles were sited and the accuracy, volume and concentration of fire that could be achieved.

5. The location of the IRA positions and their implicit purpose.

6. The unnecessary speed with which the ambush was organised.

7. The location of the Cadets' bodies and the injuries they suffered.

8. The difficulty one has killing people and the time it takes them to die.

9. The fact that until the heroic account was seriously challenged by Dr Hart in 1998 the Irish political Establishment stayed well clear of Kilmichael. Even though for more than 50 years those in power had been alive at the time and would know pretty well what happened and why.

10. It is also worth noting that Bishop Daniel Cohalan, of Cork, who was a local man, responded to the ambush by issuing a degree of excommunication on 12th December 1920 on all those who participated in ambushes, kidnapping or murder. It would be a reasonable assumption that he would know very well what had happened from the confessions made to his priests. The killing might have been going on for a year but one could speculate that as an honest Christian he considered Kilmichael was going a bit too far.

It is frequently reported, but never commented on, that the Macroom Auxiliary Company was disbanded shortly after the ambush and its members distributed to other units. To those who know about esprit de corps this is highly significant because in terms of relationships each military unit is self-contained - so the desire for revenge exists most fiercely in men's immediate comrades. Had the Macroom company been left together the chances of the victims' comrades carrying out some very politically embarrassing reprisals were too great for the authorities to overlook. Consequently they were broken up into other companies, where there would be no general motivation to actively seek revenge. In short, they were disbanded to ensure there were none of the attacks on the civilian population they were supposed to have been carrying out.

Most men shut their bad experiences up in their minds, but there is the little-known phenomenon whereby in old age a few come to terms with the actions of their youth. So it was that Liam Deasy, one of the IRA leaders at Kilmichael (whose brother was one of the three IRA killed there) broke ranks in the 1960s. He criticised Barry's account of his exploits in the glorious fight for freedom.

And if that were not enough, he spoke of D I Crake for his "soldierly humanity". As a result he was reportedly ostracised by his fellow veterans. But this happens in every culture because the glorious fiction is always preferable to the brutal facts. As to the supposedly brutal behavior of the Macroom Company toward the local people that made the ambush essential, other IRA men recalled the Auxiliaries' "decency and restraint".

Dr Hart has rightly said that Kilmichael made Barry's reputation, even though he was little more than the front man who was being both tested and used. He grabbed the "glory", first because he was so vain and stupid, but more importantly nobody else wanted it because the truth was so brutal. Irish patriots have a remarkable capacity for justifying almost any action, but Kilmichael was just too big and dangerous for those really responsible to claim credit and so he was allowed it by default. After all, who will destroy a false reputation by not only publicising an atrocity but by implication taking some personal responsibility for it?

It is true to say that in every field of human activity total incompetence is no bar to celebrity if one has a sufficient quantity of luck - and even when the luck runs out you can still achieve fame and glory.

This is particularly so in the military field and the most outstanding example would be General George

Armstrong Custer who is probably the best-known general in western history. He was an able, if somewhat reckless, cavalry commander in the American Civil War but his fame rests on the Battle of the Little Big Horn in 1876 in which he managed to get most of his command massacred.

A self-seeking publicist, he not only defied orders to avoid an engagement until he was reinforced but split his command and in his haste to grab the glory left his Gatling machine guns behind. An American writer maintained that had he survived the Little Big Horn he would have been court-martialled for incompetence and booted out of the army. Another attributed Custer's fame to the longevity of his widow who survived into the early 1930s and spent the rest of her life touring the United States lecturing about him. Consequently, anyone who might have challenged her version of the Custer legend felt honour-bound to remain silent while she lived . . . but she outlived them all.

That is not quite the case with Ireland's legendary guerrilla leader General Barry because, although he outlived just about everybody else from the period, his contemporaries had reasons other than courtesy to remain silent.

The same could be said for his other glorious victory at Crossbarry, which even a Republican website agrees was due to a substantial part of the encircling cordon going to the wrong place. Concentrating 100 plus men in a well-patrolled area of the country for any length of time is almost as stupid is General Custer taking on 2,000 men with 200 having left his machine guns behind. It would be interesting to know what would have happened to General Barry's reputation as a legendary leader and the reaction of the IRA leadership had he not been lucky that the Black & Tans had gone to the wrong place, creating the gap that allowed him to escape.

There is now no one left alive to be punished and certainly no one left alive to be compensated.

I doubt Barry was primarily responsible and, however ruthless a killer he became, I believe that on this occasion he was used by other cruel men. But in either case their guilt died with them.

We cannot continue to justify the evil done at Kilmichael and against all evidence continue to hide it behind a storm of screaming hysterical lies. Our duty, not only to ourselves, but humanity is served by simply saying - yes this happened, and it was wrong.

If that is not enough, then common decency demands that the 17 men who died there deserve a more honest epitaph than the lies of the men who butchered them, for whatever reason.

Voltaire observed that we owe honour to the living, but to the dead we owe only truth.

The men who died at Kilmicheal should receive the truth that is their due.